WITHDRAWN

INDIAN RAWHIDE

THE CIVILIZATION OF THE AMERICAN INDIAN SERIES

UNIVERSITY OF OKLAHOMA PRESS : NORMAN

INDIAN RAWHIDE

AN AMERICAN FOLK ART

BY MABLE MORROW

FOREWORD BY ALICE MARRIOTT

WITH DRAWINGS AND PAINTINGS BY THE AUTHOR

Library of Congress Cataloging in Publication Data
Morrow, Mable.
    Indian rawhide.
    (The Civilization of the American Indian series,
v. 132)
    Bibliography: p.
    1. Indians of North America—Leather work.
2. Parfleches. I. Title. II. Series.
E98.L4M67   745.53'1'09701   73–7427
ISBN 0–8061–1136–4

Indian Rawhide: A Folk Art is volume 132 in *The Civilization of the American Indian Series*.
Copyright 1975 by the University of Oklahoma Press, Publishing Division of the University. Composed
and printed at Norman, Oklahoma, U.S.A., by the University of Oklahoma Press. First edition.

Foreword

By Alice Marriott

Mable Morrow, like the Indian women of whom she writes in *Indian Rawhide: An American Folk Art*, is a superb craftswoman. A lifetime devoted to learning Indian skills in many fields has resulted in a breadth and depth of knowledge and deftness that mean from Florida to Canada, from Montana to Mexico, one thing: the words "Miss Morrow" open doors that might otherwise be forever closed.

Not only does this book tell of the preparation and many uses of rawhide; also it provides glimpses of Indian life, particularly Plains Indian life, that can be found nowhere else. It is safe to say that whatever one's specialized field of interest, it will be impossible to write of Indian life in the future without reference to this book. Its view of the life of Indian women, of their philosophy of teaching and child training, can never again be recorded.

Only one who has worked with Miss Morrow in the field, who has watched her go into an isolated community where she had no common language and go to work on a local craft, can comprehend what she has done here. Indian women surround her at such times, and she learns from them and they from her the particular skill of the area.

Mable Morrow was associated with the Bureau of Indian Affairs and the Indian Arts and Crafts Board of the Department of the Interior during her rich and full career. She now lives in Santa Fe, New Mexico, where she was formerly Director of Arts and Crafts in the Bureau of Indian Affairs school, now the Institute of American Indian Arts.

Preface

This book is about the folk art of a people who learned to use the material at hand to serve their needs. It is an examination of the buffalo-rawhide culture of the North American Indians.

There was a time on this continent when its people did everything for themselves, when they had to manufacture their necessities from whatever could be obtained from their immediate environment. That they created beautiful as well as functional objects is a reflection of their cultural heritage and their skill. Today craftsmen and artists, trained in art schools, purchase most of the materials they use: canvas stretched on wooden frames, paints, pencils, brushes, and paper. The potter may import his clay and glazes. Most weavers do not card, spin, or dye their yarns. They have forgotten—or perhaps never learned—the amount of skill and time that has gone into making the materials which they use and without which they would be unable to produce a work of art. Primitive peoples had to begin with the basic materials and develop their arts and crafts as they proceeded.

To understand and appreciate a folk art, it is necessary to understand the people who produced it and to have some awareness of their culture. Thus I have attempted in these pages to show, by words and illustrations, the development of the rawhide of the North American Indians, a folk art which reached high standards long before the settlement of Europeans on this continent.

Convincing proof of the great antiquity of the rawhide craft comes from a comparison of the characteristics of the oldest samples of rawhide, or parfleche, made by various linguistic groups. When an Indian group, whose ancestors have in times past made articles from rawhide, talk about the art of working and decorating it, there seems to be great reverence for this portion of their common heritage from the time when all Indians were "the people."

I first became interested in Indian rawhide when I was supervisor of Indian arts and crafts for the Bureau of Indian Affairs, Education Division, in the United States Department of the Interior. Since the 1930's I have examined, studied, and reproduced hundreds of rawhide parfleches and have investigated early explorers' and travelers' descriptions of them. The results of this research are recorded here.

Many of the illustrations are my own drawings and paintings of designs from the parfleches and other containers, which I drew to scale as often as possible. Measurements were made with the side flaps folded and the upper flaps open.

Completion of this book was made possible through the assistance and co-operation of a great number of people. It would be impossible to list all of them by name, but the following groups and institutions should be mentioned: the Indian women who made rawhide articles and furnished information (a partial list of informants and consultants appears at the end of the book), the museums and private collectors who preserved the specimens for study, Bureau of Indian Affairs of the United States Department of the Interior, and the Bureau's Indian Arts and Crafts Board, all of which have encouraged the revival of the old Indian arts. I wish to thank Mr. Richard Gonzalez, the Mellon Foundation, the Kerr-McGee Foundation, and the Houston chapter of Contemporary Hand Weavers of Texas for financial help that made this book possible.

MABLE MORROW

Santa Fe, New Mexico
March 10, 1974

Contents

CONTENTS

Color Illustrations

Black & White Illustrations

THE RAWHIDE PEOPLE AND THEIR CULTURE

1. The People

Most North American Indian tribes believed in a Great Spirit who was the source of all things, including the buffalo. The buffalo was venerated in dances, ceremonies, legends, myths, and the arts. The Indians who lived on the fringes of the Great Plains and those whose homes were across the mountains and who only ventured on the plains to hunt have a traditional buffalo dance which is still performed. After the buffalo no longer roamed Indian country, it was felt than any object made from buffalo had power. Natural objects commanded the respect of the Indians. Rocks, trees, sun, and stars had power to help or hinder an individual or group, and the Indians devoted much of their lives to securing the goodwill of those forces.

The head of a lodge (who was usually an older man), had one or more bundles of different sizes and shapes, which, in good weather, were placed outside the lodge on a support of three poles or, in bad weather, were hung high above his place in the lodge. These bundles contained his sacred medicines, which had been revealed to him by a mysterious spirit. The word *medicine* is not the medicine of the non-Indian but is a term applied to all natural and supernatural manifestations occurring in the owner's experience. These bundles and their contents might be sacred to him and to no other person. They might contain material expressions of symbolic manifestations revealed to him at times when he had gone to places where he could be alone to contemplate and to commune with the Great Spirit and the universe. Many Indian ceremonies are pleas to the Great Spirit for plenty, for fruitfulness, for beauty in life, for success in various undertakings, and for the realization of plans.

The Indian women were always busy. They sometimes continued with their tanning and making of rawhide when they were camped at ceremonial grounds, even at the sun dance. The Dakota women believed that they were helped in their rawhide craft by a Double Woman. They believed that she taught them how to prepare rawhide and what designs to paint on it. Anyone who dreamed of Double Woman was fortunate because she would be helped with her designs. The Arapahos had Whirlwind Woman, or First Woman, as a legendary helper with all phases of their rawhide craft, just as the Navajos had Spider Woman to teach them to weave.

The Indians did not produce art merely for art's sake. Artistry was a by-product of the tribal way of life. Nothing was left to chance. There was an orderly progression of seasonal occupations. Every act of man's daily life had its own tradition.

An important aspect of Indian life was the narration of legends and folk tales. They served as both entertainment and education. Folk tales gave meaning to their lives. The tales were not written down, of course, but were passed from generation to generation by word of mouth. Storytelling was common during the winter evenings. The narrator was usually an older man with a good memory and some imagination. Any phenomenon, from Earth Maker to the most insignificant incident, was explained by myths and legends. These legends were often long and might take several evenings to finish.

Although the greatest herds of buffalo were those on the plains, the animals were at one time found almost from coast to coast and as far south as northern Mexico and north into Canada. During the time of the great herds, nearly all Indians, no matter where they were living, hunted the buffalo and believed that the buffalo was sent to the Indian by the Great Spirit and that it was their greatest gift.

Hunting the buffalo was the way of life for most Indian tribes for many hundreds of years. Some groups traveled many, many miles to find the buffalo,as they were pushed westward or extermi-

The Dance of the White Buffalo Cow Society of the Mandan Indians. This drawing, by Carl Bodmer, shows the painted and embroidered buffalo robes worn by the Mandans when Maximilian, Prince of Wied, visited them in 1833. The drawing shows a curing ceremony. A hand drum and rattles were used, and a white buffalo hide was worn by the leader with the hair outside, while the other robes, painted or embroidered with porcupine quills, were worn with the hair inside. (Drawing by Charles Bodmer from Maximilian, Prince of Wied, *Atlas* accompanying *Travels in the Interior of North America in the Years 1832 to 1834*, American Museum of Natural History, New York)

nated by the invading white men. Indian tradition tells us that the hunters were often gone for a long time. Today reverence for the buffalo persists among young Indians, who may never have seen the Great Plains or a live buffalo.

When the white man arrived, he found that many groups of Indians had a base location which might be called "home" but that some of them were at "home" for only a short period—two or three months at most—each year. This seemed a poor idea to the white man, and he immediately began trying to teach the Indians to live in one place—on a few acres of ground where they could plant a garden and have plenty of vegetables.

The movements of the Indians especially bothered the missionary. He believed that the Indians ought to build a church and live near it. The trader was often inconvenienced when he could not find the Indians with whom he had hoped to trade. The army officer who was expected to keep order in Indian country found his police work difficult because the Indians could vanish like a chinook.

Later, when the United States government put the Indians on reservations, agents and superintendents were sent from Washington to look after them. These officials were often deeply disturbed when the Indians went off the boundaries of their reservations.

2. Rawhide: A Culture Symbol

Long before the coming of the European explorers and settlers the original inhabitants of North America developed a culture based on the use of materials which were at hand and from which they could satisfy their economic, material, esthetic, and spiritual needs. All this was achieved through

4

Piegan Blackfoot medicine bags and bundles on a tripod. The bags were placed outside the lodge as soon as it was erected. (Edward S. Curtis, *The North American Indians: Being a Series of Volumes Picturing and Describing the Indians of the United States and Alaska*, Vol. VI, plate 68; E. E. Ayer Collection, Newberry Library, Chicago)

Black Dog, of the Wichita National bison herd. This photograph was taken in February, 1913. (*American Zoological Society Bulletin*, Vol. XVI, No. 57 [May, 1913], 990; Division of Manuscripts, Western History Collections, University of Oklahoma Library)

their own labor or through the co-operation of the family, clan, or group. Each individual had a pride in his contribution, and in turn he was respected by the group for his industry and technical proficiency.

We often judge a stranger by the way he looks and what he does more than by what he says. Rawhide articles could tell other Indians something of the well-being of a strange group, its pride and skill.

Many millions of buffalo roamed the plains between the Alleghenies and the Rocky Mountains;

but before they could be made to supply the needs of a group, a primitive people with primitive equipment needed years of experimentation with this resource. Necessity forced many individuals who were masters of birchbark and pottery techniques to adapt their knowledge to a new medium, the hide of the buffalo.

From the earliest times Indian groups had used the skins of many small and several large animals —rabbit, beaver, antelope, elk, moose, deer, and others—for clothing and other necessities. Acquisition of the horse, the coming of the white trader,

6

Buffalo Hunt, painting by Allan Houser, a Fort Sill Apache. (Department of the Interior, Indian Arts and Crafts Board, Washington, D.C.)

and the destruction of the buffalo made many changes in the lives and culture of these early groups.

The rawhide craft was nearly at its peak when the white man arrived. After the Indians had procured horses, they could carry more baggage and travel farther than before. When they met strange Indians, it was important to have good baggage and to have horses decorated with brightly painted, long-fringed rawhide bags.

Before horses were brought to the plains, rawhide containers had been carried on dogs or on dog travois, and fringe, if any, was short. After the acquisition of the horse, long fringes came into vogue. The standard length of these narrow strips of rawhide, or buckskin, was determined by placement of the rawhide container on the horse. The fringe must just miss touching the ground.

When traders, trappers, and explorers came up the rivers on boats, the Indians, who had no use for money, traded goods or supplies. In general, up to this time travelers had been people who wanted information about the geography and resources of the country, or who sought the hides of fur-bearing animals.

Following these first contacts, the Indians met the men of various armies. The soldiers traded for rawhide articles, but in most cases were interested only in utilitarian pieces. They had saddlebags made and occasionally picked up a fine parfleche or bag after a battle or after the Indians had fled from the approaching soldiers.

The next group, the white immigrants, came looking for land. They brought containers different from those used by the Indians, such as iron kettles and wooden buckets.

This flat, envelope-type rawhide bag, with a long, tanned fringe, was made by the Arapahos from a buffalo hide. (United States National Museum, Washington, D.C.)

Dakota Woman and Assiniboin Girl, from a painting by Charles Bodmer. The woman is wearing a painted buffalo robe. Beautifully decorated robes were worn by the Indians when the first European tourists visited the plains. The process of tanning and painting robes such as the one in this painting developed over a long period of time. When Indian women said that making a parfleche was "easy," they were comparing the parfleche with a robe like this. The brown side of the hide was worn on the inside, and the stake holes provided decoration around the edge of the robe. (Division of Photography, American Museum of Natural History, New York)

On the Great Plains and in the surrounding areas rawhide was an essential and versatile material. There were no towns or roads or stores. Large herds of buffalo fed on tall grass and made trails across the country in their constant search for food and water. Groups of Indians hunted the buffalo which furnished their food, clothing, and shelter, and filled many other needs. Unlike the Europeans of that time, the people on the American continent secured, through their own efforts, all the things which they used in everyday living.

Just as an Indian group living in the north woods or forests by degrees learned the birchbark technique and became expert in using birchbark to fulfill their needs, so groups living in other areas learned to use rawhide. Birchbark was the material which the Woodland Indians had in abundance, and they learned to cover their houses with it, to make buckets for maple syrup, and to make canoes for traveling on streams and lakes. Rawhide was the material which many Indian groups had in unlimited supply until about 1880; the making and decorating of rawhide containers was one of the oldest American Indian industries. Indeed, the first traders and the early travelers found the rawhide craft well developed.

Some ceremonial rawhide bags still in existence can be traced back through at least eight or ten owners. The rawhide in these bags is almost like leather (tanned hide) and in good condition after being exposed to the elements for many years. The decorations show an understanding of design and the use of color. The old mineral paints are well preserved because of the finish applied to the rawhide. Any Indian craft which shows a high degree of perfection is probably very old; perfect control of a technique evolves over a long period of time. Rawhide was in use before the Indians learned to tan hides for robes or buckskin for clothing.

The Indians had a strong feeling for technical perfection. They became so experienced and skilled in handling rawhide that it was considered an easy task which everyone knew how to do and enjoyed doing. In actual fact, however, a great amount of skilled heavy manual labor was required for making a rawhide container. Skill was needed in each step from removing the hide from the animal to tying the finished bag. The Indians' methods were their own, developed through many years of experimentation with the materials which they found or traded for.

The steps in the making of rawhide might be considered the first steps in preparation for tanning. Long before the first Europeans came, the Indians tanned buffalo, elk, deer, antelope, and other hides. These were used for clothing and lodge covers. Beautifully tanned buffalo robes were painted with realistic or geometric designs or embroidered with porcupine quills. Dresses, shirts, leggings, and moccasins were made from the finest of tanned deer and elk skins. Making a handsome buffalo robe was more difficult than fashioning a rawhide parfleche. It was an advanced step in leather technique.

After the coming of the trader, an Indian woman might tan thirty or thirty-five buffalo robes a year for trade in addition to the robes used by her family. When the family's buckskin clothing is added, it is obvious that Indian women were industrious. Techniques were handed down from one generation to the next, often from a grandmother to her granddaughter.

In early times there were no such things as wrapping paper, paper bags, pasteboard or wooden boxes, suitcases, tin cans, glass bottles, cellophane, and cotton flour sacks, which are now commonly used as containers. To make all kinds of containers, the Indian used the material which he had in abundance—rawhide. When an animal was killed, it was skinned and butchered on the spot. The meat was wrapped in the hide of the buffalo and carried to camp. There the hide was fleshed, washed, and staked out to dry. When camp was moved, the dry hide was folded and transported on a dog travois. The Indian woman placed some of the family possessions on the inside of the hide for safe transportation to the next camping place. Then she gradually began to make rawhide containers of convenient sizes and shapes for packing all the family possessions. Probably the hair was left on the first containers, and there was no decoration. The beautifully decorated bags developed over a long period of time.

3. The Source of Rawhide

The American bison or buffalo was not a migrating animal until the herds became so numerous that they were forced to keep on the move in search of food and water, finally returning each year to their home grounds. They ranged chiefly from the

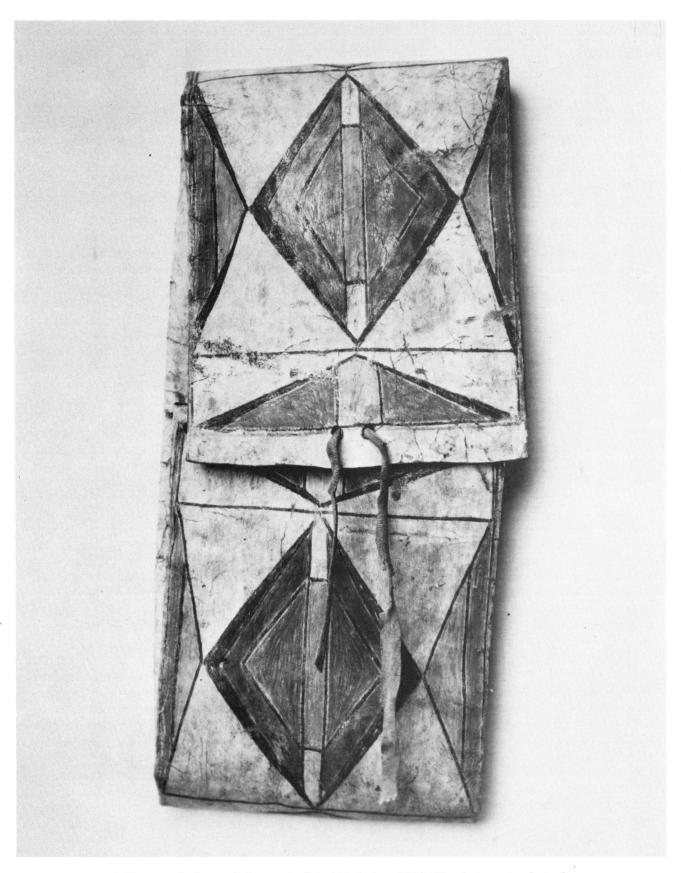

A Crow parfleche made from a buffalo hide before 1890. The design extends to the back of the parfleche. (United States National Museum)

SIZE OF PARFLECHE: 64 x 13 in. SIZE OF DESIGN: 17½ x 13 in.

11

Rocky to the Allegheny Mountains, but remains have been found from Alaska to Georgia, as well as evidence that they wandered through New Mexico, Utah, Oregon, Washington, and British Columbia and the Northwest Territories of Canada. There were never as many beyond the mountains as on the plains.

Probably the buffalo population increased from the Ice Age until the arrival of the whites despite the fact that many were killed by wolves, by breaking through the ice when crossing rivers in winter or drowning in summer, by freezing when they had taken refuge below a cutbank near a river, by starvation when very deep-drifted snows impeded their hunt for food, and by the many Indian groups that subsisted on the buffalo. It has been estimated that the number of buffalo during the latter part of the eighteenth century and early part of the nineteenth century was sixty to seventy-five million.

For thousands of years the very existence of many Indian groups depended upon the buffalo. Although there were many herds, they could not always be located when needed. Since the Indians were on foot until the coming of horses, groups could not travel great distances.

Every part of the flesh was consumed, including the liver, brains, tongue, and blood. While few wild vegetables, nuts, or fruits were found on the plains, the wild dried chokecherry, seeds and pulp, were pounded fine and added to pulverized dried buffalo meat and fat to produce pemmican. Dried chokecherries were also added to meat stew. Many Indian groups planted corn, squash, and a few other vegetables; but during the growing time they might be away hunting, and in their absence the crops were often ruined by dry, hot winds, lack of moisture, and wild animals.

Courtesy and generosity were fundamental in the Indian way of life. If a group had any food at all, it shared with others. Thus the group's own food supply might be depleted, leaving its members near starvation if the buffalo could not be located.

A majority of the Plains Indian groups lived in range of the buffalo, and other groups made yearly trips to buffalo country to hunt. At temporary camps during such hunts the Indians preserved and dried meat, tanned robes, and made rawhide containers.

Most buffalo-hunting parties consisted of the whole family, but a few groups, who lived at great distances from the buffalo, said that only the men went. In this case each man had definite duties: some men were hunters, others were hide men, who skinned the animals and staked out the hide, while still others cared for the meat, cutting, drying, and packing it for the return trip.

In July and August the animals were fat and their hair thin. At this time the skins were in the best condition for making rawhide articles. However, young heifers killed in the late fall made the best robes. Fall hunting was chiefly for pelts: the buffalo was in his prime for eating around September 1.

After the Indians secured horses, they could kill more buffalo and transport more tanned buffalo robes to the trader than with the dog travois. The Indians also venerated the buffalo and held in respect anything made from the buffalo. A rare pure white buffalo was held sacred.

A buffalo hunt was well organized and planned for the benefit of the whole group. Before leaving for the hunt, the people spent days in fasting, solemn religious ceremonies, and prayers, after which the buffalo dance was performed. Everyone had his or her part. Good hunters were selected to hunt for the old, the poor, and the needy. The old people put up drying racks, and children gathered wood for the roasting fires and clean grass on which to put the meat. No one hunted alone or only for himself. The chief selected young men to act as scouts, and the other men were all under his direction. No hunter could shoot an arrow until the signal was given.

Before the time of the white trader the kill was largely limited to that which could be eaten at the time or dried for future use. After the trader arrived, the Indians were pressed to bring in robes and dried tongues and were paid for them with rifles, ammunition, and bad whisky. Dried buffalo tongue was considered a delicacy. The trader would accept tongues in exchange for articles the Indian wanted, and he built up a demand for them among non-Indians, frequently shipping them long distances to his customers.

Soon there was a great demand for buffalo hides and robes in the eastern United States and Europe. Buffalo leather could serve many purposes. A buffalo might be killed for its hide alone by whites who came to the buffalo country to make their fortunes.

When railroads were built across the United States, the buffalo vanished quickly. During railroad construction many were killed every day, for the railroad laborers and overseers ate only the choice parts. Once completed, the railroads could not operate efficiently because a great herd of buffalo crossing the tracks stopped the trains for hours or even days. A single buffalo could easily overturn a railroad car by rubbing himself against it, especially when he was shedding his heavy coat of hair. Buffalo, indeed, spent much time rubbing against anything and everything; they rubbed large boulders until they were smooth. When trees and boulders were scarce, they used the cars of stalled trains.

About this time also came the great flood of non-Indians, seeking land in the West on which to establish ranches for raising cattle and sheep. The buffalo were doomed. By 1890 very few were left, and most of these were in captivity.

Now many Indian groups had no meat to dry, just enough to keep them from starvation. They did not like the new beef supplied by the government and accepted it only because they were hungry.

The hides from elk, moose, and cattle were not as good for making rawhide as those from buffalo. Buffalo hide was quite different from cowhide, more fibrous and elastic. Long use of a piece of buffalo rawhide made it somewhat like heavy, firm cloth. The outer, hair side was brown and moisture-proof. Buffalo bones were closer grained and were preferred by the Indians for making tools for painting the hides. The rawhide craft developed while the buffalo were plentiful. Very little advancement was made in techniques, form, or use after their disappearance.

After the buffalo were gone, much of their country was covered with a layer of white bones. Many Indians and non-Indians gathered these bones and took them to traders, who shipped them by rail to the East to be used as fertilizer.

4. The Useful Rawhide

A versatile Indian people found innumerable uses for rawhide. In their lodges rawhide made a contribution to orderly living. There was a rawhide bag for the lodge stakes which held the cover to the ground and another for the wooden pins which held the cover together in the front above the entrance. These stakes and pins were carefully packed in their respective bags when the lodge was dismantled, and when it was erected at a new place, they were again ready for use. The women could set up a lodge in three minutes. Such speed would

not have been possible unless the lodge had been taken down in an orderly way.

The Indians said that a man could never be an important member of the tribe unless he had a good wife. A good wife was industrious, and her lodge was orderly at all times. She must be ready to feed and care for visitors, as well as look after her own people and immediate family. Her family must have good clothing, and her lodge must be commodious and new looking. All of these requirements demanded a large supply of tanned leather and rawhide.

Buffalo hides were used for lodge covers, for dew cloths (the inner lining), and for bedding and floor covering in the winter. Inside the lodge there were rawhide bags and cases of many sizes and shapes. A number of parfleches were needed for food such as dried meat, berries, cherries, plums, corn, squash, wild turnips, and other fruits and vegetables. Several cases were often tied together and suspended from the lodge poles out of reach. Other rawhide bags held fire-making equipment or sewing materials consisting of sinew, awl, porcupine quills in a dried bladder, extra moccasin soles of rawhide, and any unfinished work. A woman might also have small patterns cut from rawhide which she used when making designs, or she might have a rawhide pattern with which she cut out the covers for the balls used for playing a game something like shinny. These balls were made of rawhide and were always the same size; each woman's pattern was the same. There were also rawhide cases for the best clothing and perhaps for children's toys.

There might be a rawhide cradle for the young baby and willow back-rests, made from willow sticks bound together with rawhide, for the older people. A rawhide bucket might hang from a lodge pole. There also might be a rawhide basket made over a willow frame, and a mortar, consisting of a stone set in a large rawhide bowl, used for pounding meat, cherries, and other foods. The pestle was a rounded stone with a flat side and a wooden handle. The handle was held to the stone by binding the two together with green (wet) rawhide and allowing it to dry and shrink. Knives were sheathed in rawhide. The lodge door might be made of painted rawhide with a frame of willow rods.

Some groups who lived in more or less permanent villages with lodges of earth and timber used partitions of rawhide. To keep out the cold, their sleeping compartments were enclosed by rawhide walls; buffalo robes were used for bedding.

Rawhide belts held clothing in place. Heavy

loads of firewood were carried on the back held in place by plain or decorated rawhide straps which passed over the breast or forehead (tumplines).

Rawhide was also used for cooking pots. A hole was dug in the ground and partly filled with water. Then green or softened rawhide was placed in the hole and pegged down around the edge of the hole. The rawhide was partly filled with water and the food to be cooked was put into the water. Carefully selected stones were then heated on a fire built nearby. (The stones had to be of a type that would not explode when heated and were often rough and jagged). The hot stones were removed from the fire with forked green willow sticks cut for this purpose and were placed in the rawhide pot. Steam would begin to rise, and shortly the pot of food would be boiling briskly. This cooking-pot arrangement functioned something like a double boiler in reverse, for the water in the hole underneath the rawhide kept it from getting too hot.

Food was also cooked in a whole hide which was suspended by the edge upon three poles which forked at the upper end. Water was poured into the hide, chunks of meat, ears of corn, and other vegetables were added, and then the hot stones were put in with forked sticks.

Some of the oldest and finest pieces of rawhide now in existence were used in various ceremonies. These were square or rectangular flat bags with or without long fringe, which held sacred objects. A long cylindrical case held the ceremonial headdress or other ceremonial materials. There were many kinds of drums and rattles of rawhide. In some ceremonies a large sheet of rawhide was pounded as the participants sang. The sacred dried buffalo tongues used in the sun dance were kept in a rawhide case. Some groups made ceremonial masks of rawhide.

When traveling, the Indian men and women often wore sunshades or hats of rawhide, sometimes painted and trimmed with fur. A boat of rawhide with a willow frame was used in crossing rivers. After the Indians obtained horses, they made saddles, gaily decorated horse trappings, harness, bridles, and cinches of rawhide. Rawhide shoes were made for horses when they were traveling in rough country.

Stone hatchets, clubs, and lances consisted of a stone held to a wooden handle by covering the handle and part of the stone with green rawhide and allowing it to dry. A mirror was made by gluing together a thin sheet of mica, powdered mica, and a layer of long buffalo hair. This was glued to a piece of rawhide. Messages were flashed from one group to another with this crudely made mirror.

Ropes were made by cutting spirally around a hide, so that one continuous cord or thong resulted. A rope twenty feet long made of six or eight strings braided together required a whole hide. Cord or string of rawhide had innumerable uses as fishing lines and nets, wattling for cages or fences, lacing for snowshoes or travois, or thongs for whiplashes. Early white travelers tell of seeing snares for caribou or moose consisting of twenty to thirty strands of rawhide so closely twisted that the rope had shrunk to a diameter no thicker than a cod line.

Rawhide was used instead of nails for fastening materials together. Rawhide thongs bound poles together. It is related that the Indians on the northern plains saw a two-wheeled cart imported by the Hudson's Bay Company. They copied it, using only wood held together with rawhide. No nails or other metal were used.

Equipment for games and even playing cards, almost as thin as the present paper ones, were made from rawhide.

In addition to rawhide and the many things made from it, the buffalo also furnished many of the necessities of primitive existence. As has been related, the flesh was eaten fresh and was also dried for year-round consumption. The liver was considered a delicacy and was eaten at the butchering without cooking. The Indians also drank buffalo blood. A blanket of fat on the back of the buffalo was used as a substitute for bread. Intestines were used for the storage of food. Hide scrapings were made into soup flavored with herbs when a group was near starvation. Nearly every group remembers times when they subsisted on hide scrapings, which had been dried and saved by some old grandmother for just such an occasion.

Knives were made from the bones, and the older people said that they could be very sharp. The rib bones could be used for runners on a sled. Bones were also used for awls, needles, hide scrapers, and a stylus or paint brush. Sinew was used for backing bows and for bow strings and in the manufacture of arrows, as well as thread for porcupine quill and bead embroidery.

Horns were made into spoons, ladles, cups, bowls, powder horns, and bows and were used to decorate headdresses. Horn spoons are one of the lovely pieces of folk art found in many museums. The horn was softened by boiling and was shaped into a spoon with a handle carved into an animal or an animal head. Dewclaws, strung in bunches

14

and tied to the legs of dancers, furnished music for dances.

Before burial, the dead might be dressed in their best costumes and robes and then wrapped in rawhide.

The buffalo hides were tanned with the brains and liver of the animal and made into all types of bedding, lodge covers, and clothing for men, women, and children: shirts, leggings, dresses, and robes for winter. The best clothing was kept in large parfleches. The older women say that they tanned buffalo-calf skins for towels. These were washed often and were soft as long as they lasted. The buffalo hair was made into halters, rope, and yarn for weaving belts and bags; the tail made a good fly brush. Gallstones were ground for paint. Windows were made from rawhide. Necklaces and other personal adornment were made from buffalo teeth. Dried buffalo droppings were even used for fuel when wood was scarce on the plains.

Buffalo hides, staked out and dried, were carried to the trading posts. These dry or flint hides were baled and shipped to the East where they were used for wall coverings, buggy tops, book bindings, rugs, furniture upholstery, and many other items which fitted into the non-Indian pattern of living.

The top of a worn-out buffalo-lodge skin made serviceable clothing. Over a year or more the cover rotted at the bottom where it touched the ground. It was cut off one or more times, but finally the lodge became too small for practical use. Then the upper part of the cover was made into clothing. This top had been smoked often, and the smoke combined with the elements had broken up and removed the particles which would cause it to stiffen after washing. Garments made from lodge skins could be washed over and over and still remain soft and pliable. A new lodge skin or cover was needed almost every year.

5. Birchbark, Pottery, and Rawhide

The use of rawhide likely did not originate with any one group, and it did not originate on the plains; rather, it may well have been a derivation of the use of birchbark, for the birchbark culture

Beaver Meadow Woman (Mrs. Buckshot) with a decorated birchbark baby carrier, designed for an infant up to one month old. This carrier is similar to the Comanche carrier made from rawhide. (Frank G. Speck, "Art Processes in Birchbark of the River Desert Algonquin," *Anthropological Papers*, No. 17, Bureau of American Ethnology *Bulletin 128* [1941], plate 42)

is very old. Some of the groups that made the best rawhide had been driven out of the woodland areas of the East. Other groups, such as those in the Northwest, lived where both birchbark and hides were plentiful.

In some ways the two materials, birchbark and rawhide, had much in common. They were both essential to the needs of people living under different climatic conditions. Birchbark was better suited to the moist lake and forest region where the birch was native, and was better adapted for use by a semisettled people than by a nomadic group. The hot, dry plains would cause birchbark to dry out and crack, while rawhide was at its best in dry country and could be adapted to the needs of people on the move. In a moist climate rawhide

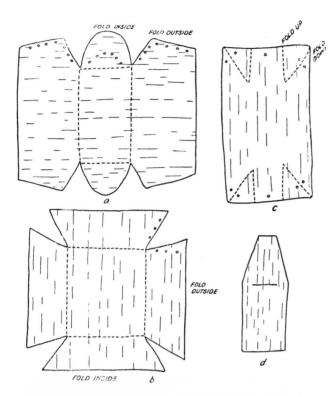

Patterns for folded birchbark containers similar to the Siouan and Algonquian rawhide boxes and trunks. The Chippewas made large folded trunks from birchbark for storage of their winter furs and buckskin clothing. The trunks were similar to the folded rawhide trunks of the Sacs and Foxes. (Speck, "Art Processes in Birchbark of the River Desert Algonquin," *Anthropological Papers*, No. 17, Bureau of American Ethnology *Bulletin 128* [1941], plate 42)

can absorb the moisture and buckle if it is not well moisture-proofed with sizing.

The Plains Indian groups did little weaving of any kind. Rawhide took the place of the woven bags and the birchbark containers of the Woodland groups, of the pottery of the Pueblo groups, and of the baskets of the Hupas, Pimas, and other western groups. Each material met the requirements of a group living in its own particular climate.

Curved lines decorated the birchbark; straight lines might cause it to crack. Straight-line designs predominated on rawhide, where they repeated the lines of the structure of the container. The Indian people thought that this was "right."

The incised parfleche and many birchbark containers show definite technical similarities. When the birchbark was stripped from the tree early in the spring, there was a layer of brown on one side of the bark. This brown layer could be partly scraped away, leaving either a design in brown

against a white background or the reverse. Later in the spring this layer adhered to the tree. Scraping away of the brown surface forms positive and negative designs in brown and light neutral color.

Birchbark was folded to make containers of many sizes and shapes—a trunk shape was much like the rawhide trunks of the Sac and Foxes. Smoked meat was stored in birchbark receptacles (in a moist climate meat kept better if it was smoked).

Many of the groups that made rawhide articles also were known to have made pottery. Louis Hennepin, a captive of the Minnesota Santee Dakotas, described their pottery. Prince Maximilian described the Mandan pottery and John Bradbury that of the Arikaras. Pottery has been made within memory of the oldest living people among the Blackfeet, Arapahos, Cheyennes, and Omahas as well as by the Pueblos and other groups.

The decoration on pottery, its shape, and the materials from which it is made are important in classifying prehistoric cultures. Pottery, characteristic of a group, has certain distinctive traits. decorated rawhide developed before the coming of the Europeans might well form another important link with the past. The decoration of rawhide is of two types, incising and painting. Both of these techniques may be carry-overs from pottery decoration. Specimens of pottery made in the plains now available for study show that the designs were cut into the pottery while the clay was still damp—what is known in pottery making as the "leather stage." The old cut decoration on rawhide was done about the same stage.

The making of pottery was discontinued by many semisettled groups when there was no longer a need for it: rawhide was easier to pack on a horse, and the iron pot of the trader was more to the Indians' liking than breakable pottery.

6. Distribution of Goods

Formerly an Indian family had a large number of painted rawhide bags and parfleches; the women spent much time in making, decorating, and caring for them. Today it is difficult to find rawhide parfleches on reservations, and those that are found may have been made elsewhere. This is due to several factors: the give-away, the system of inter-tribal trade, and the acquisition of the horse prominent among them.

THE GIVE-AWAY

To be important in buffalo country a person had to be generous. He must be known and respected not for the amount of this world's goods which he had, but for the amount and number of presents which he had given away. Thus, in studying the old painted rawhide articles found on Indian reservations or in large collections, it must be remembered that any article may have changed hands not once but several times. Most rawhide articles, however, have certain tribal and individual characteristics which identify them. Of thirty-six parfleches examined on a Dakota reservation, only four had been made by the group among which they were found. The others had been made by six other groups with whom the Dakotas had visited or traded. These old pieces of rawhide art were cherished possessions of very old Indians.

Any event in an Indian community provided the occasion for a give-away. When one tribe visited another tribe, news of the approaching visitors was heralded in the village and all the people of the village dressed in their best and went out to meet them. At the meeting place of the two groups a welcome dance was held, and the visitors were given presents. After this the hosts and hostesses escorted the visitors to the village. The visitors were loaded down with gifts when they left for home.

A Dakota man told that when he was five years old, he went with his grandfather to visit the Arapahos in Wyoming, riding from southwestern South Dakota to the Wind River Reservation in Wyoming in a wagon. The Arapahos came out a distance to meet them, and a welcome dance was held. The boy was given a stick at this time. It was a section of a branch of a tree with part of the bark on and part off. He was told to keep the stick, that it was a horse. The next morning he found a spotted Indian pony tied to the lodge where he slept. He took this pony home with him and kept it for many years. It was the nucleus of his future herd of horses. At this dance other guests received blankets, painted rawhide cases, and beaded moccasins.

In some tribes, such as the Blackfeet, when an important man died, he was dressed in his best regalia for the funeral ceremony. Then his family gave away all of his and their possessions. Among other tribes it was customary to bury all the dead person's belongings with him or to burn all of them. Sometimes after a death or at the end of the mourning period, six months to a year after the death, the relatives had a give-away as a memorial service for the dead person. A feast was held when perhaps hundreds of people were fed, and afterwards presents were given to the guests. Such events left the family stripped of all their possessions and many times actually in want.

A living person might also be honored with a give-away. At present, for example, a young man who is away in the Armed Services may be so honored by his relatives. They may walk solemnly in a circle, in front of the group assembled for the event, each one carrying his photograph, while his friends wait quietly. After this, gifts are distributed in his honor. One or more relatives may have a give-away for a student starting to a distant school. In this case the gifts, part of which may be money, are for the student.

It was customary for a whole band of Indians to go long distances to visit other Indian groups with whom they were on friendly terms. The practice of some tribes, when they heard of approaching visitors, was to erect one or more large lodges for the visitors. Everyone was expected to help supply provisions for the guest quarters. Each woman dipped into her rawhide parfleches of dried meat and other foods for the use of the guests. After the guests had eaten and rested, there would be an exchange of gifts. These formalities over, they might start trading and dancing.

The Flatheads had a gift dance in which the man or woman could ask a person of the opposite sex to dance, but the one who requested the dance had to give his partner a present. These presents could amount to as much as a horse. A young man might give a number of horses to the father of his sweetheart. This was equivalent to asking for her hand in marriage.

Among some tribes a newly wedded couple was given presents by their families, and the wife's family provided rawhide parfleches either empty or filled with dried food. Or there might be an exchange of well-filled rawhide parfleches between the bride's and the groom's families to seal the marriage.

Although all this gift-giving taxed the resources of the giver, it had its rewards. The head of the family could paint on his buffalo robe a representation of the valuable gifts which he had given. Such presents were often of great value, and the giver gained the respect and esteem of his and other groups. For each horse given away an individual had the right to paint a whip on his robe. A whip was always given with the horses, so that the number of whips on a robe denoted the number of horses which he had given away.

Before the arrival of the horse and the white trader, only Indian goods were exchanged, but after that time the most ostentatious gifts were a horse, a gun, a woolen blanket, and woolen or cotton cloth. From early times to this day a rawhide parfleche filled with dried meat is a very acceptable gift between Indians and is referred to as an Indian gift.

The potlatch of the northwest and coastal tribes differs in some respects from the give-away of the Plains and eastern tribes. Some divisions of the Salishàn, Chinookan, and Shahaptian groups have a modified version of both ceremonies today.

TRADE

One of the most interesting phases of Indian life, and one which has never been written in full, is the story of Indian trade. Some materials were passed by one group to another from coast to coast through trade. Flint from Ohio, red pipestone from Minnesota, and different types of shells used for ornaments have been found far from their places of origin.

A very interesting center of Indian trade was on the Columbia River at The Dalles. Indian groups as far east as the Dakotas and Crows traded there. Later the goods from the East might be traded to the West Coast people. The Wishrams and the Wascos stayed at home. They were the middlemen. Considerable trade came to them from the East and Northeast and the West. It was one of the greatest intertribal trading places in the whole country. The Plains groups brought buffalo robes, native tobacco, and dried meat and exchanged them for dentalium shells, dried fish, and roots.

Besides the trading center at The Dalles, there were big fairs or markets each year where Indians came to trade. These fairs were held long before there were European peoples or horses in this country. The coming of the horse allowed the Indians to bring more trade goods. Taos, New Mexico, was a well-known trading center. The Yakimas held a big trading fair out on the plains of southeastern Oregon. It is said that six hundred Indians might be camped there in a circle which was six miles around. One could trade for almost any kind of Indian goods, including blankets, horses, dried

fish, roots, buckskin clothing, shells, beads, paints, baskets, corn-husk bags, buffalo robes, rawhide bags, and parfleches.

While most of the Plains groups made goods for their own immediate use, some Columbia River peoples manufactured goods for trade. Each home was a small factory, and trade goods were not used but kept new and clean. These Indians knew the exchange value of all kinds of goods. Even dried fish was packaged in dried fish skin in different sizes with a recognized "price" for each. Probably no money ever entered into the trading. Today the people think of Indian goods in terms of trade value rather than money.

A study of trade routes and practices would tell us much about the distribution of parfleches. A well-organized system of trade over the whole country helps to account for rawhide articles changing hands more than once. Only a study of the characteristics of a parfleche will place it with the group who made it.

Among the Indians themselves, a set amount was paid for any service; for example, a buffalo hide or a wooden bowl which had been carved from a burl. After the whites arrived, the Indians still traded. A yard of silk ribbon would buy corn enough to last a man a month. For a well-tanned buffalo robe a woman might receive three measuring cups of sugar and one cup of coffee beans. A dozen steel arrowheads, which cost the trader six cents, were traded to the Indian for a buffalo robe worth five to ten dollars.

An early traveler, going by boat up the Missouri River, wrote in his diary: "I saw sacks of rawhide the shape of a quiver for an Indian head-dress, satchels, saddle bags for horses, made in the best manner of white rawhide." He regretted that he could not get any of these because he had nothing to trade. Also on the Missouri a Cheyenne man wore a very fine robe purchased from an Arapaho for ten dollars' worth of silver ornaments (probably made from German silver trade money).

The Indians paid the equivalent of ten dollars for one pound of vermillion pigment. It was possible to obtain a painted robe for five musket balls and some powder. A robe, handsomely painted, was equal in value to two not painted. The Crows, who made some of the best robes, received six to ten dollars in trade from the fur companies. The Indians traded or exchanged hides, robes, and dried tongues at the trading posts for guns, ammunition, iron kettles, mirrors, beads, and coffee. In this way the useful buffalo provided a means of obtaining things which could not be directly produced from the material at hand.

THE HORSE

The coming of the horse changed the lives of the North American Indians. They were able to follow and kill more buffalo, using the poorer horses for traveling and saving the best ones for the attack. The hunters shortened their bows because they now could get closer to the buffalo. Taking a horse from an enemy became a recreation, a sport, a test of bravery, skill, and daring. With horses the Indians could travel farther and faster, carry more baggage, visit groups of their own people, or meet strange tribes. They could carry more pelts, tanned robes, and dried meat to the trader.

The Indian men became famous for their skill in training horses. An Indian could ride into a herd of buffalo, select a prime animal, kill it, and escape from the herd without injury to himself or his horse. The owner of a very fine horse tied it to the front of his lodge at night or even took it inside. The number of horses a man owned determined his importance both in buffalo days and after the buffalo were gone.

Many of the Indian women were excellent horsewomen, but they used the slower, docile horses to ride when carrying their equipment, supplies, babies, and small children and pups. A mother might have a cylindrical rawhide bag filled with dried food from which the family could eat as they rode slowly along several miles behind the men who were following the buffalo.

The introduction of the horse gave the Indians more uses for rawhide: horse trappings were needed; more possessions could be acquired now that they could be more easily transported; and more dried meat, packaged in rawhide, could be taken to other Indian groups or to the trader.

The horse, like the buffalo, flourished on the plains because of the good grass which is very nutritious even when dry.

7. Type of Hides Used

Buffalo hide differed from the hide of any other animal. It was thicker and became soft with use,

having a texture somewhat like felted cloth. Some old buffalo parfleches can be rolled up as easily as a turkish towel. They will not curl or buckle as much as other hides. Indian buffalo rawhide was white on the outside, the brown side always turned in except in the case of incised parfleches. It was opaque whereas the commercial rawhide of today is nearly yellow and partly transparent. The Indian rawhide was whitened and softened by the method used in removing the hair, pounding it off with a stone.

During the buffalo period, when large hides were plentiful, Indian women preferred a summer hide from a fat buffalo cow which had not produced a calf in the spring. This hide would be in good condition and more even in thickness throughout. It was large, light in weight, thinner during the summer, and more pliable and easier to handle through the different processes than a winter hide. The hide of a full-grown buffalo cow might weigh forty to fifty pounds when green. A bull hide was thicker and heavier, often weighing around two hundred pounds, and was used for shields, boats, and floor coverings. In the summer the buffalo shed most of their hair except around the neck, and therefore less labor was involved in removing the hair. The outer skin or epidermis of the buffalo is browner at this time.

The rawhide worker liked to get the hide as soon as possible after it was removed from the animal in order to get it fleshed and staked out before it began to dry.

8. Rawhide and Food Preservation

Every group of people throughout the world developed ways of storing food for future use, for all had known times of plenty and times of want. The Pueblo Indian groups of the Southwest have known seasons when little rain fell and their corn did not mature. Until recent years each farmer gave a certain amount of his harvest to the tribal granary to be kept until times of actual need. These Indians developed large pottery jars for the storage of food. The Pima Indians living in southern Arizona made a very large round, ball-shaped basket of wheat straw to use for storage. Columbia River groups dried fish and wrapped it in fish skin, much like our cellophane-wrapped food. In the north country folded birchbark containers were used.

The migration of the buffalo led to the need for preservation and storage of meat for times when the buffalo was out of range. The Indian groups that hunted the buffalo and other large animals developed a near perfect way of storing food. Rawhide made from large animal hides, sized with materials such as cactus juice and folded into a portfolio-like case, were filled with dried meat and other dried food. When these cases were cached in a well-drained spot, the meat would keep for several years.

DRIED MEAT, FRUITS, AND VEGETABLES

When a buffalo hunt was successful, much meat was dried. As much as twenty-six pounds of dried meat might be obtained from one animal, and many rawhide parfleches were needed to store it. The old people said that the whole camp looked red and white. The lean meat was very red when first put out to dry, but turned almost black when it was completely processed. The white was a sheet of white buffalo "fat," called by the French *depouille*. It has been defined as follows: "It is a fat substance that lies along the backbone next to the hide, running from the shoulder blade to the last rib, and is about as thick as one's hand or finger. It is from 7″ to 11″ broad, tapering to a feather edge at the lower side. It will weigh from 5 to 11 pounds, according to the size and condition of the animal. This substance is taken off and dipped in hot grease for half a minute, then is hung up inside of a lodge to dry, and is used as a substitute for bread, but it is superior to any bread that ever was made. It is eaten with the lean and dried meat, and is tender and sweet and very nourishing, for it seems to satisfy the appetite. When going on the warpath, the Indians would take some dried meat and some 'depouille' to live on and nothing else, not even if they were to be gone for months."[1]

The Indian women were expert at drying meat, employing several methods of handling the process. Often the meat to be dried was taken from the buffalo by muscles. Some women cut the meat from a muscle in one piece by cutting round and round. Others cut it in thin sheets, following the grain of the meat. Many could cut meat nearly as thin as a sheet of paper with their sharp flint or bone knives. Thin sheets of meat dried quickly. At a distance these large pieces of meat looked like clothes drying on a line.

[1] Montana Historical Society *Contributions*, Vol. X.

The meat was dried on racks made by driving two posts, forked at the top, into the ground and placing a third pole horizontally between them. These racks were high enough to be out of the reach of dogs. The meat was hung on the horizontal pole, and when dry was packed in parfleches between layers of dried peppermint (*Mentha canadensis*) leaves, which were picked and dried on the stem. This mint was eaten with the meat. Some women said that they preferred to dry the meat in the air and sun until it was half-dry and then build a brisk fire and finish drying over the coals, which were not allowed to smoke. The weather on the plains was usually perfect for drying meat, but occasionally it had to be protected from the elements. Then it was taken inside the lodge, where a small fire was lighted to keep the air dry. Buffalo tongues were also dried, and a parfleche filled with buffalo tongues was an acceptable gift to the Indian or the white traveler.

Pemmican was often prepared. To make pemmican, the dried meat was placed between two pieces of rawhide and pounded until it was fluffy and light. It might be left plain or mixed with dried pounded chokecherries, fat, and sometimes a little sugar. It was then made into cakes and wrapped in "waxed paper," made by washing and drying the inner lining of the stomach of the buffalo. Pemmican kept indefinitely in parfleches, and a small amount went a long way. It was easier to carry and took up less space than dried meat.

The natives had no refrigeration to preserve their meat. Sun-drying was the preferred way of preserving a year's or a half-year's supply of meat or other food and the one way for many groups to keep from starving. The dried meat was stored in a rawhide case and cached in the ground or hung from the lodge poles.

During buffalo days, many of the Indian groups furnished large amounts of dried meat, processed (cured) buffalo fat, and pemmican to the trading posts, including the Hudson's Bay Company. This meat was carried long distances to the trading posts by slow-moving Indian groups. At that time the only container which would carry dried food in good condition was the parfleche or rawhide packing case, the manufacturing of which will be described in detail later.

Much of the meat was sold by the trader to the fur trappers who would be away from the post for months at a time and to the non-Indian travelers in Indian country, explorers of the West. These groups used the empty parfleches for other supplies such as sugar and flour.

THE CACHE

The Indians who had permanent or semipermanent homes made large, bottle-shaped caches underground with openings in or near their lodges. (Lodge is used here to designate any Indian home or dwelling, whether it is skin, log, earth, mat or bark, plank, or stone.) The opening of the cache was small, about twenty inches in diameter, with a hole below which might be five to seven and one-half feet deep and four to six feet in diameter. This served as a cellar, cooler, and storage room.

Ella Deloria says: "They [the Dakotas] made caches, great underground rooms which were shaped like immense jars with narrow necks. Down there in definite arrangement, the stores of several co-operating families were piled around the walls as high as might be. And, because it was necessary that each woman know her own store and not confuse it with others, her rawhide containers, which always came in pairs, were boldly painted with her own over-all design."[1]

The Omahas and other groups built large underground storage rooms or caches in which they stored all their possessions which were not carried with them on a hunt or visit. Their finest wearing apparel as well as their supply of dried meat and vegetables might be left in the cache, all usually enclosed in rawhide. The same parfleche was never used for both meat and clothing. Each one was kept strictly for one type of material.

Groups who had no permanent homes cached food and other possessions where they expected later to return. They dug a hole in a well-drained spot and piled in rawhide parfleches and covered them over with leaves, brush, and soil, carefully concealing the spot. To disguise a cache, a fire might be built over it or grass skillfully replaced or stones placed on top to keep animals from digging.

The Indians said that the buttes in eastern Wyoming known as Rawhide Buttes were so named because the Indians who traveled from the Dakotas to visit Arapaho country to hunt or make war upon their enemies often cached parfleches of dried meat in the ground in these buttes. On the way home, the travelers would unearth the parfleches and use the food for the return trip. Parfleches filled with food were also cached in hollow trees or treetops in such a way that bears could not get at them. These caches might be left for weeks, months, or even years. Sometimes their owners never returned and at times could not locate the cache when they did return.

It was commonly known to all Indians that dried meat was cached in these buttes, and any Indian, whether he owned a cache or not, could get enough meat to keep himself from starving.

---

[1] *Speaking of Indians*, 72.

THE PARFLECHE AND ITS MANUFACTURE

Introduction

Parfleche is a term probably applied by the French to Indian rawhide shields and then, by extension, to any article made from rawhide. This term is not known or used by Indian groups except where a group may have lived near or intermarried with the French. Each Indian tribe has its own names for this folded rawhide container which changed according to the material packed in it. Examples of Indian parfleche names are:

    Arapaho: *hoa-woo-na-ko, ham-wana, ham-itha*
    Assiniboin: *ho-he*
    Cheyenne: *hoem shot*
    Crow: *nes-kes-cha*
    Iowa: *oyce-x-roki* (a trunk)
    Kutenai: *a-gko-lem*
    Omaha: *we-ab-asta* (when used to carry meat)
    Warm Springs: *shup-tuk-kiah*
    Wenatchee (Salish, eastern Washington): *pun-pun-nubex*
    Yakima: *cata kai*

Sometimes the parfleche is referred to as a horse bag, meat bag, suitcase, trunk, or packing case.

Because no other more suitable term was found for use in this book, *parfleche* is used and is defined as a folded rectangular container made of buffalo or other large-animal hide which was used by the Indian people for storage and for the packing of dried meat and other dried foods, blankets, clothing, and other items. A parfleche is made by folding a large rectangular piece of rawhide, usually about half of a large hide. The first fold is made by bringing the longitudinal edges toward each other until they meet or lap, forming a long rectangle from eleven to twenty inches wide. A second fold is made by bringing the two ends toward the center, where they meet or lap.

Parfleches were made in pairs since two could be cut from a large hide. In early days they were carried on a dog travois or on the backs of humans; later one or more pairs were used as saddlebags.

The parfleche was the most useful of all rawhide containers made by Indians. It was distensible and a large amount of provender or goods could be packed into it. It was tough and would stand rough use. If a pack horse ran among bushes and trees and knocked the pack off, it was not damaged. It was difficult for a mouse to chew his way into the rawhide parfleche, and prairie rains and moisture rarely penetrated a well-made one.

1. Making Indian Rawhide Parfleches

Indian rawhide could be manufactured from the hides of large animals other than buffalo. Cow, elk, moose, deer, antelope, and horse hides were sometimes used in areas where they were available. These hides were made into rawhide in much the same way as buffalo. In the minds of the older Indians, however, it is not easy to separate parfleches, dried meat, and the buffalo. The sight of an old parfleche always brings up the subject of dried meat and the buffalo. The Indians consider the buffalo a beautiful animal and anything made from buffalo hide is shown respect.

After a successful buffalo hunt there was much work to be done. Every man, woman, and child knew his or her chore. If the Indian group was traveling or following the buffalo, even more dispatch was necessary. The men usually killed the buffalo, skinned it, and cut the meat into large pieces. After that the hide and the meat belonged to the women, and they did all the work connected with its use and preservation. Rawhide was considered woman's craft; few men worked with it.

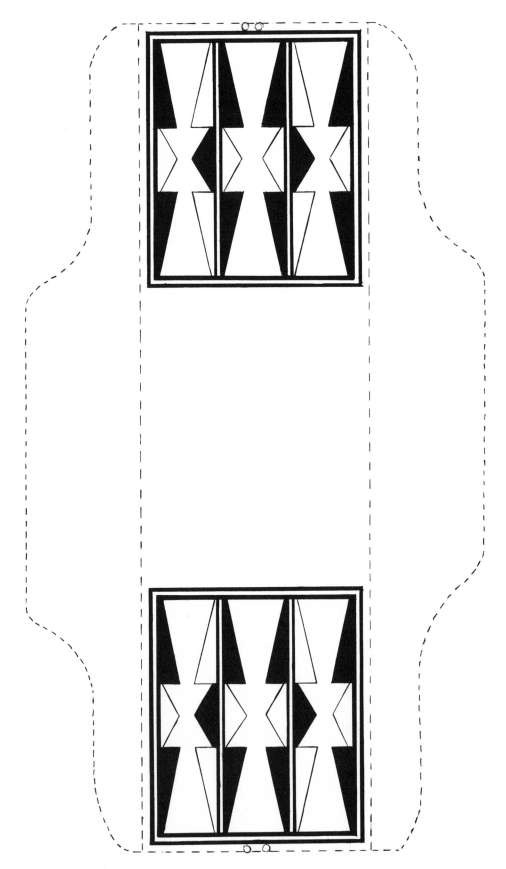

An Arapaho parfleche. The finished parfleche was packed, and the side flaps were folded toward the center and tied together. Then the upper, or end, flaps were folded to meet in the center. They were tied by means of one pair of holes in each upper flap. The decorated areas of this parfleche are not connected with colored bands, and there are no decorations on the side flaps. The design is outlined in old black. The ends of the decorated areas roll over slightly onto the back of the parfleche. This parfleche was collected in 1900. (American Museum of Natural History)

HOLES: 1 pair in each upper flap. SIZE OF PARFLECHE: 61 x 15 in. SIZE OF DESIGN: 17 x 14¼ in.

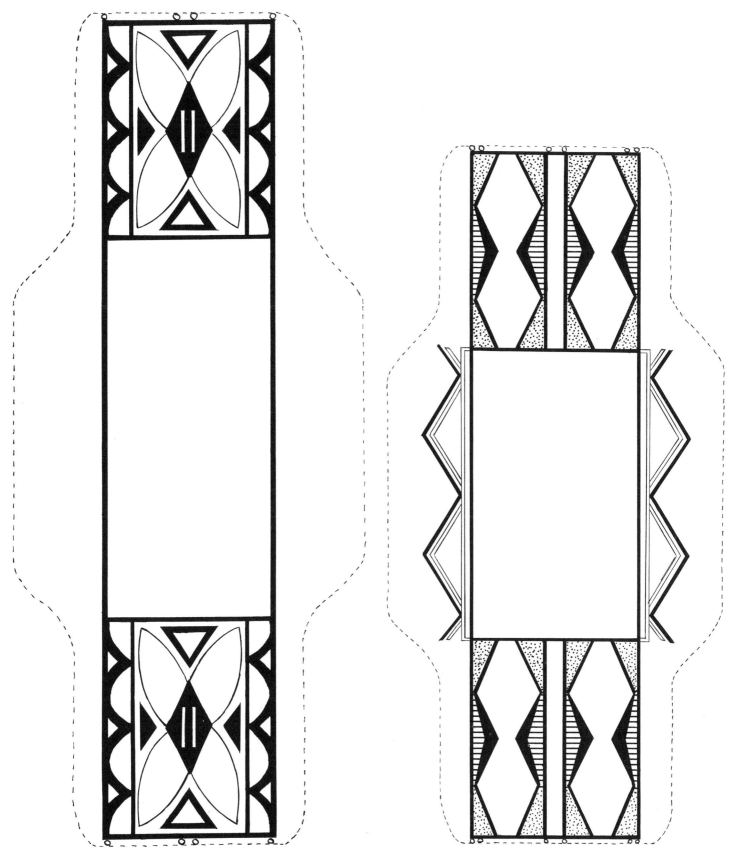

A Teton Dakota parfleche from Pine Ridge, South Dakota. The side flaps of the Dakota parfleches, such as the one sketched here, were not painted, but the upper, or end, flaps were decorated and connected by two bands of color. The decorated ends were closed and tied together. Typical Dakota colors were deep yellow, blue, green, red, and black. This design is outlined in black. (American Museum of Natural History)

HOLES: single, pair, single (see page 187).

A Klikitat meat case, probably of buffalo calf hide

The techniques of manufacturing a rawhide parfleche differed among groups and even individual workers. The exact method of working was determined by the condition of the hide, whether green or dry; the weather; the immediate need for a bag or parfleche; the amount of other work to be done (such as drying meat); and whether the group was traveling, following the buffalo herd, or living in a fairly permanent place.

Many excellent craftswomen used the following steps in making their painted parfleches. The buffalo was skinned and butchered where it was killed, the butcher knife being of stone (obsidian or flint), bone, or other material such as a beaver's tooth. It had to be very sharp to cut tough rawhide. The green hide was carried to camp and fleshed as soon as possible; then it was staked out, flesh side up. The hide was washed, worked down to a uniform thickness, and sized while it was still wet. The designs were laid out on the hide. The paints, which had been previously collected and prepared, were applied and the design outlined. The second sizing was applied, and the hide was allowed to dry slowly. When it was thoroughly dry, the stakes were removed and it was turned over, hair side up, on a thick layer of clean grass. The hair was removed by pounding with a stone. Then the painted parfleche was cut from the hide, folded, and the holes for closing burned into the rawhide.

There were many variations of this method, but skilled workers always pounded the hair off after the hide had been painted and dried. When all was finished, the flesh side was the outside of the painted parfleche.

A good worker fleshed a hide, staked it out, and washed it in one day. At least three days of work all together were required to turn a green hide into a painted rawhide parfleche under the best conditions. Usually two weeks were required, including time for slow drying.

Other methods of working were dictated by necessity. A green hide might be staked out and left to dry and bleach. The "flint" dry hide might be put away until the craftswoman had need for it or the time to work on it. The dry hide was then softened by burying it in wet sand or putting it, weighted down, into a creek.

The hide was sometimes dehaired with a kind of hoe, but dehairing in this way removed the epidermis which would be the inside of the parfleche and left it rough and difficult to keep clean. Rawhide made in this way was more liable to buckle, curl, or warp if it became damp.

Pounding off the hair with a fairly heavy stone

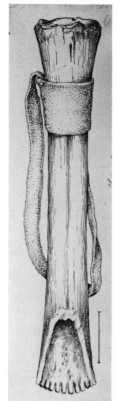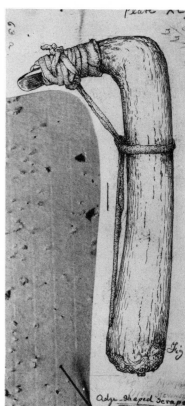

Tools used in the preparation of rawhide: left, a toothed bone fleshing tool; right, an adz-shaped scraper. (Bureau of American Ethnology)

whitened and softened the hide a little. The second method of whitening was accomplished by bleaching in the elements. Hoeing off the hair did little to soften or whiten the hide.

SKINNING

When the hide was to be used, great care must be taken in removing it from the animal, so that as few knife marks as possible would be visible. One method of removing a hide was by hanging the animal so that the hide could be pulled off. This required little or no use of the knife. Non-Indian professional buffalo skinners hitched a horse to the hide to pull it off.

FLESHING

Most of the rawhide craftswomen felt that there was a definite advantage in fleshing the hide as soon as possible after the animal was killed and before the fat and blood adhering to the hide were allowed to soak into it and dry. Each worker had her own method of fleshing. Some threw the green hide over a post and worked from the center toward the edge. Others hung the hide up by a corner and worked from the center out, hanging it by another corner when the first quarter was finished. A third craftswoman might stake out the hide a few inches above the ground and flesh it in that position, although most of the women interviewed said that they preferred to flesh the hide before staking it out. If the hide showed signs of drying before the fleshing was finished, water was thrown on it.

The flesh must be removed carefully because that side would be the outside of the parfleche. As has been pointed out, the flesh side was always outside except for the old incised parfleche in which the hair side was the exterior. Deep cuts or gouges ruined the smooth surface of the finished article and so were avoided as much as possible.

Fleshing tools were made of stone with the edge flaked off, elk antler, or bone, such as the cannon bone of a buffalo cut diagonally so as to give an edge and notched along this sharpened end. The shin bone of an elk was also used as a fleshing tool, the lower or working edge thinned and notched. Many of the fleshing tools were about the shape of a chisel and had a leather wrist loop.

STAKING OUT THE HIDE

If there were any holes or slits in the hide, a good worker mended them carefully with sinew before staking it out. Then with a sharp knife she cut slits about six to ten inches apart all around the edge of the hide. The worker learned by experience how far from the edge to cut the slits. Pegs were put through these slits and driven into the ground, and the hide was stretched to make it smooth and even when dry. It was thicker through the center from head to tail and thinner on the sides, which had been on the belly of the animal. If the hide should tear at any stake while drying, the painted parfleche might be ruined by drying unevenly.

In the days when large animals were plentiful, the hide was trimmed to an approximate rectangle; the legs and some of the thin sides were removed and discarded.

Some thought had to be given to the place where the hide was to be staked out. It might need protection from the sun, dust, or rain, or it might be placed where the worker would be protected from the wind and heat. Most workers staked out the wet hide about six to ten inches above the ground, which must be smooth, and dry grass was usually placed under the hide.

The best weather for making rawhide was clear with a light wind and without too hot a sun. Since trees were uncommon in parts of the Indian country except along the streams, the craftswoman often protected the hide from the sun by staking it out under a "shade" or in a lodge and sometimes erected a lodge over the stretched hide. Nearly every family built a shade of poles brought from along the river, using about eight uprights with several poles across the top. On these was placed a thick covering of cottonwood or pine boughs. In addition, the hide might be further protected by stretching a piece of buckskin, canvas, or blanket above it. The sun should not strike the painting while wet. Often a fence of brush was built around the hide to keep small children and animals away.

In winter the hide must be protected from freezing. Winters could be very cold, but winter was the very time a woman often was free to work on hides. More than one worker told how she had put a double cover on the lodge at night to protect the hide on which she was working and then took it off the next morning when the sun came out so that she could see to work. Two coverings made the lodge very dark.

Stakes used for pegs were made with care from ash, wild cherry, or willow; and, as few hardwoods were available in much of the buffalo country, these stakes were kept in a rawhide bag when not in use and used again and again. Each worker had a type of stake which she liked best. Some insisted on a forked stick which they said would never loosen as the hide dried. Others, however, used a straight stick and drove it in at an angle. One fork of a stake was shorter than the other. The stake was pounded in as far up as the end of the shorter fork. The craftswomen say that the drying of the hide forced this stake into the ground rather than pushing it out.

Before starting to stake out a hide, the worker inspected it to see there were no dry spots, for it must be thoroughly and uniformly wet.

Experience told the worker how much to stretch the hide. Most workers tried to have it about the same size as it was on the animal. Stretching must not all be done around the edge as that was already the thinnest part. The hide from along the backbone and shoulders was heavy and thick and should be stretched out as much as possible. The hump of the buffalo must be stretched if it was to be used. Sometimes a hide was cut through the center from head to tail and the two pieces staked out. This was done in order to assist in stretching out the hump.

The first stakes were usually placed opposite each other, one at the head and the other at the tail. After this the sides were stretched and pegged

A Dakota woman staking out a green hide, photographed about 1940. The hide was staked out several inches above the ground with large, heavy pegs, hair side down. (Photograph by Helen M. Post)

This photograph was taken after a buffalo hunt on the Upper Missouri River in 1870. Dakota women from the Cheyenne River Reservation are shown staking out a hide. The hides in the background have already been stretched. Meat has been hung to dry on poles near the lodges. (Bureau of American Ethnology)

out. If a hide was not stretched enough, it would be bumpy and have an uneven surface; if it was stretched too tight, a heavy hide would break almost any stake as it dried. There was a terrific pull on these stakes as the hide dried, and the whole hide might be spoiled if a stake broke or pulled out during the drying. The stakes shown in old photographs look large and heavy.

WASHING AND WORKING THE HIDE

Every rawhide craftswoman wanted her rawhide to be white, and the first step in producing a white hide was thorough washing. This was no easy job because a green hide from a full-grown buffalo might weigh as much as fifty pounds when the hair was dry and weighed much more when the hair was wet. A wet hide was very heavy to handle. If put in a stream, the hide would slow the current and soon be covered with silt.

The following method produced the desired results. After the hide was fleshed and staked out, water was thrown on it and then scraped off. This process was repeated over and over until the hide was clean. The washing and scraping not only cleaned the hide but helped to deodorize and whiten it as well.

The scraping was done with a dull knife or bone or by another ingenious method: the rough side of a buffalo's tongue was used to wash and scrape the tissue off the hide. The tongue was kept in a container of water beside the staked-out hide. This method of washing the hide had one advantage. It required very little water, which was scarce in many places. In summer, many of the water holes dried up, and in winter it might be necessary to melt snow.

Part of the water used on the hide could be soapy through use of the root of the native yucca, which makes a suds even in cold water. The root was pounded to release the "soap" and then whisked in the wash water. The Indians also knew how to use wood ashes for cleaning.

If the hide was dry, it might be softened and washed at the same time by putting it in a stream of running water. One end of a rawhide rope was tied to a corner of the hide and the other to a tree or bush on the bank. The hide was then placed in the stream, and the women waded in, barefoot, to place rocks on the hide so that it would stay under water. The rocks were moved often so that the hide would be thoroughly softened and washed. It was necessary to watch it constantly so that it would not be destroyed by dogs or other animals.

The women did not allow the hide to stay in the water long enough for the hair to begin to slip. In many places, however, it was not possible to put hides in running water, for many streams were completely dry in summer or so low and slow that they could not be used. In the winter they were frozen. The Indian craftswomen learned to adapt their methods to climatic conditions. It might even be necessary to bury the hide in wet sand. No matter what method was used, the hide had to be perfectly clean and worked down to a uniform thickness by scraping with a bone tool.

SIZINGS AND THEIR APPLICATION

The dictionary defines size as a "thin glutinous wash for glazing the surface of a material" and varnish as a "more or less viscid liquid, usually a solution of resinous matter in an oil or volatile liquid which, when spread upon a surface, dries either by evaporation or chemical action, forming a hard lustrous coating capable of resisting more or less the action of air and moisture."

The materials used by the Indians for sizing rawhide might be either a size or a varnish. A great variety of materials were available and were used by different groups. These sizing materials were also used in painting tanned robes but in a different way. For rawhide the entire skin was covered. For a robe only the painted area was covered or narrow white bands of sizing formed part of the painted design. Indians were using sizing in this manner when the first Europeans arrived.

At some undetermined date the rawhide craftswomen discovered that if a piece of rawhide was given a coat of size or varnish, it resisted the action of the sun, air, and moisture. Since the oldest pieces extant are covered with size, sizing must be a very old procedure. The use of sizing may have developed through a desire to protect the contents of the parfleche or, at a later date, to preserve the beauty of the painted design. The sizing on some ceremonial or medicine bags seems to be more important than the design or color.

A rawhide bag or parfleche must stand severe treatment. Sacred or ceremonial bags often hung outside the lodges except in the worst weather. All types of bags or cases might be carried on a person's back, on a dog travois, on a pack horse, or cached in the ground or in a tree where they might remain for months or even years. The contents must be kept dry and painted designs must not fade. Different groups found many ways of making these parfleches moisture-proof and color fast.

Sizings included cactus juice, hide scrapings, antler or horn glue, fish roe, the lymph from a fish, a gland from an elk or buffalo, wax from the tail of a beaver, or liquid from animal eyes. Varnish was made from resin or gum from wild cherry, piñon, tamarack, and other trees. Gallstones from a buffalo were also used.

Rawhide workers probably used more prickly pear cactus than any other material for sizing. It was common in most of the buffalo country and could be kept for some time without spoiling. Each worker had her own way of handling this medium. One said that she selected a succulent prickly pear stem and burned off the spines with torches made of sticks (the Indians had no paper at that time). The cactus was then pared or skinned and rubbed over the wet hide. When dry, the hide had a smooth, glossy finish. Some rawhide workers boiled the cactus in water for a short time, while others said that they boiled it from one to three hours. The liquid was used as a covering for the hide. When prickly pear was not available, the pincushion or other cactus was used. Various materials gave a different appearance to the finished parfleche.

A size made from hide scrapings was favored by some workers. It may have been used when and where cactus was not available. Further, cactus could not be used in winter. Hide scrapings, the thin pieces of hide which had been shaved off in the process of reducing the hide to a uniform thickness, were saved and boiled for sizing or glue. An older Indian woman said that she covered the scrapings with a little water and boiled them for a short time. This thin, gluey substance was smoothed over the wet hide. Any sizing not used was cooled and made into balls or sticks for later use. Some Indians living west of the plains used fish roe for sizing, while others used the liquid (lymph) found just under the skin of a fish.

Gum and resinous materials were collected from wild cherry bushes and various trees. These were boiled for a long time and often combined with other substances to size rawhide.

Some of the very old women told of waxing rawhide with a skinned and heated tail of a beaver. This gave the same finish that wax gives to material today. They said that they put the wax over the whole hide once and over the design twice, making the design stand out.

Two methods of applying size were most frequently found. The partly dry hide was covered with size, then the paint was applied and given a coat of size; or the designs might be painted on the unsized rawhide and the whole hide given a coat of size and allowed to dry.

The coat of size or varnish applied to the flesh side made the skin smooth and glossy. It gave the paint a luster and preserved the design. It protected the rawhide from soiling easily and kept out moisture in wet weather; in effect, it rain-proofed the rawhide. It was possible to clean rawhide parfleches with yucca root and a little water if they had been well sized.

RULERS—LAYING OUT THE DESIGN

When the washing of the hide was finished, the scraping off of moisture continued until no more could be removed in this manner. The hide must be at a certain stage of wetness or dryness before it could be sized, the design laid out, and painted. It might be necessary to allow it to dry for a time. The impressions made by the rulers told the craftswoman when the hide was ready. One informant said that the painting was started about the time the hide stopped shrinking or about the time the glue came up.

Each rawhide craftswoman owned a little bundle of peeled willow sticks which served as rulers. These were of the same diameter but of several lengths with two to four of each length. The willows were about the size of an ordinary lead pencil in diameter, and the length of each equaled the length or width of a structural part of the design. The dimensions of the willow sticks partly account for standardization of design or at least for the size of the design area. The sticks were used for curves by tying a string to the ends and bending the willow like a bow, thus providing a marker for a segment or part of a circle.

These sticks were also used in painting designs. Paint was rubbed in on large areas with the ends of the sticks, and dots were made by dipping the end of a stick in paint and then pressing it on the wet rawhide. When not in use, the willow sticks were carefully tied in a bundle and put away with the paints and other articles which the worker used. The worker might also have some triangles, squares, or other design units cut from rawhide or other material for marking out the minor design units.

The worker had her pigments, painting bones, paint pans, and rulers ready. She had her design "dreamed" or visualized and her assistants on hand. Now the painting of the rawhide began. She started by laying out, with the longer of willow sticks, the outer lines or frame of the design. For this two pairs of sticks, one longer than the other, were used. When these sticks were in the desired position, she pressed them into the wet hide with her thumb and forefinger. The impression left on the rawhide served as a guide for the painted lines. The width of the lines or bands of color in the design were determined by the diameter of the willow sticks, the thickness of the disk of color, or the point of the painting bone. After the outside lines were finished, the design units were filled with color.

THE BRUSH OR STYLUS

The bone brush of the rawhide painter is more accurately termed a stylus. It was cut from the cancellous inner part of large bones or joints. The shape of these bone brushes was dictated by the fancy of the worker, but was more or less wedge-shaped with rounded outline. Held in one way, it could be used for drawing fine lines; given a quarter turn, it served the purpose of spreading the color over a large area. These bones, being porous, picked up and held a quantity of paint. Buffalo bones were better, closer grained, than cattle bones.

One worker described the making of these bone brushes in this manner. The shoulder bone of a buffalo was split into small strips about one and one-half inches wide by three to four inches long. One end of these strips was whittled down to about one-fourth of an inch thick and the edges tapered slightly.

Dry pigment was sometimes rubbed into large areas on the wet hide with a finger or the rounded end of a willow stick.

COLOR AND ITS APPLICATION

The Indians always had a variety of pigments sufficient to execute pleasing designs. In old vocabularies words for blue paint, green paint, and red paint are found. Most of the native paint used on rawhide was made from minerals, but some vegetables and animal paints were also used. All the tribes could have yellows, reds, and blacks with little trouble. Many greenish or reddish-yellows were used, but orange almost never.

The tribes living near the Bear Paw Mountains in Montana used rose and soft violet, which they found on the side of a cliff. The Indians living near the Rocky Mountains could get almost any color that they wanted, including blue, green, and a very beautiful red. Men hunting in the Rockies often brought back paint. The red from caves near Helena, Montana, is widely known. The Dakotas used a dark blue paint which they secured near Blue Earth and Manakato, Minnesota; tribes living near the Missouri River found blue and other colors in crevices along the river banks. Rock paints were pigments found between layers of rock, having been carried there by a seepage of water through minerals. Indians living west of the plains tell of collecting paint from the high rimrocks near Mitchell, Oregon. A black stone found near Ouray, Utah, which was pounded up and used for brown-black, was widely known. Some tribes pulverized lignite and used it for paint. Iron oxides and cinnabar furnished yellows and reds, while greens and blues came from copper ores and phosphate of iron.

A dark blue paint was made by boiling white maple bark with roasted yellow ocher. A rose-red paint was made from the ripe fruit of cactus. A vegetable blue was made from wild grapes and a green from fresh algae. These faded very little when covered with sizing. Greenish-yellow was made from wolf's moss (*Evernia vulpina*), a lichen which grows on trees; ocher yellows were more common. Fungus found on trees furnished pigment in the Northwest. Some groups said that they made blue from the crushed fresh flowers of the larkspur which was plentiful in many places on the western plains and in the mountains.

Paint was an article of trade between groups or individuals long before the white trader arrived. It was expensive, held in great respect, and cared for as carefully as gold dust. Each color was kept in a separate little buckskin bag often exquisitely decorated.

The Blackfeet and other tribes had members who were known as paint gatherers, whose task it was to go for paints and bring them back to the rest of the tribe. Walter McClintock tells us that "Paint gatherers traded with their own people and with other tribes. Yellow came from a place on the Yellowstone River near some warm springs. Yellow also came from Buffalo gallstones, black from charred wood, blue from a dark blue mud, green from the scum of a lake. It was customary for women while digging for paint to pray to the Sun in behalf of some prominent Medicine Man."

Certain individuals were much better at preparing paint than others. Some groups might go to their medicine man for paint; he spent long hours preparing it and charged accordingly. Even today there are persons who know how to make paints in the old way and craftswomen who buy from them.

Any of the Indian groups could have painted rawhide with the colors found within a short radius of their lodges. Since it was not customary to use a large number of colors on any one piece of rawhide, two colors and a dark outline were usually sufficient. Pigments were combined with water, cactus juice, boiled sinew, resin, or salmon roe.

The Indians did not use much black in rawhide designs except for outlining and for very small units. Many of them realized that black outline made the colors appear brighter and clearer and gave unity to the design. Much of the black, which never faded, was a mineral containing iron ore. It was not a true black, but varied from medium brown to dark brownish-black. (Indian women usually refer to brown as black. The brown side of the buffalo hide is the "black side.") It was used to outline the figures on buffalo robes and is still used to lay out the design on moccasins.

Every worker had a favorite place where she secured black. Some said that it was always in thin veins near yellow earth. The Northern Arapahos liked that found on the banks of the Powder River; the Western Dakotas favored certain buttes in the Black Hills; the Montana Assiniboins liked to go across the Canadian line near a lake where they said the black pigment bubbled up out of the ground. Still others took their black from the bottom of certain springs of water. This black was usually found in small quantities or in thin veins which ran out or were quickly exhausted. It was soft and slimy when found, but could be dried and kept indefinitely. Certain legends are connected with the collection of black paint. One is that an individual must not talk while approaching the spot or while taking the black paint. If a word is spoken, it will go away.

Red pigment was sometimes found in an almost pure form, but some of the reds used by Indians were made. Yellow earth was collected very carefully, and all grit, sticks, and other foreign matter removed. A small amount of water was added, and the mixture was patted into thin cakes. When dry, the cakes were burned in a fire of buffalo chips. It was necessary to know how hot to make the fire, how to make a fire without smoke, and how long to keep the cakes in the fire. When the yellow cakes were taken from the fire, they might vary in color from a very bright red to a dark brownish-red, according to the skill of the worker in regulating temperature and timing. These cakes were easily pounded into a fine powder, which might be ground between stones and then between the thumb and forefinger before it was ready for use.

Other pigments secured from cliffs or caves might be ground between two stones and mixed with water. The mixture was then put in a buckskin bag, which was hung up in such a way that the pigment dripped into a second bag. Placed immediately under the second bag was a third one into which a little of the finest pigment would drain. When this was dry, it was placed in a small buckskin bag for future use.

Some Indians said that they went out on the flat prairie and dug white earth, which was made into balls about as large as a baseball and baked in a fire. The centers would then be red. After the ball had been thoroughly soaked in water, the red paint could be squeezed out.

For black, some of the groups used charcoal made by burning a certain wood or grass. This might be mixed with clay. Still others boiled the root of the black walnut tree for a long time. This last probably gave the nearest to a true black.

Many of the old rawhide pieces have more of the old brown-black than the modern ones. Formerly colors were difficult to secure and expensive to buy. Native vermilion pigment was worth four dollars an ounce in trade. Paint was very precious.

Earth paint had a quality of belonging, of being a part of the hide, not something put on top. This

O INCHES 1 2 3 4 5 6

Top: the seven disks are disks of pigment with which some workers painted on wet rawhide. The disk was held between the thumb and the forefinger, and lines were drawn and spaces filled in without brush or stylus; the disk took the place of both. Below: porous bones, or styli, typical of those used by the Indian women (who mixed their paints in clam or turtle shells). The bone was held by the blunt end and dipped into the paint. The point was used for drawing lines and given a quarter turn for spreading color over a large area. Buffalo bones were closer-grained than those of cattle. (Chicago Museum of Natural History)

quality, combined with the practice of putting the paint on the wet hide, often resulted in the finest folk art.

There were two methods of applying the paint, and the choice seems to have been an individual one rather than a group preference. For the sake of clarity we will call one of them the dry method and the other the wet method. Craftswomen who used the dry method did not need a paint pan or brush of any kind. They painted with a large disk or pencil of color made from sizing and pigment. When new, the disks might be as large as three or more inches in diameter and looked much like a large blue, red, green, or yellow cookie. Each of these was kept wrapped in a piece of buckskin so that the colors would not become mixed. In the wet method, the pigment was mixed in a liquid sizing and then painted on the wet hide.

Disks were made in different ways. One worker described her method thus: After she had secured

A Teton Dakota woman painting a parfleche with a porous buffalo bone. This photograph was taken on the Rosebud Reservation by John A. Anderson about 1890. The hide has been staked out with the hair side down. The woman has finished painting one parfleche and is working on the second flap. Her position is the typical one taken by a craftswoman while painting a wet hide. The designs are alike, as is customary on a pair of parfleches. The hide in the background has been painted and dried, and the stakes have been removed. It has not been dehaired. The hair was pounded off before the painted containers were cut from the hide.

the pigment, she obtained a large succulent stem of a prickly-pear cactus, singed off the spines, and peeled one side of the cactus stem. Then she poured the dry pigment on the peeled side of the cactus and mixed it with the cactus juice. This was scraped off the cactus and formed into a cake. The process was repeated until the cake was the desired size, and then it was dried. When she had finished a disk of each needed color, she was ready to start painting.

Another craftswoman might burn the spines from the cactus and peel both sides. She would start the disk with a drop or two of juice and pigment, then pass the cactus over it and dip it in the dry pigment, repeating the movements until the disk was quite large.

A third worker might use this "cookie" recipe. She would boil the cactus about three hours, adding water from time to time. Then she would take the pigment mixed with water and put it in a buck-

skin bag to drip. The dripped color was made into a cake and then put in the cactus juice to absorb as much liquid as possible. If cactus was not available, resin could be used, but it is more brittle and so not as good.

A fourth worker collected a number of eyes from buffalo after a hunt and used the liquid from these eyes to form the pigment into a disk. "Pencils" were made in the same way, but shaped into a short cylinder, though these seem to have been less popular than disks.

The wet method of painting required the craftswoman to have a paint pan and bone brush or stylus for each color. Some workers had six to eight mussel shells in which the pigment was mixed with a liquid and kept until used. The Dakotas often used the shells of the ornate box turtle (*Terrapene ornata*) which was found on the prairie. Turtle shells are deeper than clam shells and hold a larger quantity of paint. The shell of this turtle measures about four to four and one-half inches across and is not as flat as many other turtle shells. After the turtle was killed, the shell was removed and thoroughly cleaned and boiled before using. The paint was rather thick and the hide wet. The pigment might be mixed in the shell with cactus juice and painted on the wet hide, or it might be mixed with water and painted on the hide and then covered with cactus juice. Turtle and clam shells have been found in old caches with the paint still in them.

For both methods the worker held the bone brush or disk of pigment in her hand and drew the lines toward herself; kneeling on the ground beside the staked-out hide, she painted without any means of holding the hand steady. An accurate eye and well-controlled hand, arm, and back muscles were necessary for painting on wet hide. The lines must be right the first time since little or no changes could be made, although some workers say that a painted design could be erased or blotted out by rubbing a piece of roasted liver over it while the design was still wet. The Indians, however, did not do much erasing or changing. Their plans were definite in the beginning, and they adhered to them. This is an Indian standard today. The design is made "right" the first time and they seem satisfied with it when it is finished.

Painting on a wet skin allowed the paint to penetrate and become a part of the hide. The result was more permanent than when the painting was done on dry hide. Methods of working rawhide varied so much that it is often difficult to make a definite general statement, but almost everyone painted the *wet* hide and the *flesh* side. The women said that the paint adhered to the flesh side, took the sizing better, and was whiter. They had learned, through experience, that the dehaired side was better on the inside of the parfleche.

It would take a woman all day to paint two parfleches (a pair of the envelope type). She would start early in the morning, rest for a time at noon, and finish about dark. Since all painting on a hide must be finished before it dried, a woman desiring to paint a pair of parfleches might ask one or two other women to help her, or a mother and daughter might work together. Because the hide was large and pegged above the ground, a woman needed to move around the hide as she worked. A wet hide could not be turned. If she had helpers, she would not need to change position as often. When a woman had one or more assistants, it was necessary that they thoroughly understood the designs to be painted.

When Europeans came to the Indian country, they soon offered the people imported pigments in small wooden boxes. The old journals of trading posts list the following pigments: vermilion, red lead, chromate of lead (yellow), Prussian blue, chrome green, lampblack, Chinese white, oxide of zinc, and verdigris. The dry pigments which the Indians purchased could be used in the same manner that their own paints had been used. There was no need for a change in technique. These intense colors were generally accepted by the Indians, but they lacked the beauty of the old natural ones and the designs suffered from the lack of light and dark. The Indians still retained the old earth black and outlined the "post" colors in it. By this time, however, the decline in rawhide technique had begun.

OUTLINING

Outlining was used on many of the old parfleches. It was done after the design had been painted and was partly dry. In most cases it was the white- or natural-colored background spaces which were outlined, not the colored units of the design. The Indian was very much aware of the background spaces as an integral part of the design and frequently made use of them. The designs stood out better on rawhide when the outlining was done at the end.

Most of the outlining was done with the old earth black, which varied from a medium brown to a rusty black. This natural black was never given up or exchanged for "store-bought" paint as the other colors were. It was called ink and was the material used to draw designs on robes or outlines on buckskin before it was embroidered.

Sometimes the outline was burned into the rawhide. This gave much the same effect as the old brown earth paint, but close examination will show a depression. A painting bone or stone was heated and the outline burned with this. Lewis and Clark found the Cheyennes with designs burned on their buckskin clothing.

A few tribes used a dark blue or dark green to outline the designs on their rawhide parfleches. Green outlining was used by groups living over the mountains west of the plains, and in the eastern plains the Sacs used it on their trunks. Blue was seldom used as an outlining color, but occasionally was used as narrow construction lines with no outline. Designs without any outline were typical of some groups. The color of the outlining and the width of the line are tribal characteristics; for example, the Dakotas used intense colors with a heavy black outline. This heavy black in designs was typical of groups that lived toward the northwestern coast, along the Columbia River, and on the periphery of the plains.

DRYING

After the rawhide was painted it might have a second coat of sizing, or the design areas alone might be sized, before it was allowed to dry. For drying a painted hide, the women used sunshine without too great heat. Drying the painted hide was very important, and it took an experienced worker to know how to dry the hide slowly and evenly under all atmospheric conditions. She might give the painted rawhide two weeks or more to dry before pounding off the hair and cutting it into parfleches and bags. When it was thoroughly dry, the hair might be pounded off at the convenience of the maker.

DEHAIRING

Indian women used several methods of removing the hair from the hide: "stoning," "hoeing," and "slipping." Stoning is probably the oldest method, hoeing being typical of some pieces of rawhide made after 1880.

Dehairing by the stoning method was nearly the last step in the making of a rawhide container. After the craftswoman had fleshed, pegged out, washed, sized, painted, and dried the hide, she removed the stakes, turned the hair side up, and laid it out on a pad of dried grass or buckskin to protect the painted designs. Next, taking a rather large, heavy "water" stone with a flat side, she removed the hair by striking the hide a slanting blow with the lay of the hair; if the blow was struck against the hair, the hair was broken off short so that it was very difficult to remove. The worker began in the center of the hide and worked toward the edges. Dehairing was an important step in the making of rawhide; removing the hair with a stone after the hide was painted and dried was the secret of fine Indian rawhide.

The craftswoman who removed the hair by hoeing might do so before the hide was painted or after it was dry. The instrument used was made of an elk horn bent to resemble a hoe. It had a cutting blade about two inches wide and a handle about one foot long. The worker stood on the dry hide, almost bent double, and made short strokes toward herself with this short hoe. This method removed the hair and the cutaneous tissue while stoning removed only the hair. Stoning, however, was more desirable because it left a smooth protective cover on the inside of the container.

The Indians also knew how to slip the hair with wood ashes. A paste of ashes and water was spread over the hair and the hide buried to keep it damp until the hair loosened. The hide could also be soaked in a stream until the hair slipped.

Pounding off the hair (stoning) left the outer layer of the hide (now the inside of the container) unbroken, so that moisture would be repelled and the skin could be cleaned more easily. In addition, the finished hide was more flexible and whiter, more pliable, and not as likely to curl under ordinary conditions. Both the hoeing and slipping methods removed the hair before the hide was painted, but did not provide a means for whitening and softening the hide. The painting was done on a medium-dark rawhide; after the hair was pounded off, the design was seen against a white (or off-white) background. Pounding with a rock was the hard way, but the best rawhide was made in this manner.

FINISHING

After the hide was dehaired, the parfleches were cut from it with a piece of obsidian, flint, clam shell, or beaver tooth following the lines marked out previous to painting. A pair of parfleches would take most of one hide, but, in addition, small bags, a knife sheath, or toys might be painted on the hide. Small pieces of unpainted rawhide might be used for moccasin soles.

After the parfleche was cut from the hide, it was folded much like an envelope. The side flaps were folded toward the center to meet or lap. Among some groups the side flaps were traditionally wider than those of other groups. A second fold was made by turning the ends in toward the center until they met. Folding the parfleche the first time was quite a task because the new rawhide was stiff and heavy. The folds and corners were pounded or weighted down until the parfleche would hold satisfactorily. Indian rawhide could be folded more easily when the hair was removed by pounding with a stone, thereby somewhat softening the hide. Also, buffalo rawhide differed from that of other large animals. Usually parfleches were not made from the heavier hides.

The parfleche was not complete until the holes were burned into the flaps. Burning the holes in was much better than cutting them. The burning formed a hard edge around the hole, which kept it from tearing and spreading. The burning was done by heating a bone, stone, or piece of metal and forcing the hot instrument through the hide. Occasionally stake holes were used in closing a parfleche. When these large holes were used, the pair

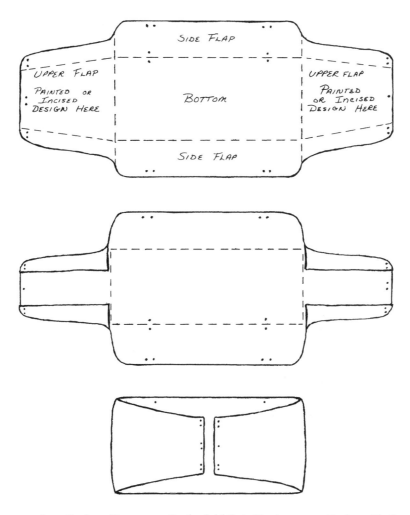

Diagrams of parfleches. Top: a parfleche laid flat. Center: a parfleche with the upper
side flaps folded. Bottom: a parfleche folded.

of parfleches had been cut from the green or wet hide and staked out separately. This method stretched out the hump and simplified the painting.

Each Indian group or tribe was fairly consistent in the combination of holes used for tying the parfleche. The number of holes and their location on the parfleche was predetermined by the tribal use of the parfleche. Today such holes also help to identify the tribe of the maker.

One method of closing the upper flaps was with one pair of burned holes in the center of the end of each upper flap. These might be tied together with a rawhide thong and then a thong was wrapped horizontally around the parfleche. One pair of holes was the method of closing used by the Arapahos, Crows, Nez Percés, and others. A variation was a double pair of holes, the second pair one inch to one and one-half inches back of the first pair. This double pair allowed for expansion of the parfleche when it was full.

Another scheme required one pair of burned holes in the center of the ends of the upper flaps and one hole at each outer corner. These corner holes could go through two thicknesses of hide, but were used as a single hole when tying. This is the method, which for the sake of brevity, is referred to as single, pair, single, or S.P.S. It is characteristic of the Dakotas, Cheyennes, Kiowas, and some other groups.

A third method consists of three pairs of holes in each upper flap, one pair in the center and a pair at the corners. It was characteristic of the Wishrams, Blackfeet, Kutenais, Sarsis, and some others. The Blackfeet burned in fourteen pairs of holes for closing their parfleches, three pairs on each upper flap, three pairs on each side flap, and two pairs in the crease where the side flap folded. All together these made twenty-eight pairs of holes for a pair of parfleches.

2. Rawhide Design

Rawhide decoration as an expression of Indian art is important since it developed before the Indians were influenced by European cultures.

In very early times the rawhide parfleche probably was not decorated. It is said that sometimes the hair was not removed; if this statement is true, some extra weight was added to the already heavy burdens which the people carried on their backs or packed on dog travois.

During the period of the great buffalo herds the type of design used on rawhide, known as parfleche or rawhide design, was rarely used on other materials or articles. The Indians painted elaborately beautiful robes, but the designs had little relationship to parfleche design. After the European trader arrived, bead embroidery made by the Crows and Osages showed some units adapted from rawhide design.

The parfleches now available for study were decorated by incising, by painting, and occasionally by burning parts of a design. Although the Indians knew about tooling leather, the technique never developed separately from painting on rawhide.

The rawhide craft passed from one generation to another. A mother taught her daughter, or a girl might act as her grandmother's assistant. An experienced craftswoman often helped other members of her clan. Women's societies controlled the rawhide craft; tribal ceremonial traditions provided the order for the procedure. A woman might have one, two, or three helpers when painting a pair of parfleches. This would mean that there were four identical designs to be painted. As described in detail earlier, the design was laid out with willow sticks, the size of which determined the size of the design and the width of lines or colored bands. Continued use of the same set of bone brushes or disks of color of the same thickness gave uniformity to the designs. Use of color varied from group to group according to the pigments available and group preference. When the women cached their parfleches together, they were not labeled, but all knew to whom a parfleche belonged by its individual characteristics.

The oldest designs on rawhide were characterized by simplicity of design, predominance of parallel lines, a large amount of neutral-colored background space, a few diagonal and curved lines for interest and accent, the use of unattached units in the design, and few colors—four or less, including the black outline, the use of earth and vegetable pigments, one of which provided dark for the design.

The designs on modern parfleches often show diagonal lines cutting the design into smaller units, larger amounts of design covered with bright colors, an increase in the number of colors used, all colors of the same value—less light and dark, more medium, with dark often missing altogether, even black outlines omitted by groups who formerly used them.

Rawhide design was not limited by the medium to the extent that a textile or a basket is controlled by techniques and materials. But to some extent the large moist hide, its bulk and weight, influenced the design. The hide was pegged out with long, heavy sticks about ten inches apart, which were always in the way, and the artist must not allow her hand to touch the wet, sized hide when she was painting.

The type of design developed by rawhide craftswomen might be considered a unit, with tribal and individual characteristics. The development of tribal patterns was partly due to the fact that certain women were recognized as being especially good at rawhide decoration so that gradually they became authorities on design and were asked to help other women. If more than one woman worked on a pair of parfleches, all must know the pattern to be painted or have the plan very clearly in mind.

The spaces decorated on the parfleches were the two upper flaps and occasionally the side flaps and back. The Crows, Arapahos, Shoshonis, and Kiowas painted only the upper flaps; the Cheyennes, Dakotas, Iowas, Kutenais, and Sarsis connected the two decorated areas on the upper flaps with bands of color; and the Jicarilla Apaches, Mescalero Apaches, Kutenais, Sarsis, Wascos, and Wishrams painted on the side flaps as well.

The space to be decorated on the upper flaps was square, rectangular, or trapezoidal. The painting of side flaps may have originated with the groups who used the trapezoidal flap—the Kutenais, Sarsis, and Blackfeet—but the Apaches and Wishrams had a rectangular decorated area and also decorated side flaps. The decorated area did not always coincide with the top of the parfleche. The decoration might be longer than the flaps and run over to the back. Thus the two entire designs would not be seen when the parfleche was closed;

40

instead, the two were then seen as one. This and the large number of vertical lines and figures give the impression of length to the design and the parfleche seems longer than it actually is.

Starting with the space to be decorated—square, rectangular, or trapezoidal—many of the designs were made by continuous division and subdivision. In this manner a surprisingly large number of designs could be worked out. Modern Crow designs are a good example of this subdivision. The Jicarilla Apaches and Upper Kutenais show less tendency to subdivide the area.

It was characteristic for all tribes, except the Mescalero Apaches and some of the Utes, to enclose the design in a band of color or a simple frame which followed closely the outline of the flap. A type of band or border was characteristic of a group:

1. No continuous band or border enclosing the designs as in some of the Mescalero and Ute designs.

2. A narrow band of one color on all four sides of the design, typical of the western groups: Shoshonis, Flatheads, Nez Percés, and other tribes to the west of the plains.

3. Two colors which form one narrow band, typical of Crow designs.

4. Two narrow bands of color with a neutral or white space between them, characteristic of the old Atsina designs.

5. Two bands of color as in No. 4 but joined occasionally by simple units of design, common on the parfleches of the Cheyennes, Arapahos, Kiowas, and related groups.

6. The more elaborate or true border used by the Siouan-speaking people, the Blackfeet and others.

Four types of lines are found on the parfleches. Parallel lines, meaning the lines in the design which are parallel, or nearly parallel, to the structural lines of the parfleche, predominate in many of the oldest designs. Genuine curves were used by a few tribes, and curved lines are found in the designs on old buffalo parfleches as well as on the modern ones made from cattle hides. Curves may have taken more skill. Some workers today are very definite in their dislike of curved lines, and they think that only straight lines should be used on rawhide. Some very pleasing designs with curved lines are found on the older pieces, however, and are characteristic of the Teton Dakotas, Mandans, Kutenais, Blackfeet, and some others.

Some free-hand lines are pleasing because they are not ruler straight, though the worker probably thought of them as straight. They always curved slightly into the design, leaving more background than if the lines were drawn with a ruler.

Diagonal lines were used more frequently on modern designs made after 1880 or 1890. These designs lost much of the simplicity and beauty of the old ones. In many groups, design can be traced from the oldest ones, with a predominance of straight lines and a few curved or diagonal lines for variety and accent, to the decline of the rawhide craft when diagonal lines divided the design into many small spaces.

Separate unattached units of design were occasionally used on parfleches. Black dots were often placed in rows, which gave the impression of a line rather than a spot. Many of the old rawhide craftswomen said that they liked black dots in a design. They used them to break up too large natural-colored spaces, to draw two parts of a design together or to make it into a unit, to lend interest, and to add dark to the design. Dots were found on the old designs from the Blackfeet, Hidatsas, Dakotas, Cheyennes, and Arapahos. White dots were sometimes used as negative designs to break up a painted area which the worker considered too large to be pleasing.

Often the side flaps did not seem to be as carefully painted as the upper flaps. Some workers seemed to use the color which was plentiful on the side flaps and reserve the rarer colors for the upper flaps. The designs on the side flaps had little or no relation to the design on the top of the parfleche. This seems to indicate that the decoration on the side flaps were for a different purpose than that on the upper flaps; some Indians said that the decoration on the side flaps was the more important. When bands of color connected the designs on the upper flaps, they often formed a base for the side flap decoration.

Types of decoration on the side flaps varied from group to group. Very wide flaps which overlapped had decoration on one flap only. Other decoration included two like bands of decoration, one on each flap, not attached to the other designs: two unlike bands not attached to the other designs; a design, not a border, attached to the colored bands which connect the designs on the upper flaps. All of these types are lengthwise of the side flaps, but others consisted of short horizontal designs made up of a number of small, short units of design. Another type of design is made up of lodges, hunters, animals, and trees, the type usually painted by the men. Some painting on the side flaps might have been for decoration only, but it appears that much of it was important or symbolic.

The decorated areas on the upper flaps were made up of units of design: bars, triangles, rectangles, squares, dots, and lines. The diamond or lozenge was not a favorite and was seldom used alone. Sometimes it is found as the center unit of a design or in a panel, but it usually has triangles attached to the points making the diamond into a double X or the diamond may be split through the center which divides it into two triangles. The Crows were an exception to this rule, often using the lozenge prominently in their designs. They said that it represented the sand lizard, their talisman. Kiowas call the lozenge the "parfleche design." Occasionally a diamond, cut symmetrically by both horizontal and vertical lines into four triangles, was made asymmetrical by the use of color. Asymmetry was common on parfleches made by the Blackfoot Confederacy, the Dakotas, and some of the tribes living northwest of the plains.

Filling a unit of the design with hatching and crosshatching was seldom done except on the old incised parfleches. The Indians said that it was used occasionally on modern pieces when a worker was short of colors. The crosshatching gave variety to her design, but it was only done as a last resort and was scorned by most craftswomen.

Rawhide as a medium discouraged elaborate design. Realistic design was very seldom used on parfleches, except occasionally on the side flaps, but a highly conventionalized flower design sometimes appeared. A certain amount of irregularity in parfleche painting was pleasing, but irregularity when carried to any extent looks like careless, poor work.

3. Symbolism

Many of the Indian women have said that they painted designs on their parfleches because they wanted them to be "pretty." In modern times many of these designs were purely decorative; the women used parfleches to beautify their lodges or to dress their horses when traveling or on parade.

Often the Indian women referred to drawing or painting a design as "writing" and to crosshatching as "scribbling." Their painting bones they called pens or pencils, and the old brown-black earth paint, ink. In times past, as now, the painting of rawhide was one way of self-expression. More than one old craftswoman said that the design on her bag or parfleche told what was in it; a certain type of design was used for certain possessions such as clothing, feathers, or dried meat.

In some groups a minor unit of design might have a name. For example, the small white or natural-colored squares or rectangles enclosed in a colored area was known by the Arapahos as "the place where the buffalo came into the world" (this was always in the mountains). This white space might be a negative design. The Dakotas used it and said it represented "the place through which the sun shines" or "where the light shines through." The cross in the center of a design or a panel was not a cross but a star, according to the Dakotas, Cheyennes, Arapahos, and Kiowas. The diamond was a turtle. Formerly eight-sided, it gradually developed into the diamond. Long lines were "trails."

Some designs themselves have names, but these may have no symbolic significance. The name may have been acquired after the article was finished in much the same way that colonial coverlets and quilts received names. Coverlet designs such as Whig Rose, King's Flower, and Lee's Surrender are well known. Names for rawhide designs were often acquired in the same way or from their fancied resemblance to an object. One old Dakota rawhide design was recently renamed the "bridge" design. It made the women think of the long bridge across the Missouri River. When the design was made, years ago, there were no bridges of this type. Another design was called a "train." In no way did the design resemble a train. The name came from glimpses of the sky or scenery seen between the different cars as the train passes by. This was interesting because these spaces might be background spaces in the design. In discussing a design with an older Indian, one expected her to talk about the painted area and was surprised to find that she was referring to the design made by the unpainted background. Other examples of designs with names are Rainbow from the Dakota and Butterfly from the Warm Springs Reservation.

The same unit of design has a different name on different reservations. For example, the black dot may be referred to as buffalo, coyote, or horse tracks, campsites, or people. Alfred L. Kroeber commented: "The series of six spots, which is repeated four times, denotes that Whirlwind Woman successively sat down in six places around the bag that she was painting with this design."[1] Whirlwind

[1] "The Arapaho," American Museum of Natural History *Bulletin*, Vol. XVIII, Part 1.

Woman is a mystical character who made the designs on Arapaho painted rawhide. A group of these small black triangular-like figures on the old Arapaho parfleches were always "bear hands," and the line of color in the corners of the borders of the Cheyenne parfleche might be termed the "life" symbol. The long, pointed, brown-earth triangles on Jicarilla Apache parfleches were called "fringe." Some designs belong to a clan, for example the fish design on a Fox trunk.

When an Indian wished to paint a rawhide, she did not work out a design on paper, but instead "dreamed" or visualized the design. Indians seemed to have more than an ordinary ability to form a mental image of the design in its entirety before they began to paint. After they had it clearly in mind, the strokes were firm and sure. There was no erasing or changing.

Dreams also enter into designs in a slightly different way. For example, a Dakota might say of a certain woman, "She ought to make good designs because she had a dream about Double Woman." This dream is considered very fortunate for anyone who has designs to make because she will have the help of Double Woman, a Dakota mystical character.

The men seldom helped with the painting of rawhide, but they sometimes made suggestions about designs. In a Dakota tale, a young warrior who was lost from his party hid in a clump of bushes to avoid the enemy. He was tired and went to sleep and was awakened by the morning sun shining in his face. When he looked up, he saw that a spider had woven a very beautiful web in many colors above his head. He lay there a long time studying the designs in the web. When he finally reached home, he helped the women make many rawhide designs from the patterns in the web.

A "dreamed" parfleche design found among the Oglala Dakotas was explained by the maker's friends. The old woman who made it died about 1891. She was known among her friends as Wase-O-Cin or Mrs. Begs-Paint. She acquired this name because she painted many rawhide parfleches and often ran out of paint. She called this design "karmni-mni-la." It was made after she had dreamed that she was in a very beautiful country where there were many beautiful lodges and all around them were flowers and butterflies. The next day she interpreted her dream in this design. The red triangles were the lodges and the blue diamonds in the white panels were butterflies.

Many of the older rawhide designs probably had symbolic significance to the originator, but only the maker could give an interpretation; others would be able only to generalize. The Crows said that the diamond on their parfleches represented the sand lizard and was a protection for the owner.

Symbolism in design was stronger among the Dakotas, Cheyennes, Wishrams, Arapahos, and Crows than in other groups. The Dakotas said that their concept of life included bravery, fortitude, generosity, and integrity and that they worked constantly to attain these qualities, which are listed in the accepted order of importance. Children learned early in life that one is respected according to his attainment of these attributes. They also learned that it was desirable to be respected.

A Dakota parfleche design often seen is very old and is known as the bravery design. The red diamond is a turtle, the stripes in the diamond are of heraldic significance, badges of distinction. They could be used by a family whose head was known to have distinguished himself in two ways. He might have been known for his bravery in battle and his generosity (he might have given away all his possessions one or more times). If his group recognized him as brave, generous, and a man of his word (integrity), his family could use three stripes in the decoration of their possessions.

On another parfleche, a fairly modern design was called the Distant View. It refers to the revered Black Hills. The blue triangular units at the sides of the panels represented tree-covered hills nearby. The yellow in the Dakota rawhide designs is a symbol for rocks as an example of something which lasts throughout the ages. To the Dakotas rocks and mountains were animate and objects of veneration. Leaders of the Indian groups went to the rocks to meditate, to look into the future, to receive strength for a difficult mission, and to ask help and protection.

4. The Incised Parfleche

A hide with a brown or browned epidermis was necessary for the manufacture of incised parfleche. The decoration was made by carving and peeling off small pieces of the dark outer layer of brown-pigmented skin. The design showed as light and dark only; no color was used. Buffalo hide lent it-

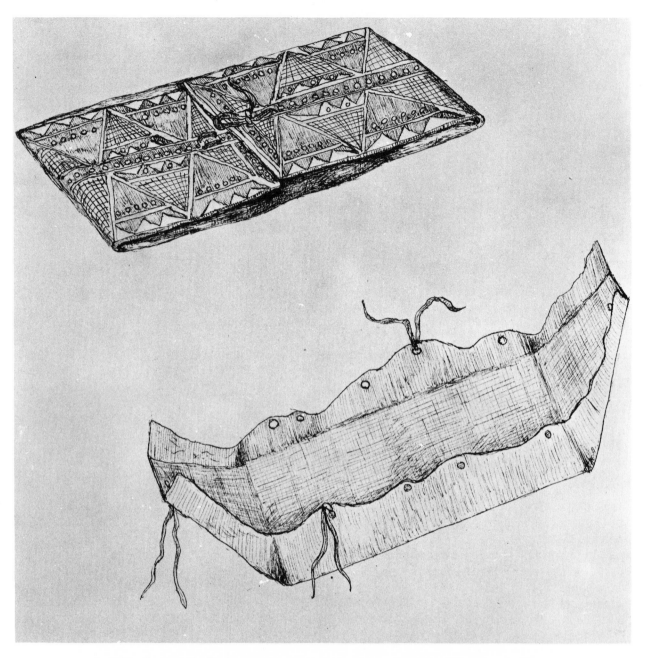

A design from an incised parfleche. The sketch below shows the parfleche open and the holes for closing. (Herman Haupt, Jr., "The North American Indians," unpublished manuscript, E. E. Ayer Collection, Newberry Library, p. 182)

self to this type of decoration because the outer layer of skin was brown. The summer hide was darker than the winter hide since the buffalo had shed most of its hair, thus exposing its hide to the sun.

The Indian tribes of the Northwest said that they sometimes used elk hides for making incised parfleches when buffalo hides were not available. The epidermis of the white elk hide was dyed or painted brown by rubbing in blood or blood mixed with other ingredients.

The older people of this region valued the in-cised parfleche highly and said that as long as they could remember these were used to hold surplus dried food. All this seems to indicate that the use of the incised parfleche is very old. It was certainly a definite and important part of these Indians' lives, and incised parfleches were in use until the present time in some of the far western groups. It may be that incising originated with the Columbia River group, the easternmost people of the Chinookan family, or among the Shahaptian groups and that the Plains people learned the techniques from them, carrying it from west to east. The Crows and

Incised parfleche. (Denver Art Museum)

45

other Plains groups went as far west as Oregon to trade. Some of the older women among the Dakotas said that they knew how to make incised parfleches but definitely liked gaily painted containers better.

Characteristics of the incised parfleche vary from tribe to tribe among the Columbia River groups. All the typical Northwest characteristics are found: the horizontal divisions in the designs, the use of a heavy stick to keep the parfleche distended when packed on a horse, one set of holes for tying when the parfleche was full and another pair of holes for use when it was empty. Crosshatching was common. On the plains crosshatching was said to be a Crow characteristic, but it has not been found on the painted Crow pieces available for study. Some of the incised parfleches show curved lines as well as straight ones, and it is often difficult to tell which part of the design was the background and which the design.

In preparation for an incised parfleche, the hair was removed with great care so that the outer brown layer of the buffalo hide was not marred. Skill was necessary in each step of the manufacture. Timing was important, and each step was determined by the condition of the hide: for example, the incising must be done while the hide was still damp and finished before it dried. Lines were made by cutting the damp hide with a sharp instrument. These cuts opened as the hide dried, exposing the white inner portion. In other units of the design the dark outer skin could be peeled from the hide after the sections had been outlined with a knife. Small dots were common in the designs in either white or brown.

A number of Crow women reported that they used a sharp bone knife for incising. The older women in the Northwest said that a sharp piece of obsidian was used and that they worked while kneeling beside the hide, drawing the lines toward themselves. For the incised parfleche they seem to have cut the hide into two pieces and staked these out separately, making it easier to reach the design area. Incised parfleches were made in pairs as were the painted ones.

The incising technique may be older than painting and may have originated with the people who made pottery or birchbark containers. In fact, they may have adapted the birchbark technique to rawhide. Birchbark was available in the Columbia River area and the Northwest. Archaeological evidence for the antiquity of incised work is provided by a Chinookan mummy which was found wrapped in an incised rawhide.

Herman Haupt, Jr., discussed the parfleche thus: "To carry the dried meat and other portable articles the Dakota Indian has recourse to the parfleche, or so to speak Indian trunk. It is a piece of raw buffalo hide folded so that it will form a rectangular package. The hide is first folded along two sides in parallel lines. The opposite edges are perforated and thongs of buckskin fastened to them by which the edges are tied together. The ends are then folded in toward the center and a thong is passed through holes in the middle line by which the parfleche is tied shut. The upper surface of the parfleche is ornamented in any way the fancy of the maker may dictate. Most frequently they are daubed with red, blue, green or other colored paint. More rarely the markings are burned or cut in the rawhide while green. Such is the method employed in ornamenting the one in the author's collection: the lines and points are cut with a knife on green hide. The parfleche is made from the skin of a buffalo calf and was procured at the 'Crow Agency' in Montana and was the only one so marked among a lot of fifty that were all of them painted. The cut or engraved specimens are extremely rare. Being rawhide they are almost indestructible and last an Indian almost if not quite a lifetime."[1]

Frank G. Speck told of the use of folded birchbark among the Algonquins for preserving dried and even fresh meat and also for storing clothing. These same Indians also used green elm or cedar bark for storing foods such as dried beaver tails and dried fish. Larger trunks of folded birchbark were used to store fur clothing in the summer. Says Speck: "The similitude of these bark folders to the parfleche of the Plains area is a feature of comparative ethnology not to be overlooked. It lies in their constructional simplicity and in their adaptation to the same economic purposes; namely, the preservation of dried meat and the storage of clothing. The textual quality of the wet green birchbark or elm bark closely resembles that of green rawhide, a fact not without interest in consideration of resemblances between Woodland bark containers and Plains Folk Art."[2] One of Speck's illustrations, Plate 32, shows a birchbark baby carrier used the same way as rawhide cradles.

The following groups are known to have made the incised parfleche: Wascos, Wishrams, Teninos, Tyighs, Nez Percés, and others.

[1] "The North American Indians" (unpublished MS in the Ayer Collection, Newberry Library), 182.
[2] "Art Processes in Birchbark of the River Desert Algonquin," *Anthropological Papers* No. 17, *B.A.E. Bulletin 128*, p. 239.

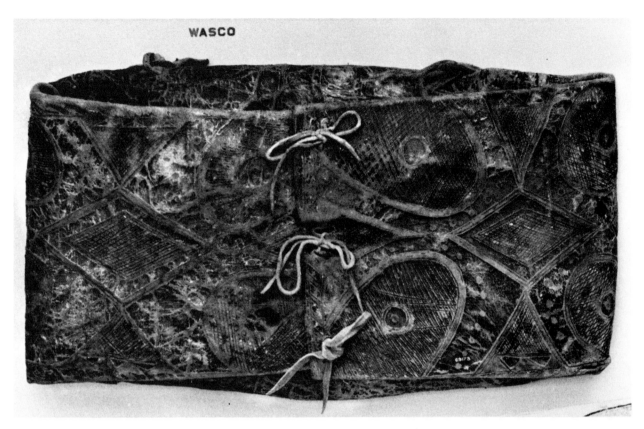

A very fine old Wasco incised parfleche, showing a combination of curved and straight lines. The skin is probably elk, browned with blood. (Chicago Museum of Natural History)

NOTES ON THE TRIBES

:×≡×≡×≡×≡×≡×≡×≡×≡×≡×≡×≡×

1. Algonquian Family

:×≡×≡×≡×≡×≡×≡×≡×≡×≡×≡×≡×

ARAPAHOS

The Arapahos are an important Algonquian-speaking group who have lived on the plains for a long time. They wandered over the Dakotas and Wyoming until 1876, when the parent group was assigned to the Wind River Reservation in western Wyoming and the group now known as the Southern Arapahos was settled on the Cheyenne-Arapaho Reservation in western Oklahoma. The Arapahos have been closely associated with the Cheyennes for over a century.

The use of rawhide is considered ancient by the Arapahos. There are stories woven into their mythology of "First Woman" or "Whirlwind Woman" teaching them how to make designs and use color on their parfleches. Elderly Arapaho women said that the five-block design on their parfleches was very old and that the design was known as "Wal-say-dad," or "Bear Hand," and could be made with or without claws. "Wal-say-dad" is an old Arapaho word. In the 1940's only the oldest people knew the word.

The Atsinas, an Arapaho group, broke away from the mother group a long time ago. The oldest surviving parfleches of the Arapahos and the Atsinas have similar designs. These may have been made before or soon after the groups separated.

Arapaho designs underwent changes as the Arapahos lived near other groups or were friendly with others. Some of the modern, or late, parfleches the Arapahos made have certain units of those of the Teton Dakotas of the same period, while the Atsinas adopted some of the characteristics of the Crows. The Arapahos themselves said that some of their designs came from the Apaches, but this statement does not seem to be substantiated by the many specimens studied.

There is little difference between Northern and Southern Arapaho parfleches. The two groups lived together during most of the time that buffalo rawhide was being made and visited each other after they were put on different reservations. Their parfleches are greater than average in length and quite wide. One pair of holes for tying was made in the center of the outer edge of each upper flap. The parfleche then was wrapped several times with a long rawhide thong and was secured to the saddle cinch with another thong. The Arapahos occasionally painted a number of blue bands horizontally across the backs of their parfleches. These may relate to the thongs with which they bound the parfleches.

Each of the upper flaps was painted with the same design, which was enclosed by a narrow border made up of two narrow bands of color with a neutral space between. A very simple bar connected the bands at the center of the top, bottom, and sides. The two designs on the upper flaps were not connected across the back, but narrow bands were painted on the side flaps.

The very old Arapaho designs were made up of blocks, but on modern parfleches the structural design was made by dividing the area vertically into two, three, or four panels, though two panels are by far the most common. Indeed, the most common types of modern structural design comprised two panels with four very long triangles or three panels with six long figures. On the Arapaho parfleche the painted area seems longer than it really is because of the longitudinal divisions and because of the number of lines in the design which are parallel or nearly parallel to the structural lines of the parfleche. This appearance is further enhanced by the absence of horizontal lines. The painted flaps are rectangular, and when the two are tied together, the completed parfleche has the appearance of length. Many of the lines are straight or what might be termed freehand straight lines. The women always called them "straight." The decoration on each upper flap averaged sixteen

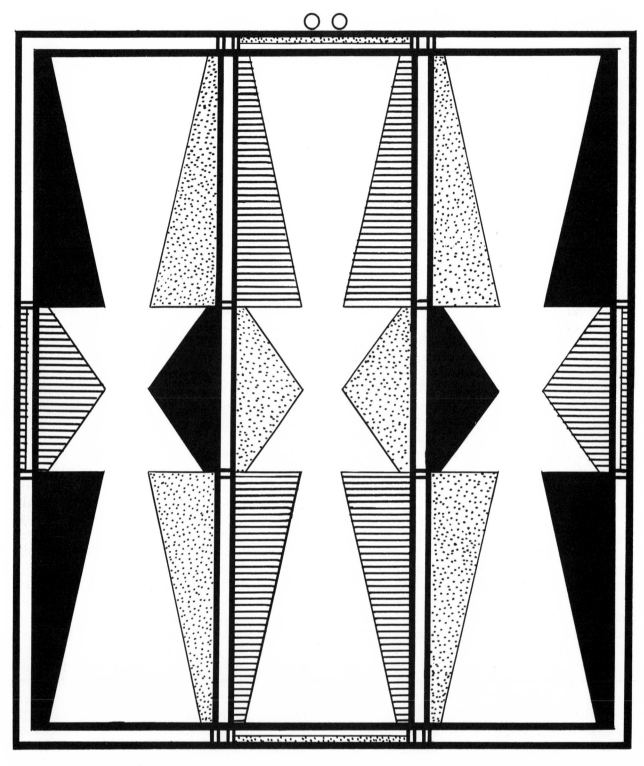

An Arapaho parfleche. The design is outlined in old black. (Milwaukee Public Museum)

HOLES: 1 pair. SIZE OF PARFLECHE: 54 x 15 in.

PARFLECHES

ARAPAHO (Northern)
(*Algonquian linguistic family*)
(See Chart of Parfleche Characteristics)
This design is from a parfleche (called *ham-wang* or *ham-itha*) of buffalo hide from
the Wind River Reservation, Wyoming. It was collected in 1900. (Chicago Museum
of Natural History)

HOLES: 1 pair in each upper flap, 3 pairs in each side flap. SIZE OF PARFLECHE: 62 x 15½ in.
SIZE OF DESIGN: 16¼ x 15 in. SIZE OF FOLDED PARFLECHE: 31 x 15½ in. BORDER: No. 5.

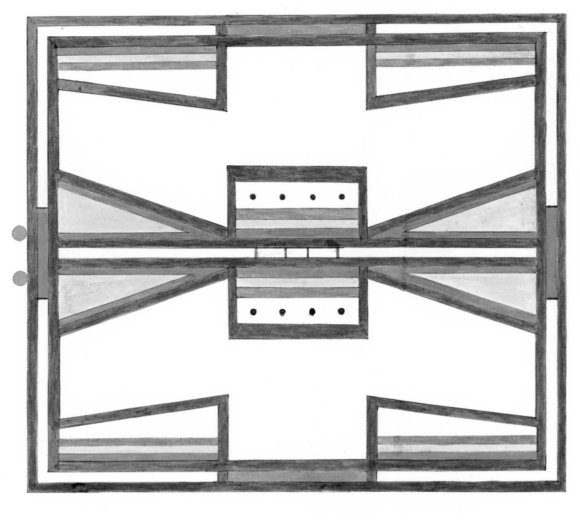

ARAPAHO (Southern)

A design on a buffalo hide. (Chicago Museum of Natural History)

HOLES: 1 pair in each upper flap, 3 pairs in each side flap. SIZE OF PARFLECHE: 62 x 16½ in. SIZE OF DESIGN: 18¼ x 15¾ in.

ATSINA

(*Algonquian linguistic family*)

This design, from an old parfleche of buffalo hide, is the five-block design known as Was-e-keck, or Bear Hands. It is outlined with old mineral brown and has small units of the same color. The parfleche belonged to White Eagle, or Short Man, who was drowned in the Musselshell River in 1882. White Eagle had carried it on his back when he went on war parties, and in it he could pack all the things he needed: dried meat, fat, berries, new moccasin soles, sinew, and an awl for repairing his moccasins. Mrs. Julia Schultz, Fort Belknap Reservation, acquired the parfleche from her mother in 1902.

HOLES: 3 pairs in each upper flap. SIZE OF PARFLECHE: 60 x 15 in. SIZE OF DESIGN: 16 x 13 in. BORDER: No. 4.

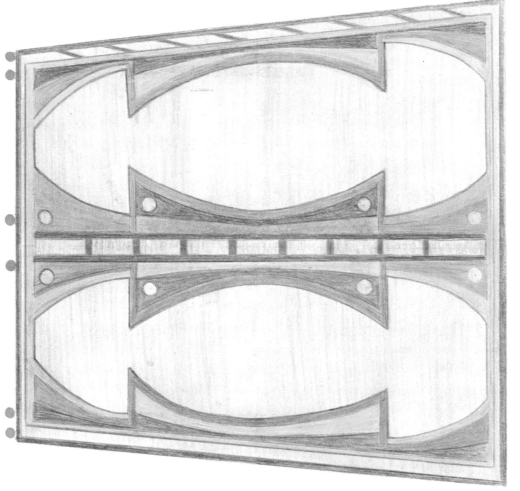

BLACKFOOT

This design is from a cylindrical ceremonial bag, made from one upper trapezoidal flap. It was labeled Crow Water Bundle (named for the bird, not the tribe). It is characterized by interesting curved lines and small negative circles. The background spaces are outlined in brown, and the whole bag appears to have been browned.

HOLES: 3 pairs. SIZE OF DESIGN: 16 x 16 x 17½ in. STRUCTURAL DESIGN: A.

BLACKFOOT
(*Algonquian linguistic family*)

This design is from a large parfleche owned by Mrs. Temma Pierre, a full-blood Blackfoot, born in 1874. The design is characterized by much white background. The main interest is the center of the design, which is common among parfleches of the Blackfeet, the Dakotas, the Crows, the Yakimas, and the Kutenais.

HOLES: 3 pairs. STRUCTURAL DESIGN: G.

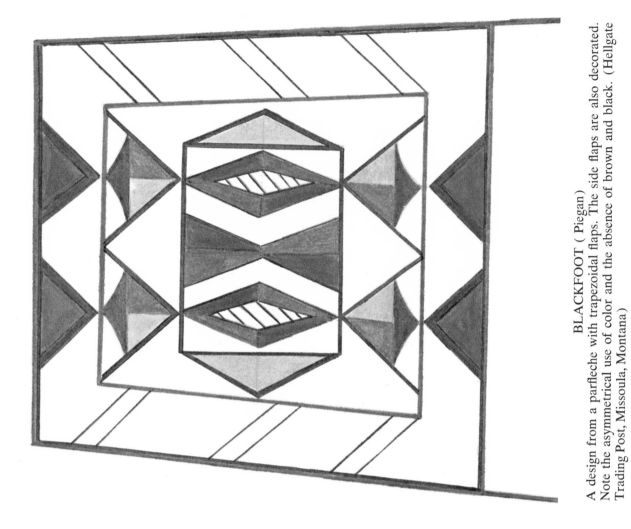

BLACKFOOT (Piegan)

A design from a parfleche with trapezoidal flaps. The side flaps are also decorated. Note the asymmetrical use of color and the absence of brown and black. (Hellgate Trading Post, Missoula, Montana)

HOLES: 3 pairs in upper flaps. STRUCTURAL DESIGN: G. BORDER: No. 6.

BLACKFOOT (Blood)

This small trapezoidal design is from an old parfleche from the Northwest Territory, Canada. It is outlined with the old brown earth paint, and small units of brown appear in the design. (Blackfeet Craft Shop, Browning, Montana)

HOLES: 3 pairs. SIZE OF PARFLECHE: small. STRUCTURAL DESIGN: A. BORDER: No. 5.

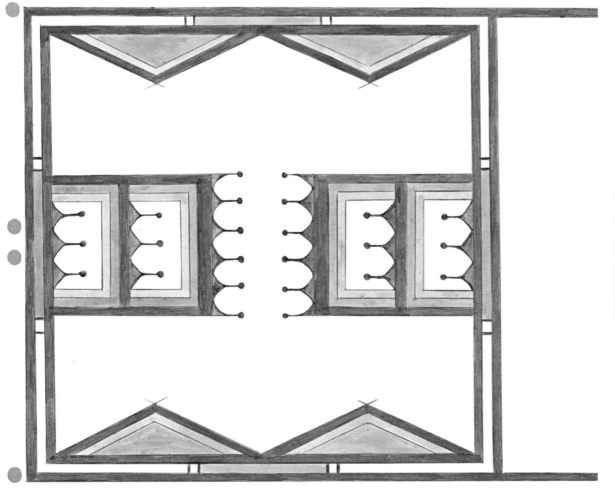

CHEYENNE (Southern)
(*Algonquian linguistic family*)

A design from a parfleche with the typical small brown figures and the brown outline with a simple border. Blue bands across the back connect the two decorated areas on the square upper flaps. (Museum of the American Indian, Heye Foundation, New York)

HOLES: single, pair, single. SIZE OF PARFLECHE: 51 x 15 in. SIZE OF DESIGN: 14½ x 14 in.
STRUCTURAL DESIGN: I, attached to the border with undecorated space in center. BORDER: No. 5.

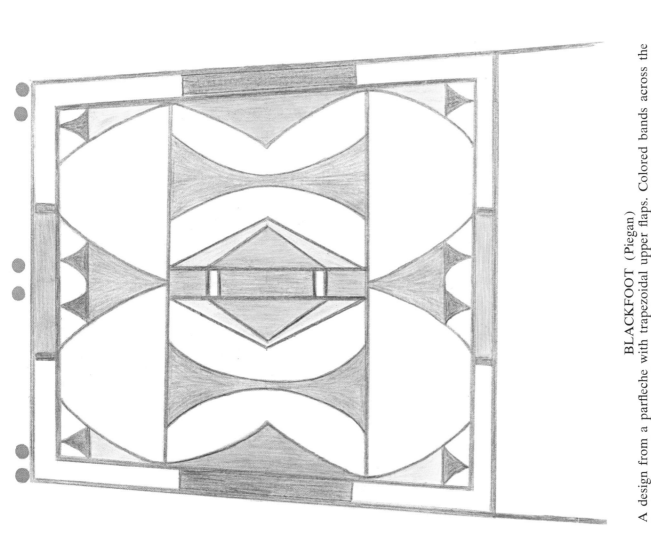

BLACKFOOT (Piegan)

A design from a parfleche with trapezoidal upper flaps. Colored bands across the back connect the decorated areas on the upper flaps. The side flaps are painted with a simple design. There is no brown outlining. The curved lines form interesting back-ground spaces. (Taggert Collection, Museum of the Plains Indians, Browning Montana)

HOLES: 3 pairs. STRUCTURAL DESIGN: F. BORDER: No. 5.

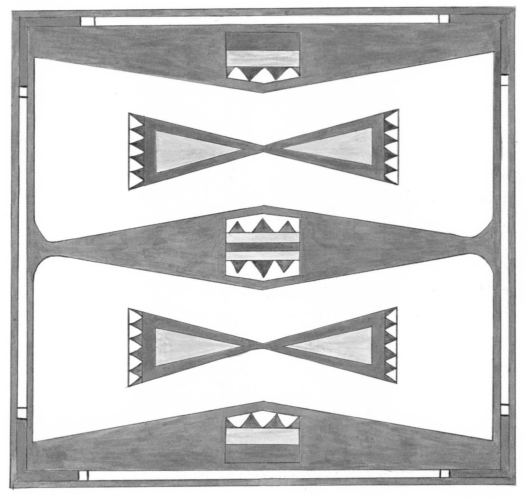

POTAWATOMI
(*Algonquian linguistic family*)

A design from an old buffalo parfleche from Kansas. It has brown outlines and simple brown units. The very long green triangular units are attached to the border and almost become a part of it. The same design runs through the center. Two long, free X units are filled into the large remaining neutral area. This parfleche had been folded into a trunk, and the holes had been removed. (Museum of the American Indian, Heye Foundation)

SIZE OF PARFLECHE: 17 x 14½ in. STRUCTURAL DESIGN: H. BORDER: No. 4.

KICKAPOO
(*Algonquian linguistic family*)

A design from an old parfleche which had been refolded into a trunk-shaped container by the Foxes. The outlines and small figures are brown. (Museum of the American Indian, Heye Foundation)

HOLES: single, pair, single. SIZE OF PARFLECHE: 61 x 17½ in. SIZE OF DESIGN: 16½ x 17 in. STRUCTURAL DESIGN: A (both panels painted alike). BORDER: No. 5 (green). (slightly wider than long).

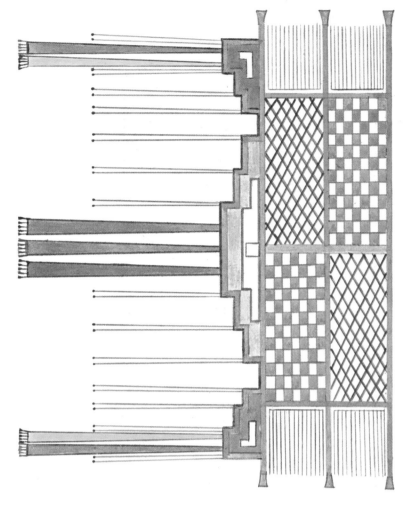

APACHE (Mescalero)

In this design there is no real border. When the parfleche is closed, the designs are seen on each end with no decoration in the center. There are no holes for closing; probably the parfleche was tied with a long thong. The parfleche is small with wide side flaps. Only the side flap that shows when the upper flaps are opened is decorated. The design is outlined in dark brown. It was found in Taos, New Mexico. (Museum of the American Indian, Heye Foundation)

SIZE OF PARFLECHE: 48 x 12 in. SIZE OF DESIGN: 11 x 12 in.

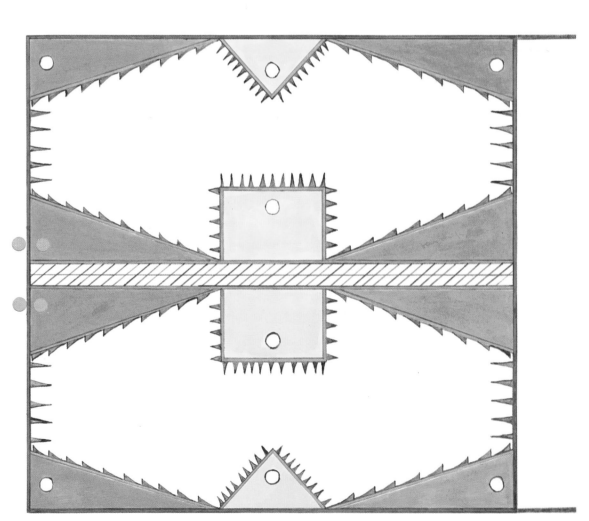

APACHE (Jicarilla)
(Athapascan linguistic family)

This design, from an old parfleche, shows the typical Jicarilla Apache characteristics: a simple border with colored bands across the back and many small brown units. Jicarilla Apache parfleches are so large that they appear to have been made from a whole hide rather than one-half a hide, as was the usual custom in other tribes. (Denver Art Museum, Denver, Colorado)

HOLES: 1 pair on one flap, 2 pairs on the other flap. SIZE OF PARFLECHE: 81 x 17 in. SIZE OF DESIGN: 18 x 17 in. STRUCTURAL DESIGN: A. BORDER: No. 2.

APACHE
Sections of unlike designs from the two side flaps of an Arizona Apache parfleche. The neutral areas are outlined in heavy black. They are not seen when the parfleche is closed. (M. G. Chandler Collection, Southwest Museum, Los Angeles)

APACHE (Mescalero)
A design on the border of the upper side flap of a parfleche. It is outlined in dark brown. This type of design is seldom seen on rawhide. (Denver Art Museum)

PAWNEE
(*Caddoan linguistic family*)

Design from a parfleche collected in 1902. It is outlined in brown-black and has a few small units of the same color. (Chicago Museum of Natural History)

HOLES: 1 pair. SIZE OF PARFLECHE: 62 x 17 in. SIZE OF DESIGN: 19¾ x 16½ in. STRUCTURAL DESIGN: B. BORDER: No. 5.

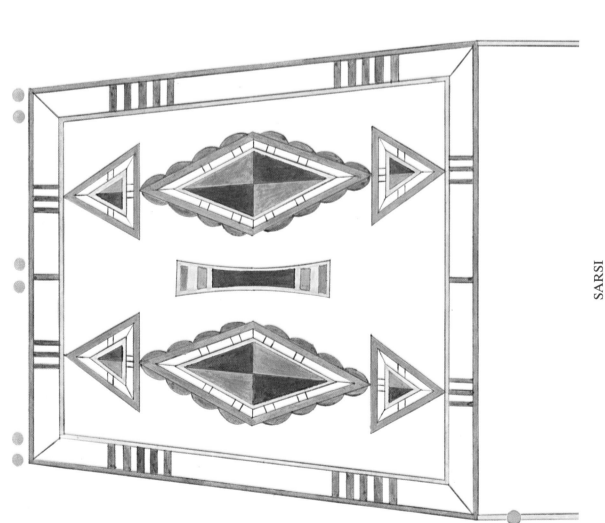

SARSI
(*Athapascan linguistic family*)

The buffalo parfleche from which this design was taken has the following characteristics: trapezoidal upper flaps, decorated side flaps, decoration on the upper flaps connected across the back by bands of color. Small brown figures are appended to the larger units of the design. The parfleche was collected in British Columbia, Canada. (American Museum of Natural History, New York)

HOLES: 3 pairs. SIZE OF PARFLECHE: 58 x 16 in. SIZE OF DESIGN: 15½ x 16 in. and 15½ x 12½ in.

61

WASCO
(Chinookan linguistic family)

This design, from a large parfleche collected in 1905 at the Warm Springs Reservation, looks old. It is outlined in the old earth brown-black and has some small brown units in the design. Note the unusual curved lines on the center block. (Chicago Museum of Natural History)

HOLES: 3 pairs for closing the upper flaps. STRUCTURAL DESIGN: C. BORDER: No. 2.

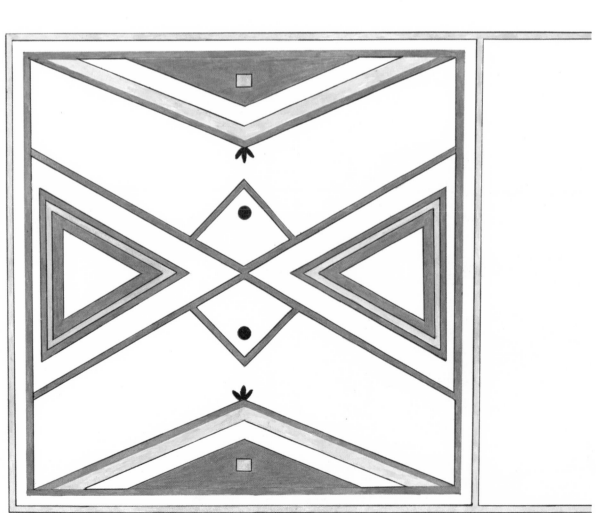

WICHITA
(Caddoan linguistic family)

A design from an old parfleche, collected in Oklahoma in 1901. This large parfleche had been made into a large, flat bag for storing corn. The original folds are clear. The background spaces are outlined in black. The outer band of yellow connects the two decorated areas on the upper flaps. A large X design fills the center. The parfleche is well browned by use and smoke. It was sketched from the case and was not drawn to scale. (Chicago Museum of Natural History)

BORDER: No. 4.

WASCO

Design from the upper flap of a Warm Springs Reservation parfleche. It is outlined in green. (Chicago Natural History Museum)

HOLES: One pair. SIZE OF PARFLECHE: 59 x 14 in. SIZE OF DESIGN: 16 x 13¼ in.

WISHRAM
(*Chinookan linguistic family*)

This design is from the upper flap of an old parfleche made from the hide of a young buffalo. The side flaps are decorated with designs interpreted as human beings. This type of figure has been used by different groups in many parts of the world and reaches far back into prehistoric times. The upper flaps are joined by green bands. (Museum of the American Indian, Heye Foundation)

HOLES: 3 pairs. SIZE OF PARFLECHE: 53 x 13 in. SIZE OF DESIGN: 18 x 13 in. STRUCTURAL DESIGN: B.

KUTENAI
(*Salishan linguistic family*)

Above: This freehand design, painted on wet rawhide, required skill, experience, and perfectly controlled muscles. The parfleche designs have much in common with those of the Sarsis and the Jicarilla Apaches. The small brown figures are also found on Sarsi and Jicarilla Apache parfleches. Note that there are both curved and straight lines. The use of color in this design is particularly interesting.

Below: The design on the side flaps. Blue bands extend across the back of the parfleche to join the two decorated areas on the upper flaps and also form a base for the decoration on the side flaps. (Taylor Museum, Colorado Springs, Colorado)

HOLES: 3 pairs. SIZE OF PARFLECHE: 55 x 14 in. SIZE OF DESIGN ON THE TRAPEZOIDAL FLAPS: 13½ x 14 in. STRUCTURAL DESIGN: G. BORDER: No. 2.

KIOWA
(*Kiowan linguistic family*)

This design is from a parfleche which had been refolded into a Fox trunk. It is brown from smoke, like all Fox trunks, but the folds can be seen. It was made from a buffalo hide before 1840. It has distinctive Kiowa characteristics: it is slightly smaller than average and has a square upper flap, a free, unattached design in the center of each panel, transposition of color in the border, and a meager use of blue. It is outlined in old dark brown. (Collection of Roy Robinson, Chicago)

HOLES: single, pair, single. SIZE OF PARFLECHE: 55 x 14 in. SIZE OF DESIGN: 14 x 14. BORDER: No. 4.

64

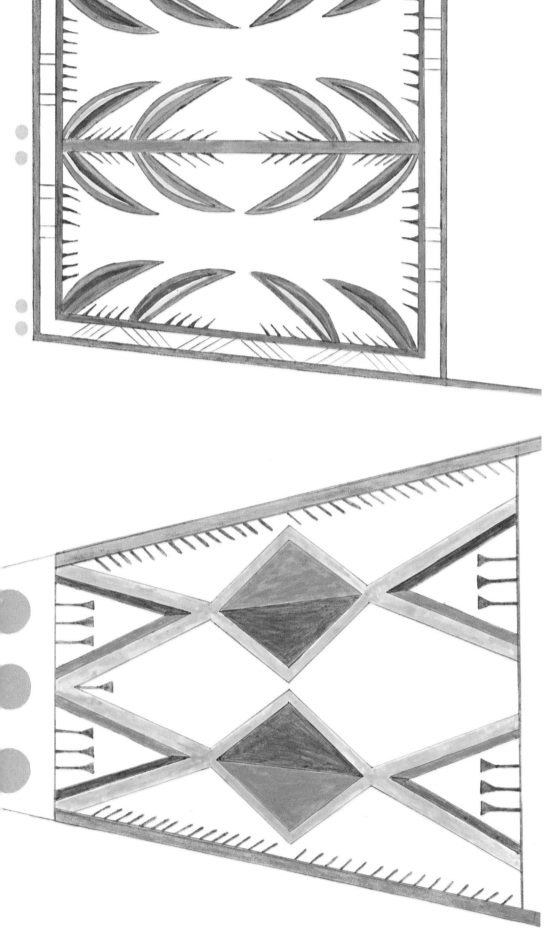

KUTENAI

This design is from a parfleche collected in British Columbia. Bands of color connect the two trapezoidal flaps. The side flaps are decorated. The design is outlined in brown and has small brown units attached to the structural lines, like the designs of back connect the two decorated areas on the upper flaps. (Museum of the American Indian)

HOLES: 3 pairs. SIZE OF PARFLECHE: 52 x 14 in. SIZE OF DESIGN: 13 x 11½ in. and 13 x 14½ in. STRUCTURAL DESIGN: B. BORDER: No. 5.

KUTENAI

This design is from a parfleche collected in 1897. The upper flaps are trapezoidal, and the ends are narrow. When the flap is trapezoidal, the design must be adjusted to the given area. The side flaps are painted in a realistic design. Colored bands across the back connect the two decorated areas on the upper flaps. This parfleche was cut from the hide and staked out while the hide was wet. No cutting or trimming was done after the hide was dry. Much of the old brown-black earth paint was used to outline the design and in small units in the design. The two pairs of holes near one side crease held a stick for extending the bag when it was packed on a horse. (Chicago Museum of Natural History)

HOLES: 3 large stake holes, 2 stake holes near the edge of each side flap, 2 pairs near one side crease. SIZE OF PARFLECHE: 63 x 17 in. SIZE OF DESIGN: 15 x 15 in. and 15 x 9 in. STRUCTURAL DESIGN: H. BORDER: No. 1

65

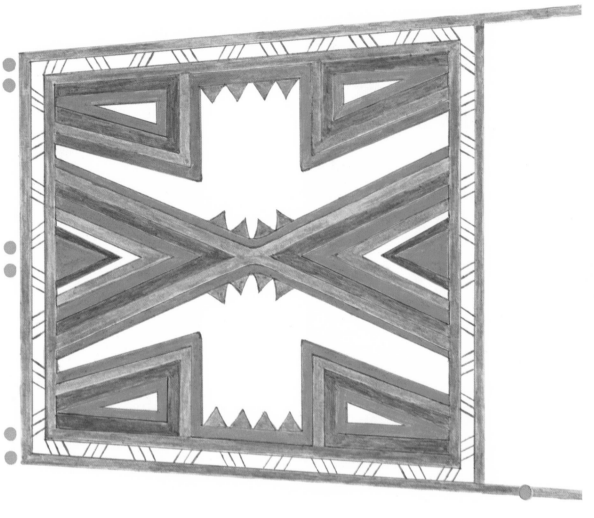

KALISPEL (Pend d'Oreille)
(Salishan linguistic family)

The Kalispel parfleches I examined were made from the hides of mature buffaloes and were rather thick and heavy. In the parfleche whose design is shown here, the side flaps have both stake and burned holes. The unpainted parts of the design are outlined in old brown earth paint, and there are some units of the design painted the same color. (United States National Museum, Washingotn, D.C.)

HOLES: 3 pairs on the upper flaps, stake and burned holes on the side flaps.
SIZE OF PARFLECHE: 58½ x 15¾ in. SIZE OF DESIGN: 13¾ x 15 in. and 13¾ x 13½ in.
STRUCTURAL DESIGN: H. BORDER: No. 6.

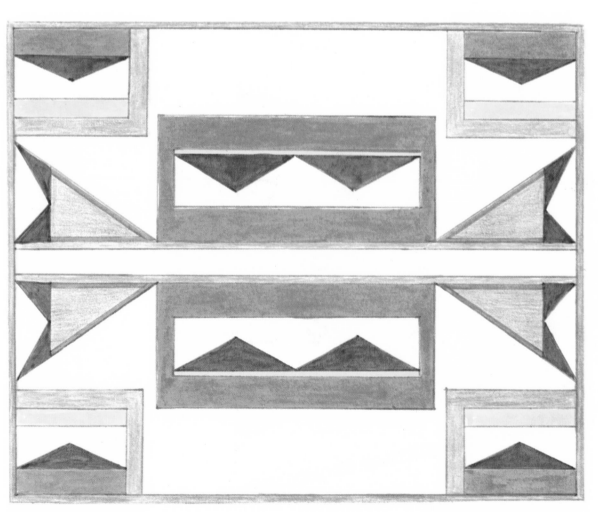

FLATHEAD
(Salishan linguistic family)

This design is outlined in the dark green·typical of the parfleches of the Northwest groups. Green bands connect the two decorated areas; there is no decoration on the side flaps. The Shoshonis said that the Flathead parfleches could be identified by the repetition of fours. (Collection of Mrs. Eneas Granjo, Arlee, Montana)

HOLES: 3 pairs, plus 2 pairs in one side flap used to hold a stick when packed on a horse.
SIZE OF PARFLECHE: 62 x 15 in. SIZE OF DESIGN: 16 x 13½ in. STRUCTURAL DESIGN: C.

NEZ PERCE
(*Shahaptian linguistic family*)

A modern type of design from a parfleche owned by Philip George, a Nez Percé from Lapwai, Idaho, who used it as a container for his dance costume. Part of the design is repeated on the edge of the flaps so that when the two upper flaps are tied together there is one continuous design with no break in the center. The side flaps are rather wide.

HOLES: 1 pair in the upper flaps, 2 pairs in the side flaps. SIZE OF PARFLECHE: 57½ x 13 in. SIZE OF DESIGN: 16½ x 12½ in.

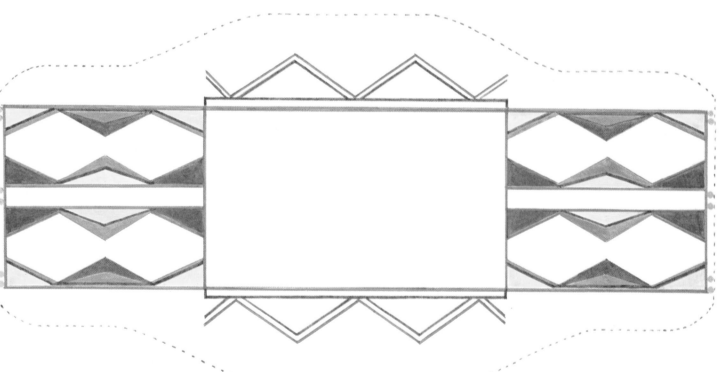

KLIKITAT
(*Shahaptian linguistic family*)

A sketch of a parfleche as it appears before folding. The decorated areas on the two upper flaps are joined by colored bands, which form a base for a simple design on the side flaps. The upper flaps are tied together by the three-pair method. (American Museum of Natural History)

HOLES: 3 pairs. SIZE OF PARFLECHE: 55 x 13 in. SIZE OF DESIGN: 15 x 13 in. STRUCTURAL DESIGN: A.

67

TYIGH
(Shahaptian linguistic family)

A design from a parfleche, or Shup-tuc-kai, made by Tyighs living on the Warm Springs Reservation. The method of closing is a variant of the one-pair method: a double pair of holes on each flap allows the extension of the flaps when the parfleche is filled with blankets or other soft items. When the parfleche is tied together, all the large triangles point in the same direction. (Collection of Josie McCorkle, Warm Springs Reservation)

HOLES: 2 pairs. SIZE OF DESIGN: 14⅛ x 11 in. STRUCTURAL DESIGN: B or E.

TENINO
(Shahaptian linguistic family)

A design from a parfleche from Warm Springs Reservation, Oregon. It has the narrow green border typical of parfleches designed by the groups west of the Plains. The corner blocks are unbroken, while the other five blocks are divided into triangles. (Collection of Josie McCorkle, Warm Springs Reservation)

HOLES: 3 pairs. SIZE OF DESIGN: 15 x 12½ in. STRUCTURAL DESIGN: D.

A Northern Arapaho rawhide bag, collected in Ethete, Wyoming, in 1891. The flap of this bag has been embroidered with beads. (United States National Museum)

by fourteen and one-half inches, and the folded parfleche thirty-three by fifteen inches.

The Arapaho craftswoman preferred a simple design with a large amount of unpainted surface. At a distance these would show to good advantage. Often each unit of a design had a name.

A light or medium blue was favored and used more than other colors. The old women said that it was the Arapaho color. The Cheyenne and Dakota people call the Arapahos the "Sky-blue People." Green was a second choice.

Sticks or willows were used for laying out the pattern on the wet rawhide, and colored disks were used for painting. Earth paint was gathered in a reverent and respectful manner. The old brown-black used for outlining was secured near the Powder River on the Cheyenne reservation in southeastern Montana. This black was like ink. Held in a shell, it was applied with a sharpened edge of a bone brush. Small black triangles and dots were sometimes used. The design was outlined after it had been painted in order to intensify the color and the design.

There was a certain amount of specialization among the Arapaho women. When a skin lodge was made, one woman might cut the skins, another would lay out the pieces as they were to be sewed, still others did the sewing and made the ornaments, while another placed the ornaments on the lodge.

When a woman wanted to make painted rawhide parfleches, she might seek the aid of specialists, and more than one woman might work on one pair of parfleches for there were specialists for every step. One woman might specialize in cutting out the parfleche after it was painted, dried, and the hair pounded off; another might burn in the holes. Such specialization helped to standardize the characteristics of the group. As was pointed out earlier, a hide could not be turned since it was pegged down. Two parfleches were made from one hide, and two to four women might do the painting in order to complete the work while the hide was in proper condition; that is, before it dried.

About two-thirds of the fifty Arapaho parfleches examined had a few small minor units of design—dots, triangles, or bars painted with the brown-earth paint.

The disks of color were made from dry pigment held together with a glue made from boiled shavings from the thick parts of the hide that had been removed.

Arapaho children were given playthings which were small copies of adult possessions. A grandfather might make a small girl a hide scraper to fit her hands, and as she grew, he would make larger scrapers. By the time she was fourteen years of age, she was expected to do good rawhide work.

An older woman on the Arapaho reservation said: "My grandmother used to have a bunch of rawhide parfleches in which she put dried squash, corn, and meat. She never used the dried food in the parfleches except in cases of dire need—would not open these parfleches unless there was no other possible food, and then she took out just enough to keep us from hunger, then she tied up the parfleches and put them away."

Another informant said, "Dried meat, dried cherries, fat back and peppermint leaves were all put together in one rawhide parfleche, and *that* made good eating."

The Arapahos made many parfleches and said that the design told the contents. A very unusual design decorated a parfleche said to be used for storing feathers. When not in use, a feather headdress was dismantled and the feathers washed, dried, and then laid in this parfleche until needed, when they were quickly arranged in the headdress.

ATSINAS

The Atsinas or Gros Ventres of the prairie are an Arapaho tribe who broke away from the main group in the seventeenth century after they came to the plains. For a while they lived with the Piegans, a tribe of the Blackfoot Confederacy and considered themselves a part of the Blackfoot Nation.

Like other tribes that depended for their existence on the buffalo, they moved about to a certain extent but spent much time in western Montana near the present town of Augusta. There they met the tribes living in or west of the Rocky Mountains, who came by way of Codotte Pass to camp on the Sun River and hunt on the plains. The western groups brought bitterroot and camas to trade with the Indians of the plains for dried meat.

The Atsinas now live on the Fort Belknap Reservation in north-central Montana. A number of very old women living on the reservation, who made rawhide when they were younger, said that after the parfleche was no longer needed for dried meat (when the buffalo were gone), they were used as decorations in the lodge when the tribe gathered for a ceremony. These women said that the old Atsina five-block design may have originated with the Arapaho people.

This old parfleche had three pairs of holes in each upper flap for closing. The women said that

An Atsina woman with a travois made of lodge poles, on which can be seen a parfleche with a five-block pattern. (Curtis, *The North American Indians*, Vol. V, plate 140; E. E. Ayer Collection, Newberry Library)

A design from the dewcloth of a lodge belonging to Mrs. Julia Schultz, an Atsina of the Fort Belknap Reservation. This very large dewcloth was painted with the personal histories of four Atsina men. This rider is leading another horse, which he has taken from an enemy, while bullets rain around him. The horse is painted red; the rider, orange.

A design from an Atsina parfleche (see page 55).

there was a stick in the upper edge of the parfleche when it was packed on a horse. This kept the bag extended and also kept the holes from being torn. Thongs were tied through the holes over the stick and then fastened to the packsaddle. When a stick was used in a parfleche, there were two pairs of holes on the side fold or crease. This method of packing a parfleche might be considered a far northwestern trait learned when they lived with the Blackfeet.

To size their rawhide, the Atsina women used resin off the chokecherry bushes boiled in water until it was very thin, or they used cactus juice. They said that they burned in some of the outlines for the designs. The hair was pounded off with a rather heavy water stone, which was round with a slightly flattened side and one slightly pointed end. This softened the hide, making it somewhat like a tanned skin.

The Atsinas decorated all the things which they used with porcupine quills or paint or feathers. The men painted the inside linings or dewcloths of their lodges with their war histories. The women said that the lichen on the rocks "were the work of the spirit people." Anyone who did not decorate his possessions on this earth had to "ornament the rocks before he could pass into the happy beyond."

A very interesting old buffalo parfleche, made before 1880, was seen on the reservation. It had belonged to Short Man, or White Eagle, the son of a brother of Curley Head, one of the headmen, who was the keeper of the sacred pipe. White Eagle was drowned in the Musselshell River about 1882. This parfleche had seen much use before that time. It was used by White Eagle and was carried on his back when he went on a war party. It contained everything he would need for the trip: dried meat, fat, berries, new soles for moccasins, sinew, and an awl for repairing his moccasins. It had been used until it could be rolled up like a flour sack, and although it had been cleaned with yucca root, the painted design was still clear.

This parfleche was large and had rectangular painted areas. The Atsinas of Fort Belknap called green "Bad Water" from the algae growing on top of stagnant water. Green predominated in their designs, with smaller amounts of red and dark blue. Designs were outlined in brown and a few brown triangles were placed on the center block. The designs on the oldest parfleches were a five-block construction and had almost the same characteristics as the oldest Arapaho parfleches.

BLACKFOOT CONFEDERACY

The Blackfeet were a large Algonquian confederacy of the northern plains consisting of Blackfeet (Siksikas), Bloods, and Piegans, and were closely associated with the Sarsis, an Athapascan group, and also at one time with the Atsinas, an Algonquian group. The Atsinas broke away from the Blackfeet during the period between 1850 and 1861. Nearly half of the Blackfeet now live in Montana and the others to the north in Canada. On the west their reservation joins Glacier Park.

Buffalo hunters and skin-lodge dwellers, the Blackfeet had access to a large variety of earth and vegetable paints in the Rocky Mountains. There were certain men in the tribe who made a vocation of gathering and preparing paints for use by others.

If a woman had no pigment and started out to get enough to paint a parfleche, she might travel 150 miles in collecting it. This is not much of a trip today, but if one walked or rode horseback over rough trailless country, one would understand why paint brought a good price or had good trade value.

The old dark blue (a blue mud) came from the mountains just north of the Canadian line. A beautiful bright red, known by many tribes, was found near what is now the town of Helena, Montana. The brown used to outline the designs could be secured near a spring on the reservation or on the banks of the Cutbank River, north of present Cutbank, Montana.

Colors were prepared for use as paint by mixing the pigment with glue obtained from boiling the hooves of buffalo. This glue was also used as sizing. The craftswomen said that they never had any "store paint" until Glacier Park was opened in 1910. On most of the old pieces they used the brown-black outline, but in late years it was sometimes omitted. This may have happened after they acquired the "store paint."

The Siksikas used a stone for outlining with the old rusty black paint; they said that this stone almost cut a ridge in the rawhide. One may become aware of this technique by running a finger over the outline. Clam shells were used as paint pans.

The Blackfoot women said each woman had her own designs, which were different from those of all other rawhide craftswomen, and that she never copied or used the designs of others because she liked her own better. When asked about making parfleches, Good Victory, an old craftswoman on the Blackfoot reservation, said: "Now I may look like an old rusty tin can which has been stepped on,

The interior of a Piegan Blackfoot lodge. The photograph shows a painted dewcloth, typical costumes, and rawhide bags and bundles hanging from the lodge poles. (Curtis, *The North American Indians*, Vol. VI, plate 18; E. E. Ayer Collection, Newberry Library)

but once upon a time I made as good parfleches as were made anywhere; and what I say about making parfleches was true, and I do not want anyone to say that it is not true. I could use the designs made by other people if I liked them well enough, but I liked my own designs best."

A lodge design belonged to the head of the lodge, or family; no one else would use or copy it. Occasionally a person might buy a design or buy the use of one, or he might hire a medicine man to paint a lodge cover; however, the Blackfoot design as a whole differed from designs of other groups.

The Blackfoot parfleche was short, smaller than the average, and proportionally wide compared to

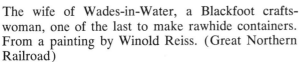

The wife of Wades-in-Water, a Blackfoot crafts-woman, one of the last to make rawhide containers. From a painting by Winold Reiss. (Great Northern Railroad)

Mrs. Louisa Croft (Berry Child), a Blackfoot raw-hide craftswoman. Mrs. Croft told me during World War II that it made her "lonesome" to look at her old buffalo parfleche because it had no meat in it. "All we have to put in it now are coupons and ration points."

its length. Most of the Blackfoot craftswomen used trapezoidal flaps. The form of this parfleche and the method of closing made it very compact. The side flaps were laced together with about six pairs of holes; the upper flaps were tied by a thong of rawhide or buckskin through three pairs of holes in the end of each flap. There was one pair of holes

near the crease of each side flap as well as two pairs for tying in a stiffening stick when the parfleche was to be packed on a horse. A loop of buckskin or rawhide was placed in each side of the pairs in the crease of the side flap. The holes on each of the upper flaps were tied together and fastened down to the side flaps by tying through the loop. This type of closing required the use of sixteen pairs of holes for one parfleche.

This short, compact parfleche could easily be packed on a travois or horse. On a journey often very little of the horse could be seen when it was loaded with travois buffalo robes, painted parfleches, and children. The baby carrier and baby hung from the saddle or the ends of the travois poles, and a child might be asleep on top of a well-packed travois.

One outstanding characteristic of the Blackfoot design was the curved lines. At one time these Indians lived in the eastern woodland country, where they made pottery and decorated birchbark with curves. Later they adapted the curves to rawhide and to bead embroidery. In their designs they liked a large natural-colored background to set off the design, while the Dakotas, who also used curves, liked much of the background painted with color. The older parfleches show more curves than the modern ones.

The Blackfeet often made use of dots in decorations, either dark on a white background or as a negative white design in a painted space. They also used spots or elongated dots, which they placed in rows to fill a long, narrow space. These dots were made with a pencil or crayon of pigment.

The Blackfeet furnished large amounts of dried buffalo meat, pemmican, and tallow to the Hudson's Bay Company, and such provisions were packed in rawhide for transportation. Some of the Blackfoot trade went to trading posts through middlemen, the Crees and Assiniboins. Early trading posts established in Blackfoot country were Fort Piegan 1831, Fort Mackenzie 1832, and Fort Benton 1847.

CHEYENNES

The Cheyennes are an Algonquian group, who at one time lived in permanent villages, planted and harvested crops, made pottery, and used birchbark. After 1700 they moved west and south from the northern Minnesota area. Lewis and Clark found them in the Black Hills in 1804. Later they separated into two groups. The Northern Cheyennes now live on the Tongue River Reservation in southeastern Montana, while the Southern Cheyennes live on the Cheyenne-Arapaho lands in west-central Oklahoma. These groups lived together much of the time when the making and painting of rawhide was an important industry. A check of many parfleches shows little difference between those of the two groups.

The Cheyenne parfleches are closed and tied by

A Blackfoot Indian camp at Two Medicine, Glacier National Park. (Great Northern Railroad)

the single, pair, single method. A pair of holes was burned into the center and one hole on each corner of the edges of the upper flaps. The two upper flaps were brought together and tied through the center pairs of holes with a thong. Then they took a long thong and made a knot in one end of it, laced the other end through the single hole in one outside flap, then brought the thong across the back and laced it through the single hole on the other side of the parfleche. The thong was then knotted securely. This was repeated on the other flap. This method tied the upper flaps firmly to the parfleche. If the parfleche was placed on a pack horse, this thong was fastened to the cinch. A matching parfleche was tied on the opposite side of the horse in the same manner, and the two were tied together under the belly of the horse.

In common with the Dakotas, the Cheyennes used two bands of color across the back of the parfleche to join the two design areas. These bands were most often dark blue on the Dakota rawhide and green or turquoise blue on the Cheyenne.

The organization of craft work among the Cheyennes was probably responsible for the superior articles produced. Each craft was controlled by a society of women who were specialists in their field. Besides teaching the techniques of the craft, they interpreted the symbolism of color and design to the tyro. A woman was admitted to a society only after she had paid the heads of the society with costly presents and feasts. The rules of each society were rigid. The rawhide craft had seven women at the head of the industry. When a woman wished to paint a rawhide, she notified one of the leaders

A Piegan Blackfoot parfleche, collected in 1903. The bands extend across the back. There is no black outlining. Note the prominent curved lines. (American Museum of Natural History)

HOLES: 3 pairs and 2 pairs. SIZE OF PARFLECHE: 55½ x 14 in. SIZE OF DESIGN: 15 x 11 in. and 15 x 14 in. STRUCTURAL DESIGN: B

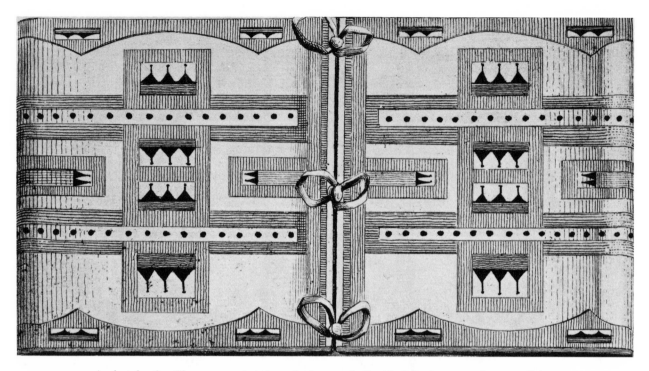

A sketch of a Cheyenne painted parfleche, made by Carl Bodmer on the expedition of Maximilian, Prince of Wied, 1832–34. Parfleches were not given much attention in the records of the period because European travelers had nothing to trade for rawhide, and trade was still the common method of exchange among the Indians. The Cheyennes say that this is definitely a Cheyenne design. Little Woman, the wife of Bull-Looking-Around, of Watonga, Oklahoma, was one of the best rawhide crafts-women living in the 1940's. Her designs show many of the characteristics of this one. (Maximilian, Prince of Wied, *Travels in the Interior of North America*; American Museum of Natural History)

and plans were made. One or more of the head women directed the work. Cheyenne design types remained fairly constant over a long period of time as a result of this arrangement.

The Cheyenne designs were delicate and the colors pleasing. The women often used a light to medium green with accents of rose-red, yellow, and brown. The thin coat of paint that was applied partly accounts for the delicacy of color. Turquoise blue sometimes took the place of green. Indeed, the Cheyennes were the only group that used turquoise as the main color, and it may have had ceremonial significance; others seldom used it except for filling in small spaces. The color has been found on the rawhide of tribes living in or west of the Rocky Mountains.

The Cheyennes used color in the corners between two bands of green, which formed a simple border around the outer edge of the decorated area. Rose-red was most common, but yellow may be found. These two short lines of color met at right angles in the corners and were referred to as "the life line."

The fine light-brown outlining and the small brown units of design on Cheyenne rawhide were nearly always burned into the hide with a sharp instrument of bone, stone, or metal to make an incised line which can be felt by rubbing the finger over the design. Brown triangles with a brown dot above the apex of each triangle were characteristic of the Cheyennes and were also found on a very few old Arapaho pieces.

The decorated areas on the upper flaps of the parfleche are very nearly square. They are enclosed by a simple frame and divided longitudinally into two or three panels with long, narrow, triangular units attached to the divisional lines. Simple curved lines are found occasionally, and frequently there are large uncolored background spaces.

An older type of design is among the most beautiful of all rawhide painting. It has two single,

78

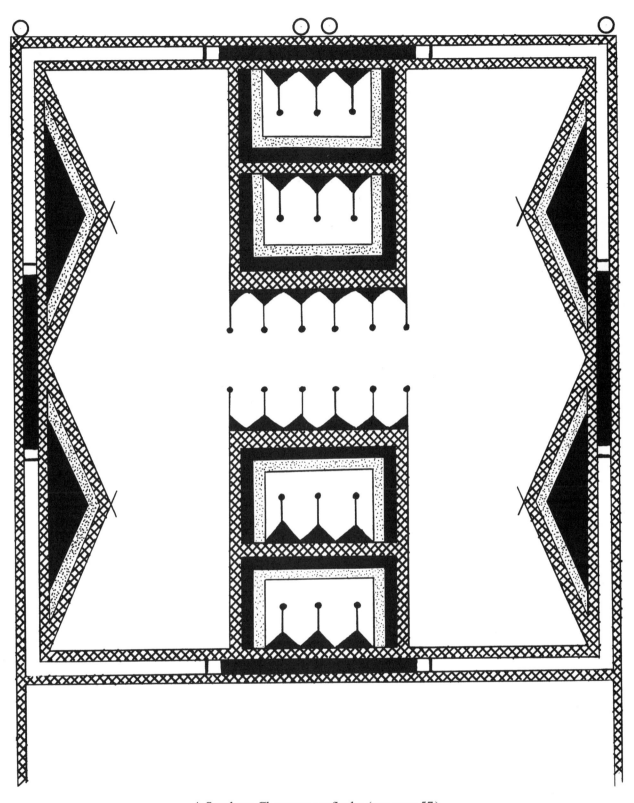

A Southern Cheyenne parfleche (see page 57).

A two-wheeled cart used by the Hudson's Bay Company on the Red River expeditions. The wheels are bound with rawhide. (Hudson's Bay Company, Hudson's Bay House, Winnipeg, Canada)

narrow bands of color divided by a neutral color space for a border, with red lines in the corners and short yellow lines at the center of each side. The design is made up of two blocks, one attached to each end of the enclosing border with two long triangles attached to the two sides. These blocks and triangles are divided and subdivided in different ways, but all have small units of brown. The Cheyenne artists said that a parfleche with this design was never used for storing dried food. Some of the old block-triangle designs have as many as six blocks, three attached to the top and three to the opposite border.

A sketch of an old parfleche from Maximilian's *Travels in the Interior of North America*, made in 1832 to 1834 by Charles Bodmer, artist with Maximilian's expedition, shows a Cheyenne parfleche with typical tribal characteristics.

Cheyenne rawhide is exceptionally well made, and the surface well sized. The craftswomen used hide scrapings for sizing their rawhide and sometimes the resinous substance found on the wild cherry bushes.

Tribes living near the Cheyennes liked to obtain their parfleches and make them into trunks. These trunks were a little wider than the parfleche, and the original parfleche folds are discernible. Some of the oldest and most interesting specimens have been found folded into trunks.

When one studies the history of the Cheyennes, one wonders how a people who lived through such tragic times could continue to make such beautiful designs and such good rawhide. An old Cheyenne woman, a rawhide craftswoman of great dignity and poise, who checked the Cheyenne designs used in this book, was a child of three years at the time of the Sand Creek Massacre. She said that she hid in a ditch and was overlooked by the soldiers.

Some of the parfleches which do not seem typical or seem hard to identify may have been made to commemorate an event or to honor a person.

80

This may be the reason that women often made rawhide parfleches at a sun dance. The Cheyennes had several types of design on their parfleches, and evidently each type was in some way connected with its use. For example, a two-panel design in the Chicago Museum of Natural History was explained by the Cheyenne women as the type painted to commemorate a battle or other event. It seemed to be a record of the year as well as the event. The Dakotas also said that parfleches were made to commemorate events.

CREES

The Crees are a large Algonquian group, many of whom live in Canada. Rocky Boy's and Big Bear's bands live on the Rocky Boys Reservation in the Bear Paw Mountains in Montana, and other bands live in North Dakota.

The Crees were among the first Indian tribes to trade with the Hudson's Bay Company. Their movements were governed by the food supply and the trapping of fur-bearing animals. They never depended entirely upon the buffalo for their subsistence.

The first two-wheeled carts seen by these Indians were imported by the Hudson's Bay Company in order to facilitate the fur trade. In time the Crees, who trapped and hunted through Montana and the Canadian country to the north, made their own two-wheeled carts in imitation of the European ones. They used the materials at hand, cottonwood and rawhide. These carts were made without nails, bolts, or bands of iron. The wheel was four to six feet in diameter; the sections as well as the spokes were drawn together with strips of green rawhide and held in place with dried rawhide. The advantage of this method was that repairs could be made anywhere at any time. The harness was of rawhide, a material the Indians knew how to use.

The Crees traveling in caravans over the northern plains in their carts could be heard for five miles as they creaked and screeched and shrieked over the prairie. For sport the drivers often chose a steep hillside rather than the more level trails around the hills, and many spills occurred during a day. The cart box might be full of dry hides for the trader with the women and children on top of the load, drawn by a shaggy, unkempt horse.

A. G. Lant provided a graphic picture of such carts: "Another picturesque feature of the fur trade was the long caravan of ox-carts that used to creak and jolt over the rutted prairie roads between Winnipeg and St. Paul. More than 1,500 Hudson's Bay Company carts manned by 500 traders with tawny spouses and black-eyed impish children, squatted on top of the load, left Canada for St. Paul in August and returned in October. The carts were made without a rivet of iron. Bent wood formed the tires of the two wheels. Hardwood axles told their woes to the world in the scream of shrill bag pipes. Wooden racks took the place of a cart box. In the shafts trod a staid old ox guided from the horns or with a halter, drawing the load with collar instead of a yoke. The harness was of skin thongs. In place of the ox sometimes was a 'shagganippy' pony, raw and unkempt which the imps lashed without mercy on the slightest inconvenience to the horse."[1]

The Crees did not make as many painted parfleches as other groups. They liked to store their dried meat in flat rawhide bags. A parfleche or packing case was used to keep their best clothing clean and dry.

The few Cree parfleches now available for study have a trapezoidal flap with three pairs of holes at the end of each upper flap and one pair near the crease of the side flap. The method of closing was the same as among the Blackfeet.

Painting rawhide was never a major craft with the Plains Crees. Their favorite paints were yellow, red, and black found in the cutbanks along the streams. The pigments were collected, pulverized, mixed with water, and formed into little flat cakes which were baked in a fire of buffalo dung until they were red hot. Later the pigment was scraped off the cake and mixed with hot grease for painting their lodges.

KICKAPOOS

The Kickapoos are an Algonquian group now living in Oklahoma and Kansas. In the years 1852 and 1863, dissatisfied with life in the United States, part of the Kickapoos went to the state of Chihuahua in Mexico. Some returned, but the rest are still living there and lead much the same life as they did in the United States many years ago.

Excellent old buffalo parfleches have been collected among the Kickapoos, often changed into trunk-shaped containers. The creases of the old parfleches can easily be seen, and after many years these old trunks have acquired a beautiful brown color. After the buffalo were gone and the parfleche was no longer needed for meat, the Kickapoos probably found the trunk shape better suited to their changed living conditions.

[1] *The Great Company of Beckles*, 198.

A Plains Cree parfleche. The Atsinas and Crees were together during much of the period when this parfleche was made. It was probably used for clothing rather than for storage of meat. (Chicago Museum of Natural History)

The old buffalo parfleches show the single, pair, single method of closing the upper flaps. The designs are outlined in rusty black and contain some small black units. The parfleches are large, without decoration on the side flaps and with a few very slightly curved lines. The border differs little from borders used by many of the other Algonquian tribes, usually two narrow bands of color divided by a neutral space. These bands do not cross the back to connect the two decorated areas. The old colors, including a very dark blue, were natural mineral or vegetable pigment. The design area on

A Kickapoo parfleche which had been made into a trunk. The following information was attached to the bag: "Fox, Tama, Iowa, Kickapoo." (Museum of the American Indian, Heye Foundation, New York)

the upper flaps was often wider than it was long.

The Kickapoos also made an unpainted rawhide trunk. An old undecorated one from Coahuila, Mexico, was made of bear hide. Other trunks found in Mexico had the same type of design as those belonging to the Fox Indians at Tama, Iowa, and probably were made by them. The Kickapoos have a close linguistic connection with the Sac and Fox Indians.

POTAWATOMIS

The Potawatomis are an Algonquian group. According to their tradition, the Potawatomis, Chippewas, and Ottawas were originally one people. In

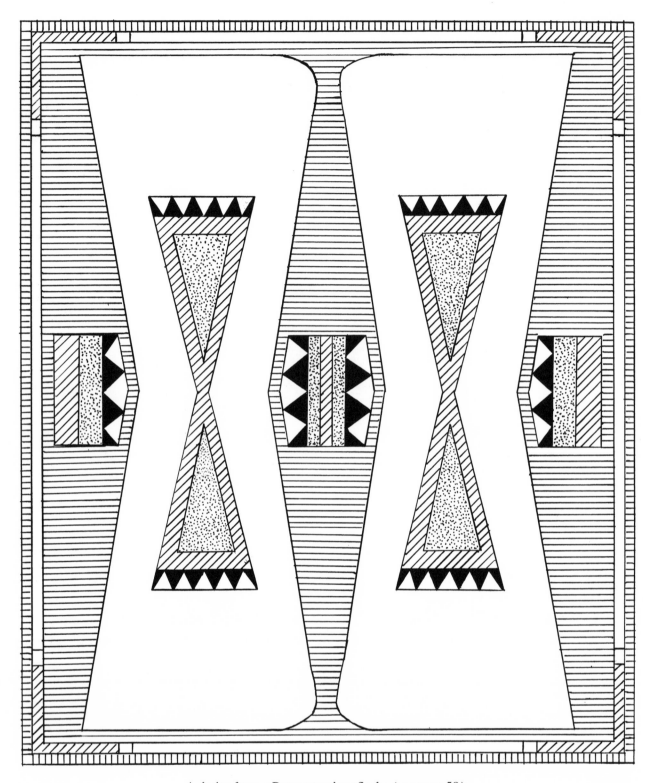

A design from a Potawatomi parfleche (see page 58).

1641 they were at Sault Ste Marie; by the end of the seventeenth century they were near the region now known as Chicago. In 1846 they were given 567,000 acres in Kansas, but at the present time they live in Kansas, Oklahoma, Michigan, and Wisconsin.

The Potawatomis were excellent craftsmen and worked in a great variety of mediums. Painted raw-

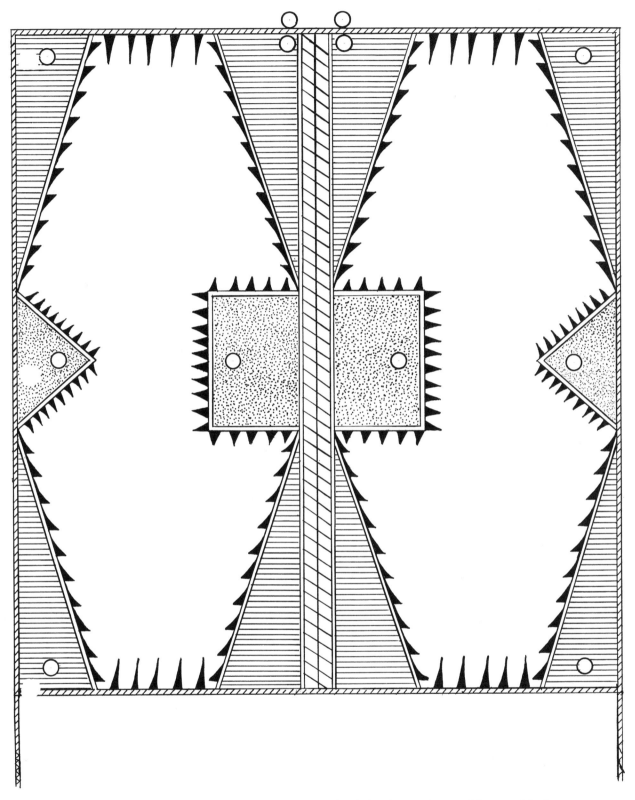

A design from a Jicarilla Apache parfleche. The design is very large, with many black units. The side flaps are also decorated. (Denver Art Museum)

HOLES: 1 pair on one flap; 2 pairs on other flap. SIZE OF PARFLECHE: 40¼ x 17 in. SIZE OF DESIGN: 18 x 17 in.

85

hide probably was not a major craft, and little if any rawhide was painted after 1890. The women said that when they wanted to paint a hide, they asked permission of the head of the tribe, as they did when they wished to harvest rushes for a mat, and he sent paint to them. After a woman received permission to paint a pair of parfleches, she paid the head of the rawhide craft a buffalo hide to lay out the patterns and to indicate colors on the damp hide. When these things were done, other women would paint in the colors.

While each design belonged to a clan, the designs had certain features in common with those of the Cheyennes, except that the Cheyenne design areas on the upper flaps were square while those of the Potawatomis were rectangular. Design units were outlined in brown-black and included some small brown-black units. Designs were enclosed in a border composed of two bands of color separated by a band of neutral or white. Most of the lines were straight or nearly straight. No bands connected the two decorated areas, and no decoration was used on the side flaps.

The Potawatomi women said that they used a clam shell and at least one bone brush for each color; paints were mixed with glue made by boiling the hide from the forehead of a buffalo. Black was made from charcoal.

These Indians also used folded containers (trunklike) made from hides with the hair on, as well as painted parfleches. In very early times, the tribes of the Chicago region carried the parfleches on their backs, from four to eight being considered a load. Potawatomi parfleches were quite large, and the design indicated what each contained.

2. Athapascan Family

APACHES

The Apaches are fairly recent immigrants to the Southwest, having traveled down from western Canada several centuries ago. In the seventeenth century the Jicarilla Apaches lived along the Cimarron River, and during buffalo days they traveled east and southeast to the plains to secure meat and hides. At the present time they reside on a reservation near Dulce, New Mexico.

Jicarilla parfleches are easily distinguished from others. They are large, probably consistently larger than those made by any other group. Typical ones measured eighty-one inches long when open and forty and one-half by seventeen inches when closed. On the parfleche of many other tribes the side flaps narrow, being just wide enough to meet in the center and cover the contents when the bag was packed full. On the Jicarilla parfleche, each side flap was nearly as wide as the parfleche, so that when the first folds were made, the contents would be covered with two pieces of rawhide; after the second folds were made, there would be five thicknesses of rawhide over the contents and one underneath.

Another distinguishing Apache characteristic is the many, many little brown triangular appendages to the edges of the units of designs. Rawhide workers from other tribes who saw the Jicarilla designs always remarked, "They must have had several workers on those designs." They meant that it would take such a long time to paint the complicated designs that the hide would dry out before they were finished unless more than one person worked on them. By actual count there were 202 little brown figures on each upper flap of a parfleche. The older Jicarilla people call these figures "fringe," and they seem to have religious significance. Fringe consists of very long, narrow, brown triangular-like painted small units attached to the border and to units of the design. The designs are outlined in brown and may have other small brown figures besides the fringe. It is interesting that small brown figures much like those of the Jicarillas are also found on the parfleches from Sarsi, Kutenai, and Columbia River groups and were also used by the Foxes on their trunks. The side flaps may also have elaborate decorations.

The Jicarilla Apaches said that they used a root to make red paint. This might have been wild madder (Galium). They used mineral paints a long time ago, but used their basket dyes after moving to Dulce, New Mexico. A bone brush was used when painting rawhide.

These Indians often used stake holes for closing the parfleches instead of burning in holes for tying. Stake holes were found on the upper and side flaps. This means that the hide was cut into two pieces and each piece staked out separately. This method was convenient in working out the hump of the buffalo. The smaller pieces of the wet hide were easier to paint and size, but the worker must determine the exact measurement and shape of the parfleche before the pieces were staked out.

A Chiricahua Apache parfleche. No holes were burned in for closing the upper flap; the rawhide was slit, and ties were threaded through the slits. One side flap was painted. Note the geometric flower designs. (Denver Art Museum)

The Mescalero Apaches live in southern New Mexico. Their parfleches have the very wide side flaps found on the Jicarilla parfleches, but there the resemblance stops. The Mescalero parfleche is small. Only one of the side flaps is decorated, the one which shows when the upper flaps are lifted.

Mescalero designs on the upper flaps are in a class by themselves; they do not cover the entire flap, only the folded ends. There is no design in the center when the parfleche is closed. The designs are not enclosed with a border. Some parts of the designs are incised and then painted. Some rectangles

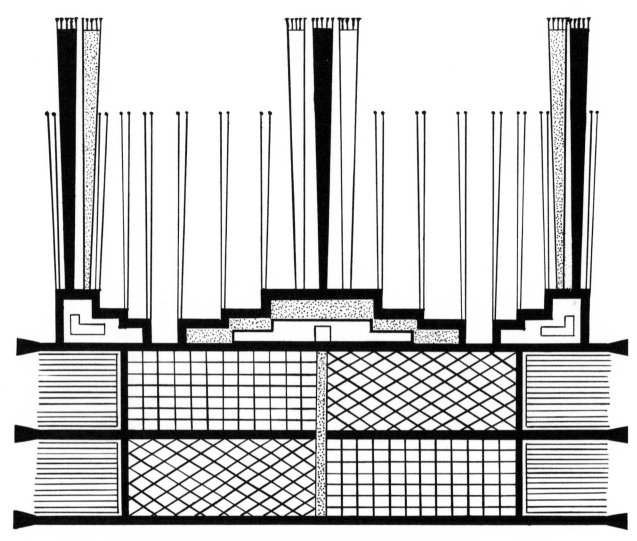

A design from a Mescalero Apache parfleche (see page 59).

are filled with checkerboard squares or crosshatching. One parfleche shows highly conventionalized flowers above a checkerboard base. Colors in the designs are green, red, yellow, and brown, with very little blue. The parfleches are quite white and the rawhide well made and smooth.

No round holes were burned in the upper flaps for closing the parfleche. Either one thong was sewed to each of the upper flaps with sinew or a slit was made in the hide after it was dry.

The San Carlos Apaches now live in Arizona. Formerly they used skin lodges and planted crops in the early spring and hunted the buffalo on the southern plains after the harvest. Most of their parfleches were large, so very large that when unfolded they look as if they were made from a whole

hide, whereas usually a pair of parfleches was made from one hide. The side flaps were wide and on them were painted colored bands of unlike designs. Stake holes were often used in tying the parfleche. San Carlos parfleches had much in common with Jicarilla designs in structure and color.

SARSIS

The Sarsis, an Athapascan group, belong to the Blackfoot Confederacy, and were one of the leading tribes that traded with the Hudson's Bay Company. Today they live in Canada to the north and west of the Blackfeet, and while the two groups have been closely associated, the Sarsis maintained their identity and their own language.

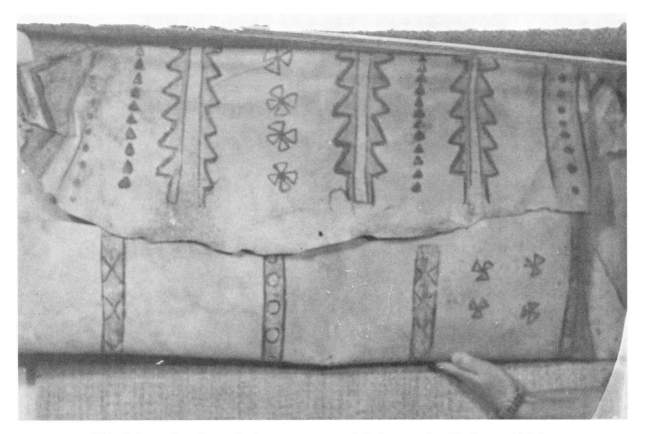

This Arizona Apache parfleche opens to reveal designs on the side flaps, which lap but are not as wide as those on the parfleches of the Jicarilla and Mescalero Apaches. The designs are at right angles to the side of the parfleche, while the other consists of one wide band parallel to the edge. Unusual colors appear on this parfleche: red-brown, red, blue, and genuine yellow. (M. G. Chandler Collection, Southwest Museum, Los Angeles, California)

The Sarsi parfleche has some characteristics in common with that of the Blackfeet and also with the parfleches of the Jicarilla Apaches and Kutenais. The old brown-black outlined the designs, and brown-black figures were common, with small half-ovals appended to the edge of the units of design. The upper flaps were trapezoid, and the side flaps had simple decoration. Three pairs of holes on each upper flap were used for closing a medium-sized parfleche. Both straight and curved lines made up the painted design. A true border was fashioned of narrow bands of color, usually two; and colored bands across the back of the parfleche connected the two decorated areas. Sarsi designs often showed an asymmetrical use of color.

3. Caddoan Family

ARIKARAS

The Arikaras, a Caddoan group closely related to the Pawnees, were farmers and buffalo hunters. They hunted the buffalo in the winter time and returned to their dwelling places in the early spring to plant their gardens. They lived in earth lodges. War and smallpox reduced the tribe and forced them to join the Hidatsas and Mandans on the Mis-

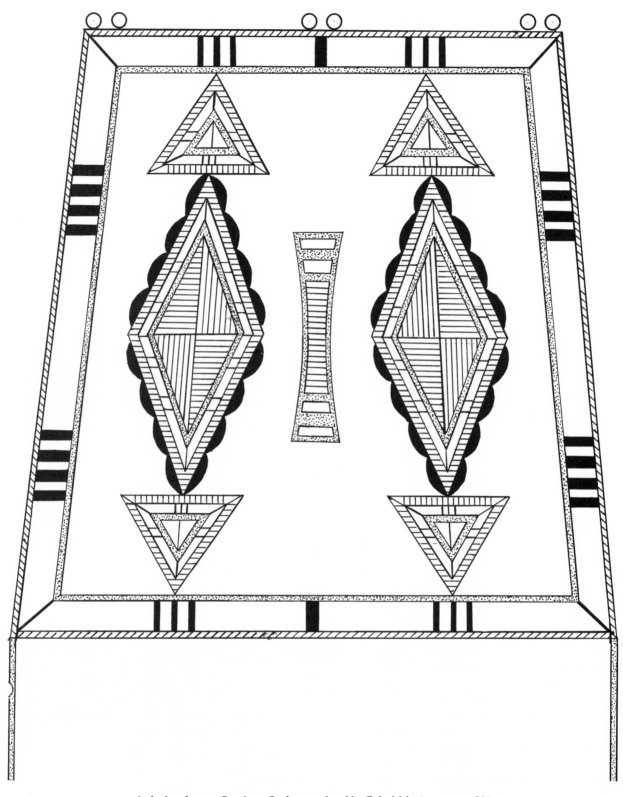

A design from a Sarsi parfleche, made of buffalo hide (see page 61).

90

Pawnee burden straps of buffalo hide, painted and incised. (Chicago Museum of Natural History)

souri River at the Fort Berthold Reservation, North Dakota. Both corn and the buffalo held prominent places in their ceremonies.

They claim that they invented the bullboat, and they used it for crossing the Missouri River and for gathering wood. This boat had a willow frame covered with a large buffalo hide with the hair side inside.

The Arikaras met the white trader about 1770. Lewis and Clark visited them in 1804, and Rudolph Kurz made many sketches of them and their villages while working at a nearby trading post. Maximilian, Prince of Wied, saw them in 1835.

The Arikaras melted large glass beads, secured from the trader, and poured the molten glass into molds to make ornaments. They also made baskets, using the techniques which are found among the Indians of Louisiana.

Very few rawhide parfleches were found for examination. The ones seen were probably made after the beginning of the nineteenth century when these Indians were living near the Hidatsas and Mandans, for their rawhide showed some of the Siouan characteristics.

PAWNEES

The Pawnees belong to the Caddoan family, closely related to the Arikaras. Coronado met the Pawnees in 1541 on the plains. They traded at St. Louis and moved to their present location in Oklahoma in 1876. They grew corn and dried green corn which they stored in rawhide bags for winter use. Corn was considered a sacred gift.

The men painted their personal histories in realistic designs on their robes, shields, and lodge covers. The Pawnees built permanent earth lodges, which are said to have been sixty feet in diameter, but lived in skin lodges while hunting buffalo. They were among the best horsemen of all the horse tribes and expert with bows and arrows and firearms.

Their parfleches were quite large with some of the characteristics of those of the Arapahos. The Pawnees used one pair of holes for closing, outlined in brown-black, and small units were also painted in this color. The parfleches had a narrow border made up of two bands of color divided by a natural band in which colored black or rectangular units were used to connect the two colored bands. The lines were straight or very slight curves, with no decoration on the side flaps. Green was a predominant color.

Their buffalo hunts were organized in an orderly manner so that each family received a share of the meat, which they dried and packed in these large rawhide parfleches.

Besides painting rawhide, the Pawnees also made pottery, baskets, and woven articles.

WICHITAS

The Wichitas, a Caddoan group, are closely related linguistically to the Pawnees. About the time Coronado went through what is now Kansas, they were hunting in central Kansas; at present they live near Anadarko, Oklahoma. These people were agriculturists who raised corn, squash, and other vegetables and hunted the buffalo. They used painted parfleches, but no modern ones were found. The old ones are large, some of them having three stake holes at the ends of the upper flaps. These holes were used for closing the parfleches; the slits for the stakes had been cut into the hide while it was quite wet. The designs, like most of the old ones, are simple with much neutral-colored hide showing. These parfleches were used for dried vegetables as well as dried meat.

The Wichitas lived in villages of large dome-shaped grass-thatched lodges, thirty to fifty feet in diameter, except when they were hunting the buffalo when they used skin lodges.

4. Chinookan Family

WASCOS

In the summer of 1856, eight or nine hundred Wascos, John Days, Tyighs, and Des Chutes were sent to live with the Warm Springs or Tenino Indians on the Warm Springs Reservation. All except the Wascos belonged to one division of the Northern Shahaptian stock and used the same dialect. These groups became closely united politically and considered themselves one people.

The Wascos are a Chinookan tribe living on the south side of the Columbia River, near The Dalles. The Wishrams, who were practically identical in language and culture with the Wascos, were placed on the Yakima reservation.

The Wascos hunted buffalo in southern Oregon. Buffalo were never as plentiful there as on the Great Plains, and they were gone fifty years before

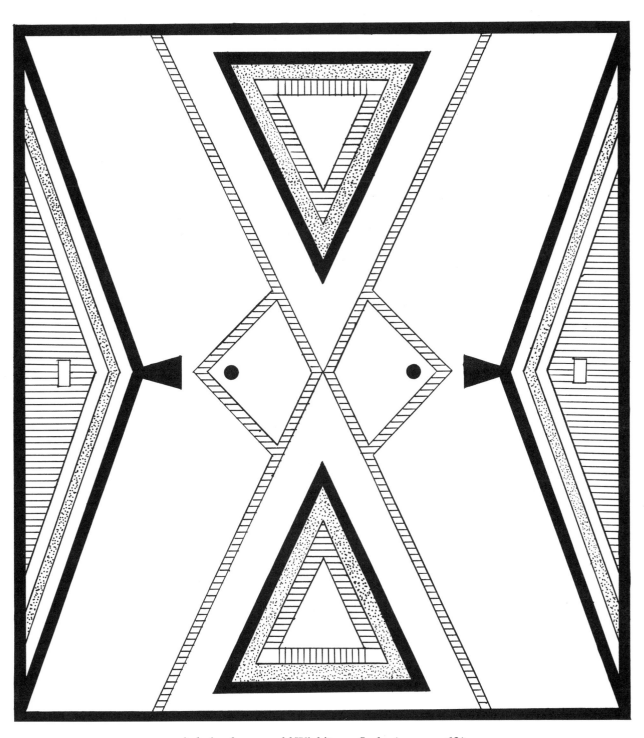

A design from an old Wichita parfleche (see page 62).

A design from a Wasco parfleche from the Warm Springs Reservation, acquired in 1905. The parfleche is of buffalo hide and shows evidence of being much used and often washed. The hide is very soft. (Chicago Museum of Natural History)

HOLES: 1 pair. SIZE OF PARFLECHE: 55 x 13 in. SIZE OF DESIGN: 15½ x 12 in.

they disappeared from the plains to the east. These people also used bear robes and hides of other large animals for rawhide and buckskin.

The Wascos used the old incised parfleche for storing meat and the painted parfleche for blankets, shawls, cloth, and clothing. There are still some of both types on the reservation. The Wascos, Teninos, and Tyighs called the painted parfleche "shup-tuc-kiah" or "shup-ta-kiah," which means "to put something in," and the difference in the words might tell what was in the container.

Among these Indians a marriage agreement was sealed between the parents of the bride and the groom by an exchange of presents. A woman who had one or more sons started early to make or collect painted rawhide parfleches and fill them with blankets, shawls, calico, and other "soft things." A woman with a daughter who would soon be of the age to marry made or traded for a number of large cornhusk bags. These would be filled with dried roots such as camas and wild turnips. The parents usually selected the mates for their children. When all parties had agreed to the marriage, the groom's parents gave the bride's parents a number of painted rawhide parfleches, each filled with "soft things." If all was well, in return the bride's family sent an equal number of large cornhusk bags filled with dried roots. Sometimes as many as twenty parfleches were prepared, but the average was less. This was not a purchase price. It was a formality which put the stamp of approval on the marriage, made it binding, and gave social standing to the young people. The marriage could not be a hurried affair because time was needed to get these presents ready.

When the "shup-tuc-kiah" was full, the ends were tied with three pairs of holes found on each upper flap. The Indian women said that certain designs on the "shup-tuc-kiah" indicated their use or contents and that the parfleches were often carried on the back. Six or eight filled ones were considered a load for a man. A stick used inside the parfleche to spread it was a custom of the Columbia River groups.

The old parfleches were medium to large in size, with the background spaces outlined in dark brown to black. A few small units of brown-black were in the old designs. The side flaps were decorated.

An old Indian woman sitting on a buffalo robe at a celebration on the Warm Springs Reservation was chosen as a good informant. The younger people said that she was too old and that she did not speak any English. However, when she was

shown a photograph of an incised parfleche, she looked at it a long time and then through an interpreter asked where it came from. Everyone became interested as she told the story of how it was made from elk hide, painted with blood and pitch from the trees, and how the design was cut on it with a sharp Indian "knife." Many of those in the group around her said that they had such parfleches at home which they used for meat.

WISHRAMS (TLAKUITS)

The Wishram (Tlakuit) Indians, a Chinookan group, who live on the Yakima reservation in the state of Washington on the north side of the Columbia River, made both incised and painted parfleches. They speak the same language as the Wascos, who live on the south side of the river.

Besides hunting the Wishrams depended on fish, roots, and seeds for their existence. Dried fish was pounded and packaged in dried fish skin for trade with other tribes. Their parfleches were used for storage as well as for packing on horses. Most of the old parfleches examined were made from buffalo calf or elk hides.

The painted designs used no brown or black as outlining or as part of the design. The rectangular decorated area on the upper flaps was enclosed with a single green band (a western characteristic), and green bands across the back connected the two decorated areas. The designs on the upper flaps may be mere decoration, but the designs on the side flaps are old and symbolic. One parfleche had three old-type conventionalized units on each side flap which represented people; another had symbolic fish designs. These designs have also been found among some of the oldest cultures around the world.

Rawhide was not as important with the Wishrams as with the Plains Indian groups, but it was a very old tradition with them as shown by the type of design and naming of the units of the design. They have very old words in their language for blue and green as well as other colors. They used natural mineral and vegetal pigments before the arrival of the Europeans.

The Wishrams made the incised parfleche from elk and other animal hides. For this type of parfleche it was necessary to have a hide with a brown layer of tissue. When buffalo was not available, an elk hide was covered with a sizing made of blood mixed with pitch from the trees, which turned the epidermis dark brown.

95

A Wishram parfleche closed (above) and open (below), showing the design on the upper flaps. The designs on the side flaps (below) are interpreted as persons. (Leslie Spier and Edward Sapir, "Wishram Ethnography," University of Washington *Publications in Anthropology*, Vol. III, No. 3 [1930], plate 9)

5. Kiowan Family

KIOWAS

The oldest Kiowa tradition locates these Indians at the head of the Missouri River in the vicinity of Virginia City, Montana. They were one of the earliest groups to have horses and became excellent horsemen. They were placed in their present location in western Oklahoma in 1868.

Their parfleches were about medium size. The design area on the upper flaps was square or only slightly rectangular. The end of each upper flap had a single hole in the outer corners and a pair in the center. This is the same as the Dakota and Cheyenne (single, pair, single) method of closing.

Kiowa designs were outlined in brown, and a few small figures were found, which might be a little more than a thickened line. Most of the designs showed some slightly curved lines, but most of the lines were straight. White negative designs, squares, rectangles, triangles, and other shapes broke up the colored areas. The design was en-

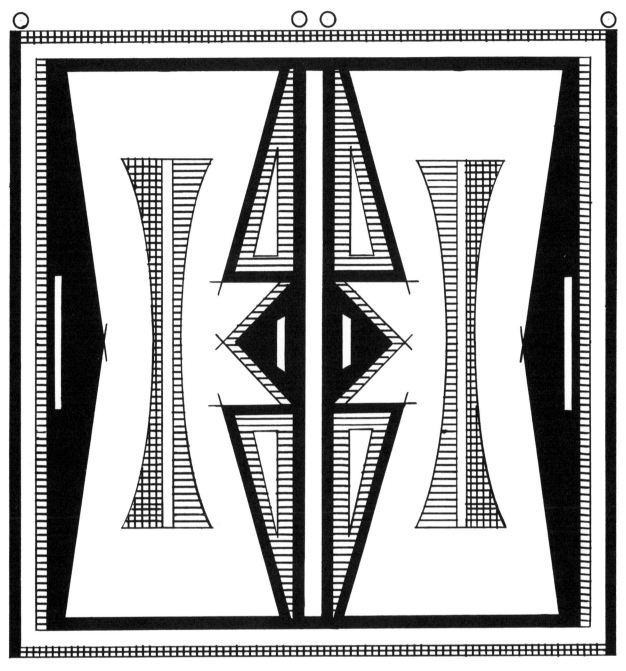

A design from a Kiowa parfleche, made of buffalo hide (see page 64).

closed in a narrow border made up of two narrow bands of color with a white area between. The outer band might be red on the sides and yellow at the two ends. On the inner band the colors were reversed. These bands were connected with a few brown lines or short band of color.

The square or rectangular design area was divided into two panels with smaller units attached to the sides of each panel. No lines connected the two decorated areas, and the side flaps were without decoration.

The older people said that the parfleches were painted blue and red with a minimum of yellow and black, and they called blue the parfleche color, although little blue has been found on the parfleches available for study. They said that they made blue from wild grapes and covered the painted area with sizing. It may be that the predominating color on a parfleche showed the contents. As a whole the designs were delicate rather than bold and showy.

A design from a Kutenai parfleche (see page 64).

6. Kitunahan Family

KUTENAIS

The Kutenais, a Kitunahan group, originally lived east of the Rocky Mountains and were great buffalo hunters. They said that they were driven west over the mountains by the Siksikas (Blackfeet), but continued to make trips to the plains to hunt. They now live in northwestern Montana, northern Idaho, and British Columbia.

Their realistic painting is like that of the Plains Indians, and some distinct differences in styles can be noted in the parfleches made by the three groups.

Kutenai parfleches were about medium size with trapezoidal upper flaps and three pairs of holes for closing. The upper flaps of some of the old ones were narrower than those of any other tribe. The side flaps often had elaborate decorations, frequently using much of the old brown paint. This color was plentiful and never as expensive as other colors, and it also may have had traditional significance. Other natural colors were used and uncommon color combinations, for example, yellow and green or rose-red and brown, both with small accents of blue. The coating of paint was rather light with the skin showing through. A large number of triangular-like brown figures were often attached to the construction lines. The use of these rusty-black figures was also common with the Jicarilla Apaches and Sarsis.

The Kutenai groups living in Idaho and British Columbia had more curved lines on their parfleches than the Montana group. Bands of color connected the two decorated areas, and usually the design area was enclosed by a narrow band of color rather than a true border.

7. Salishan Family

FLATHEADS

The Flatheads, a Salish tribe, live in northwestern Montana near Flathead Lake. Formerly in the summer they crossed the mountains to the east by way of Codotte Pass to hunt buffalo on the plains. It is true that some of the buffalo crossed the mountains, but they were few and they were gone from this region fifty years before they disappeared from the plains. When they could still be found in great herds on the plains, the Flatheads camped each summer on the south fork of the Sun River and hunted to the east. After they obtained horses, they took the poles for their lodges with them; the small ends of the poles were tied to the horse's shoulders and the large ends dragged on the ground, making a wide trail on which grass has never regrown.

The Flatheads came to hunt and brought bitterroot, camas, and many rawhide parfleches to trade with the Atsinas, Piegans, and Crows. It is generally presumed that the Flatheads learned to make painted rawhide parfleches from the Plains groups. Whether or not this is true, older Atsina women said that the Flatheads brought quantities of parfleches to trade. The Shoshonis, Nez Percés, and other groups also came to the plains to hunt and trade.

The Flatheads spent the summer drying meat and preparing buffalo hides and then returned to their homes in the Flathead Lake area with meat and rawhide for themselves and for trade with the groups on the Columbia River.

These Indians made an excellent parfleche and painted it with beautiful earth colors. Their red was superior; green was used for structural lines and a very dark green or blue-green for outlining. Blue was often used for short bands or triangles. No brown or black was used.

Four was the sacred number to the Flatheads, and everything was done in fours. In ceremonies four songs were sung or four times four songs. This feature often distinguished their designs from those farther west. For example, blue triangles might be found in fours or a multiple of four, while some of the Columbia River groups used three or a multiple of three. Green outlining was a western characteristic, seldom used on the plains parfleche but found on some of the painted rawhide trunks of the Sacs.

The Flathead design was rectangular and enclosed by a single band, usually green. The side flaps were not decorated. One pair of holes in each upper flap was used for closing the parfleche; extra holes may have been burned in at a later date when they were used by other people. Two pairs of holes on one side flap adjacent to the folded edge are a

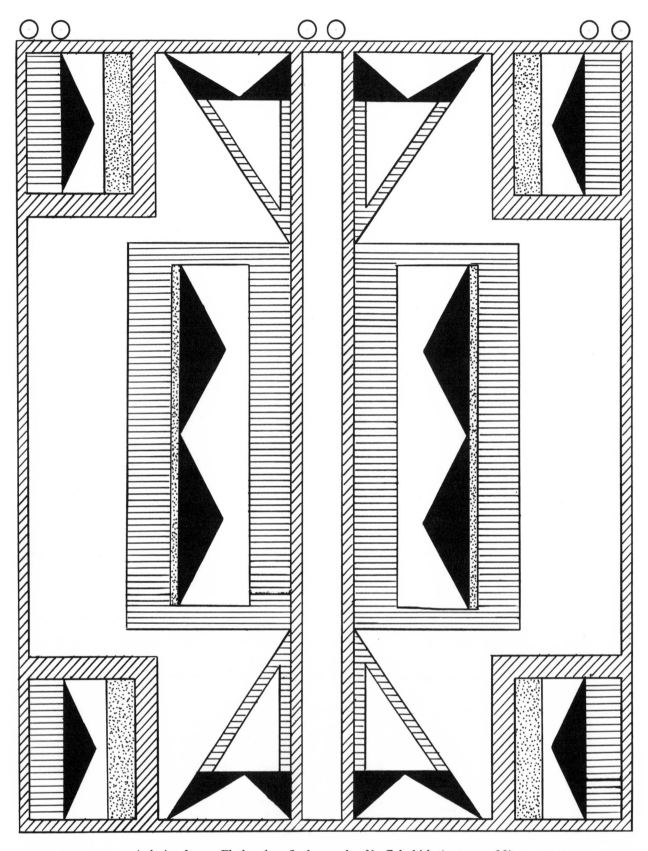

A design from a Flathead parfleche, made of buffalo hide (see page 66).

A design from a Klikitat parfleche. The design is characterized by straight lines and the absence of curves. Earth colors were used on this parfleche, and the borders are black. Rose bands across the back connect the two upper flaps. (American Museum of Natural History)

HOLES: 3 pairs. SIZE OF PARFLECHE: 60 x 15¾ in. SIZE OF DESIGN: 15¼ x 15 in.

distinguishing feature. This means that a stick was tied inside the bag to strengthen it when it was packed on a horse. A thong was tied through the two pairs of holes and inserted under the side flap.

This method of packing a parfleche on a horse was also used by the Atsinas, Wascos, and other Columbia River groups.

KALISPELS (PEND d'OREILLES)

The Kalispels, or Pend d'Oreilles, are a Salish tribe now living on the Kalispel reservation in northeastern Washington near the Idaho line and on the Flathead (Jacko) reservation in western Montana and at the Colville Agency, Washington.

Their parfleches were of medium size with slightly trapezoidal upper flaps. Green was the most important color; one or two bands of green formed a frame for the design, and the design areas on the upper flaps were connected with bands of green. The old mineral black was used for outlining and for smaller minor figures in the design. Designs in bright colors filled most of the decorated spaces.

Kalispel parfleches seemed heavy; the rawhide was thick, as if made from a mature animal. Most of the specimens available for examination were made from buffalo hides.

OKINAGANS

The Okinagans are an important division of the Salishan family. They live on the Colville Reservation in northeastern Washington and in British Columbia. They used parfleches for packing on horses, taking them on trips into the mountains, on fishing trips, or just to pack supplies from the store to the ranch. A packhorse-load of up to two hundred pounds could be put into three or four pairs of parfleches, depending upon their size. The parfleches were packed on the horse with a diamond hitch. This method of tying was noted for keeping the pack in place even if the horse "spooked," ran away, or bucked.

Okinagan parfleches were medium to large in size and showed many of the far northwestern characteristics, such as the narrow green border around the design and green bands across the back of the parfleche connecting the decorated areas on the upper flaps.

8. Shahaptian Family

KLIKITATS

The Klikitats, now living in the Columbia River valley in the state of Washington, were important traders between the West Coast Indians and those living to the east.

On the Klikitat parfleche there was no black outline, but units of design and even structural parts were sometimes painted a true black. This black and the way it was used were both uncommon. The red was a bright rose. Green, customarily used by the far western tribes, was little used by the Klikitats. Bands of red or dark blue connected the decoration on the upper flaps and often made a base for the decoration on the side flaps. Klikitat parfleches, of medium size, were made of good rawhide with attractive colors of mineral and vegetable pigments. Designs were made up of straight lines, and three pairs of holes were used for tying together the upper flaps.

NEZ PERCÉS

The Nez Percés are a part of the Shahaptian family. Lewis and Clark found them occupying a large area in what is now Idaho, Oregon, and Washington states. The present-day Nez Percé live on the Lapwai reservation in Idaho and at the Colville Agency in Washington. They secured horses about 1700 and became good horsemen. They knew the plains and made a trip each year to hunt buffalo.

Rawhide was not a major craft with the Nez Percés, but in modern times they made a great amount of painted rawhide for use and trade with other tribes. Their parfleches had characteristics in common with those of the Crows and Shoshonis and to some extent the Warm Springs group. Their parfleches do not look as narrow as those of the Crows. One pair of holes on each upper flap was used for closing. No black was used for outlining or for any small units in the design. No lines connected the decorated areas, and there was no decoration on the side flaps.

The decorated area on each upper flap was enclosed by narrow green bands or a double band with green on the outside and blue just inside the green. The structural lines were nearly always dark blue, and the blue in the border may be considered a structural line. Both light and dark blue were used in the same design.

Horizontal structural divisions of space are found mostly among the western groups and were more common in Nez Percé designs than in those of the Shoshonis or Crows. The Nez Percés sometimes cut the hide into two pieces from neck to tail before stretching it out. A pair of parfleches (mates) were painted at the same time. This may have made the painting easier, but it took ex-

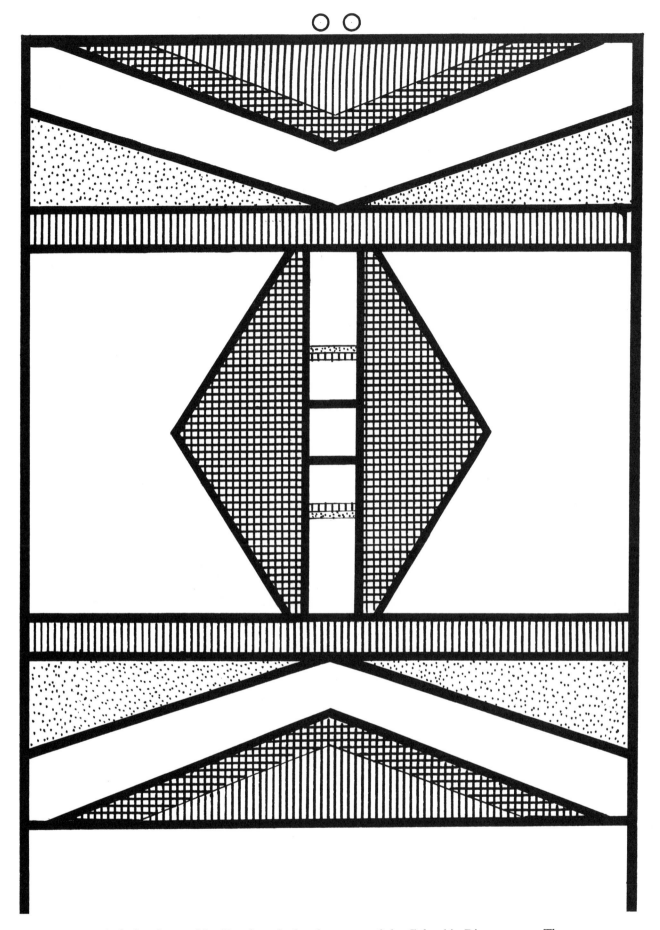

A design from a Nez Percé parfleche, from one of the Columbia River groups. The side flaps are decorated, and blue bands connect the upper flaps.

HOLES: 1 pair. SIZE OF PARFLECHE: 29¼ x 13½ in. SIZE OF DESIGN: 16½ x 13¼ in.

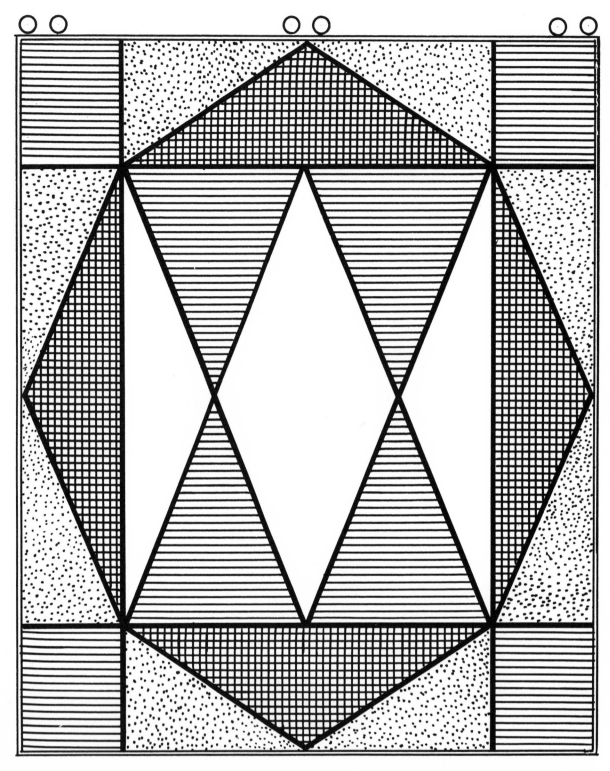

A design from a Tenino meat case (see page 68).

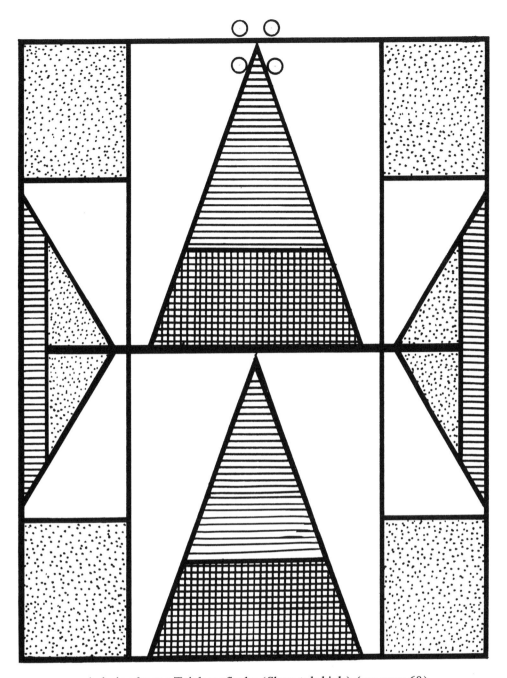

A design from a Tyigh parfleche (Shup-tuk-kiah) (see page 68).

perience and skill and left the scraps of rawhide in smaller pieces.

An illustration of the movement of parfleches from one Indian group to another was given by a Nez Percé man. A young woman of the Nez Percé tribe might wish to marry a young man from a neighboring tribe. Before the marriage was sanctioned by the families, the young man's family would take a number of painted parfleches which were filled with blankets, shawls, and calico to the young woman's family. If the young woman's family accepted the parfleches, they would return the same number of cornhusk bags filled with dried roots, and the marriage would take place. This custom indicated that there would be a number of parfleches on the Nez Percé reservation which had not been made there and would not show Nez Percé characteristics. The excellent cornhusk bags woven by the Nez Percés had nothing in common with the rawhide technique or design.

A design from an Umatilla parfleche, from the Umatilla Reservation, Oregon.

HOLES: 1 pair. SIZE OF PARFLECHE: 55½ x 11½ in. SIZE OF DESIGN: 14¾ x 11¼ in.

TENINOS AND TYIGHS

The Tenino and Tyigh Indians are two Shahaptian groups that live on the Warm Springs reservation. They both speak the Tenino dialect. It is difficult to separate the parfleches of these two since they have lived together in this location for over one hundred years. These groups made and used both the incised and painted parfleches.

Many of the Columbia River groups said they used mineral pigments from the sides of the cliffs or rimrock when hunting in the place now known as Ochoco Forest. They said that they could shoot the pigment out of veins in the rimrock which they could not reach in any other way. This pigment was powdered by pounding and then mixed with boiled sinew and resin from the trees.

The craftswomen said that before they had soap they put an alkali in the water when they washed their hides. They said that it was customary to pound the hair off the hide after it was painted and dried.

UMATILLAS

The Umatillas are a Shahaptian group living on the Umatilla reservation in eastern Oregon. The making of articles from rawhide continued long after it was given up in other areas. This may have been due to several factors. First of all, the Umatillas used the decorated rawhide on their horses, and the opportunity to display their horses, horse trappings, packing cases, and the beautiful costumes of the riders at large Indian gatherings was an incentive. There was also an economic factor: they could always trade or sell painted parfleches, which were in demand by other tribes. After the buffalo were gone, they used the hides of elk and other large animals.

In studying the rawhide of any group that made parfleches for sale as well as for their own use, it is difficult to find the true parfleche characteristics unless some old parfleches can be found in museums or private collections or treasured by an older member of the tribe. One old buffalo-hide parfleche was probably made before 1880 or at least before 1890. Parfleches made since that time, of cattle, elk, or other large animals, were usually used for storing clothing and personal articles and may have been traded or exchanged many times.

The designs on Umatilla parfleches were not outlined in black but might have black in the design. Three pairs of holes were used for closing the upper flaps, and stake holes were often found on the side flaps. Curved and straight lines were used, and the area on the two upper flaps was a rectangle enclosed by a narrow band of old green paint. No bands of color across the back connected the decorations of the end flaps; side flaps were not decorated.

WALLA WALLAS

The Walla Wallas belong to the Shahaptian family and are closely related to the Nez Percés. They now live on the Umatilla reservation in Oregon. Some rawhide parfleches are still painted in the old way. This is one of the few places where the women continue this craft, probably because of the demand and the supply of large hides in the area. Also, many Indian people live remote from good roads in widely scattered groups in Montana and Idaho, Washington, and on into Canada. They ride horseback to the general stores for supplies and still use rawhide containers for "packing." This has been a way of life for many years.

The Walla Walla women selected an old parfleche design for this book which they said was typical. The design is enclosed with a narrow blue band, though very little blue was used in the design, which was made up of triangles attached to the band at the two sides. Two rather small, long unattached motifs were in the center. No black outlining or black figures were used, but some units were outlined in green or blue. The side flaps were painted. Paints came from natural substances.

YAKIMAS

The Yakimas are an important Shahaptian group now living in the southern part of Washington State. They are related to the Nez Percés, who probably made many of the modern parfleches found on the Yakima reservation. The old Yakima parfleches are quite different from the modern Nez Percé ones, and it is possible that the Yakimas made very few parfleches after 1910.

Designs on the old Yakima parfleches show the neutral or background spaces outlined in heavy black, and black was also used in the design. Green and ocher yellow were predominating colors, red and indigo blue being used in small amounts. There were words for blue and green in their ancient language. The designs were made up of straight lines, and often a large block in the center was divided into many small units.

Parfleches were medium to large in size. The upper flaps were tied together by three pairs of holes on each upper flap. Stake holes sometimes may be found on the side flaps, showing that a pair of parfleches were cut from a wet hide and staked out. This required a skill not needed when the whole hide was staked out.

9. Shoshonean Family

BANNOCKS

The Bannocks belong to the Shoshonean linguistic group and are related to the Shoshonis, Nez Percés, and Utes. Their culture is much like that of the Wind River Shoshonis.

The making of parfleches and other rawhide articles persisted among the Bannocks after it had been discontinued by many other groups. After the loss of the buffalo, the Bannocks secured the hides of other large animals. Being horse people,

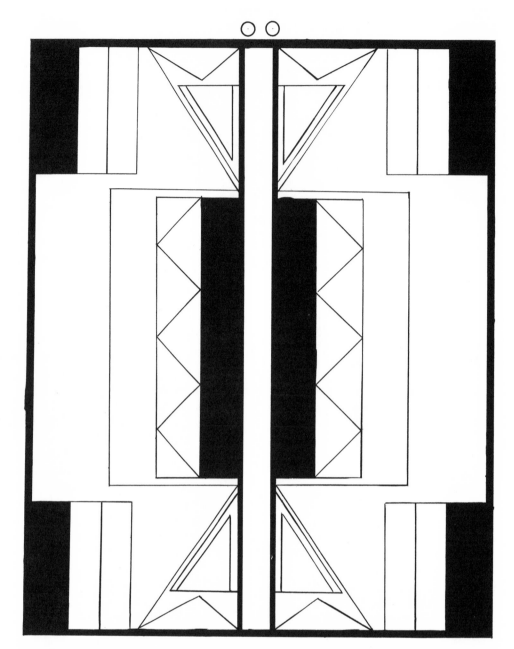

A design from a Walla Walla parfleche. This design was sketched from the case and was not drawn to scale. The parfleche is unusually long. (Chicago Museum of Natural History)

HOLES: 1 pair.

they needed horse trappings and gaily painted rawhide containers when attending the large Indian gatherings which are still a basic part of the lives of the Indians of this area.

Their parfleches were painted with rather simple, bold designs that could be seen to a good advantage at a distance. The upper flaps were tied together by one pair of holes on each flap and three pairs on each side flap. Designs often showed a definite horizontal division of space with a second-ary vertical division. The design was enclosed with one narrow band of color, often green. Two or more hourglass figures were commonly used to fill the center area. There were no black outlines or small units of black in the design. Green was often used for structural parts.

COMANCHES

The Comanches are of Shoshonean stock, closely related to the Shoshonis of Wyoming, and have

A design from a Yakima parfleche, marked "Yak Sah Yakima Res., 1913." Blue bands connect the two upper flaps. (American Museum of Natural History)

HOLES: 1 pair. SIZE OF PARFLECHE: 57½ x 12½ in. SIZE OF DESIGN: 15¼ x 12¼ in.
SIZE OF DESIGN: 14¾ x 12½ in.

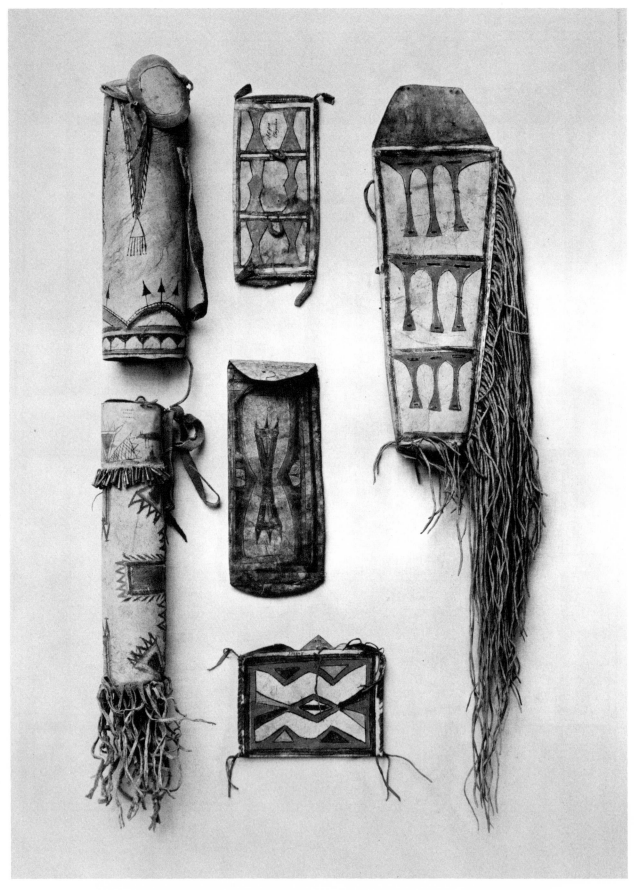

Some types of rawhide bags. Upper left: a cylindrical bag typical of those of the Comanches. Lower left: a cylindrical bag typical of those of the Arizona Apaches. Center, top: a Cheyenne flat bag. Center, middle: a Kiowa bag. Center, bottom: a Dakota bag. The bag at the right with the long fringe is marked Sioux. (United States National Museum)

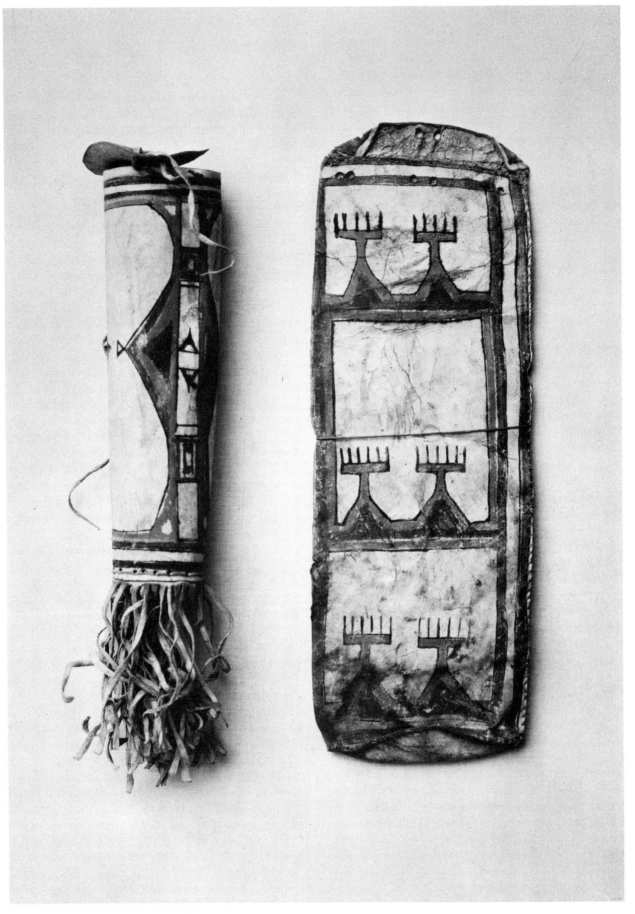

Comanche rawhide bags. Left: a cylindrical bag with a rawhide fringe. Right: a woman's workbag with a tanned elliptical piece of skin in the lower end. (United States National Museum)

been confederates of the Kiowas since 1795. For many years they were nomadic buffalo hunters, and they became known as the finest horsemen of the southern plains. They now live in southwestern Oklahoma near the Kiowas and Kiowa Apaches.

They made and used many rawhide containers, but comparatively few have been preserved for examination now because of the custom of burying the deceased person's belongings with the body or giving them away or burning them.

The utilitarian parfleche, used for meat and other dried foods, was not painted. Painted parfleches were used for clothing and shawls. Heavy black and deep, almost U-shaped, curves were found on many of their flat bags, cylindrical cases, and parfleches.

The older Comanche women said that they removed the hair from a dry hide by rubbing it with a flat sharp-edged rock or a sharp pole. Tools for removing the hair from deerskin might be made of a horse rib.

In Comanche the folded rawhide case is called a "pa-keep," meaning something which can be cached in the ground.

SOUTHERN PAIUTES

The Southern Paiutes, a Shoshonean group, now live in southern parts of Colorado and Utah. They have made little rawhide since 1880. Their old parfleches examined were large and not outlined in black, but a few small black triangles were found in the painted areas.

The Paiutes said that they dug a fine gold-colored earth on the desert which was made into balls and fired, after which they were put into a bucket of water and allowed to stand for two days. Red paint could then be squeezed from the balls. One tablespoon of this red paint could be traded for a blanket, which was valued at twelve dollars or more at that time.

The lymph or colorless fluid found between the skin and the flesh of a fish was used for sizing their rawhide; rubbed into the hide, it made the surface smooth.

Three pairs of holes were burned into each of the upper flaps for closing the parfleches. The decorated area was nearly square. The lines in the Southern Paiute designs were straight, and the border enclosing the design was very simple. No bands of color connected the decorated areas, and there was no decoration on the side flaps. The parfleche design in the accompanying illustration is made up of many triangles or triangle within triangles.

WIND RIVER SHOSHONIS

The Shoshonis are composed of two divisions; the Wind River Shoshonis, known as Washakie's band, who make their home near the mountains in western Wyoming, and the Northern group, who live on the Fort Hall Reservation in southern Idaho. They belong to the Shoshonean linguistic family and are closely related to the Bannocks, Comanches, Hupas, Paiutes, and Utes.

Formerly the Wind River Shoshonis hunted buffalo in Montana as far north as the headwaters of the Missouri River and on the plains to the east of there. After the buffalo were gone, around 1877, the Shoshonis went to Jackson Hole to hunt elk and to make rawhide from elk hides. Little rawhide was made after 1910, and many of the old rawhide pieces were buried with their owners.

A craftswoman living on the Wind River Reservation told of helping her aunt make rawhide parfleches. If not immediately made into parfleches, the green hide was staked out with the hair side down and left to dry; when ready to use it, it was soaked by tying a rope to a corner of the hide, putting it in a stream, and fastening the rope to a tree on the bank. The woman said she waded out barefoot to put rocks on the hide to keep it under water and changed the rocks often to allow all parts of the hide to become soft. The hide was not allowed to stay in the water until the hair slipped.

After soaking, the flesh was removed if it had not been before. Then the hide was staked out again and bleached by throwing water on it and leaving it to dry in the sun. The Indian woman wanted the hide to be white. The Wind River Shoshonis had plenty of water, for there were many streams from the mountains. This method was probably employed when the hide could not be worked on immediately after it was removed from the animal.

Paint in little wooden boxes could be purchased from a trader who had been on the reservation for many years, but he said that the women never used it; he sold it to the men for sun dance paint.

A Shoshoni informant said that the first painted rawhide was colored with earth colors which could be found along the streams, on the sides of hills, or in the mountains and caves. It was easy to get black, yellow, and bright or brownish reds, and it was also possible to find small deposits of dark blue and green, which the informant referred to as "mud." There were also hot mineral springs on the reservation near which deposits of colored minerals could be found.

Indian paint was pounded or ground between

A design from a Paiute parfleche (see page 119).

rocks, mixed with water, and put in a buckskin bag. This bag was hung up so that the pigment dripped into a second bag and from a second to a third. The finest paint was in the third bag.

After the buffalo were gone, the government sent in cattle, which were butchered near the agency and distributed to the Indians on "ration days." An old Indian man who years ago had helped with the butchering, said that the old women were always there early to get the eyes from the cattle. The liquid from these eyes, mixed with pigment, formed into cakes, and dried, was used to paint rawhide containers. Cactus juice was used for sizing the hide.

The rawhide parfleches were all decorated by the women; the men decorated their robes with their personal histories. The men used symbolic and realistic designs and the women abstract ones.

A design from a Shoshoni parfleche from the Wind River Reservation. The parfleche is quite old but shows no signs of use. It has no holes. The predominant color is a yellow rose shading to salmon. (Wyoming State Museum, Cheyenne)

SIZE OF DESIGN: 14¾ x 12½ in.

The women said that rawhide work was easy compared with tanning a robe; and many said the old way of removing the hair was with a stone after the painting was finished and the hide dry.

The modern Wind River Shoshoni parfleches might be mistaken for those of the Crows, but a more detailed study shows that Shoshoni parfleches are slightly wider and a little shorter. Both groups used one pair of holes in each of the upper flaps for closing the case. The Shoshoni design was more often enclosed in a narrow band of one color, green preferred, while the modern Crow design had a band of blue or a narrow band of blue inside a green one.

The nine-block structural design was common to the Wind River parfleches; a block in each corner and one on each side, with a larger one in the center. A framed square or rectangle in the center of the design is a Wind River characteristic. The Crows often used a diamond in the center of their design. Rose-red was used by the Shoshonis instead of a bright red. No black was used by either tribe for outlining or for design units. Lines were straight—the Shoshoni craftswomen did not approve of curves; the structural lines were usually blue and might be narrower in Shoshoni work than in Crow work. The Crows often traveled through Shoshoni country and may have acquired similar traits through this contact. They learned to use the nine-block design; this is older with the Shoshonis.

The Shoshonis said that in times past the Indians could tell which tribe made a parfleche by the direction of the stroke of the brush used when painting the design. For example, one group might use a horizontal stroke and another a diagonal one when filling color into a given area. This would seem to be discernible only to the initiated. The Shoshonis made a stroke parallel to the long edge of the parfleche while the Arapahos made a diagonal stroke.

The Shoshonis said that dried meat was packed into the parfleche with layers of mint leaves; the meat kept well, but the women occasionally took the parfleche off the horse and opened it out to examine it.

The people all tell that when Lewis and Clark came to this area, the Indians gave them parfleches filled with dried meat, and declared that the Lewis and Clark party ate of it "for two or three days without stopping."

Sacajawea, a member of the Wind River Shoshoni tribe, guided Lewis and Clark on their trip west from the Missouri River. When on their return trip they came to the first band of Shoshonis, of which her brother had become chief, Sacajawea acted as interpreter and enabled the expedition to obtain horses, without which they could not have crossed the Continental Divide.

An old Shoshoni woman said that meat was dried for a time in the sun. The flavor was improved if the drying process was completed by hanging half-dry meat on racks over a fire. The meat was not smoked, however, since a brisk fire was kept burning. This method was necessary because the air was not as dry as on the plains. After the meat was dry, it was pounded and put in parfleches.

FORT HALL SHOSHONIS

The Fort Hall parfleche had some traits in common with the Wind River work; there was one pair of holes for closing the upper flaps; no brown or black was used for outlining or for parts of the design; and the design was enclosed in one narrow band of color. Basic structural lines differed, however: Wind River people often used a nine-block design while the Fort Hall workers might use a three-panel; all lines were straight, and there was no decoration on the side flaps.

The Fort Hall Shoshoni group continued to make the parfleche after the Wind River group had ceased to do so. This may be due to a demand or use for the parfleche, or perhaps they dried meat from other large animals after the buffalo were gone. Indian groups to the west also provided a market for their rawhide.

NORTHERN UTES

The Utes, a Shoshonean group, are linguistically related to the Paiutes and Bannocks, but their parfleches show characteristics quite different from other western groups. One type of design from the Uinta group shows designs on the upper flaps, which are not enclosed in a continuous band of color. This design was made up of four blocks with the apexes of four small brown triangles touching the end of each block. When the small triangles were used by other groups, it was the base of the triangle which was attached to the larger unit of design. The designs were outlined in the old brown-black. Occasionally a curved or diagonal line was found, but in general, Ute designs were made up of straight lines. One interesting feature was the use of blocks inside of blocks; large rectangular designs were filled in with small squares and rectangles rather than with triangles or diagonal lines.

The Ute craftswomen said that for sizing they

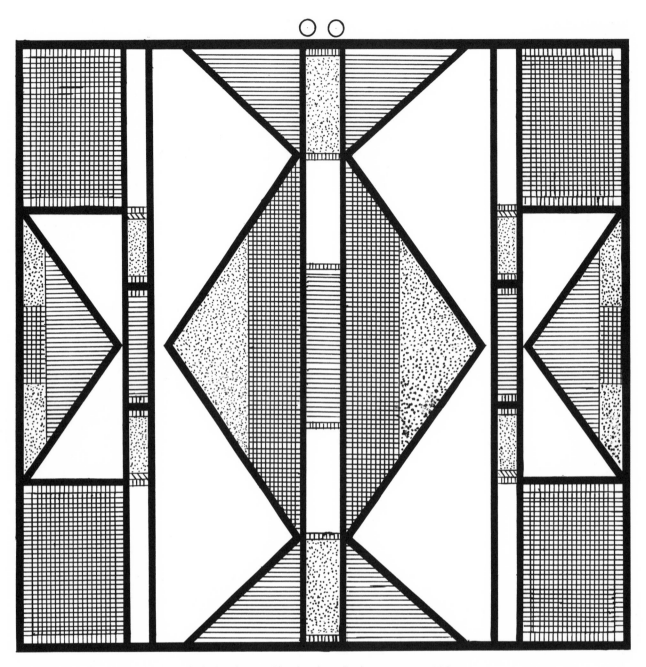

A design from a Shoshoni parfleche (see page 120).

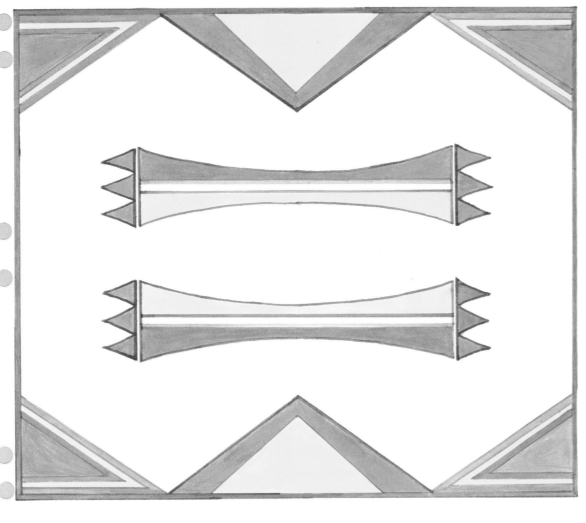

WALLA WALLA
(*Shahaptian linguistic family*)

This design is very old. It is enclosed in one narrow band of blue, but there is very little blue in the design (outlining with different colors is unusual). The side flaps are decorated. This parfleche was sketched from the case and was not drawn to scale. (Chicago Museum of Natural History)

HOLES: 3 pairs in the upper flaps. STRUCTURAL DESIGN: G. BORDER: No. 2.

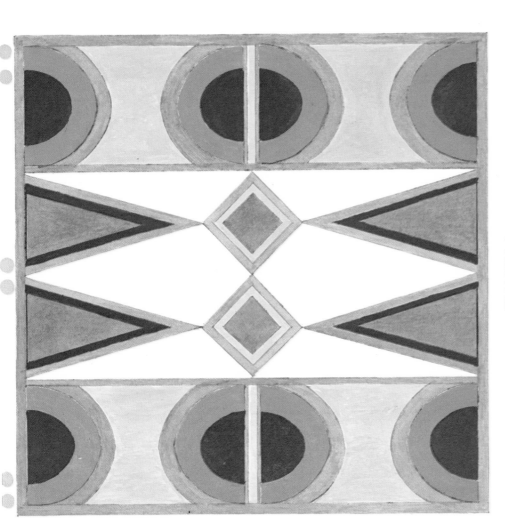

UMATILLA
(*Shahaptian linguistic family*)
(See Chart of Parfleche Characteristics)

The pointed triangles contrasted with curves give a contemporary look to this parfleche design, but it has been in the University of Pennsylvania Museum for many years. It shows an unusual use of the three-panel vertical structure, with black in the design but no black outlining. The border is of the old natural green typical of the parfleches of the area. (University of Pennsylvania Museum, Philadelphia)

HOLES: 3 pairs for tying the upper flaps, stake holes on the side flaps. SIZE OF PARFLECHE: 54 x 13¼ in.
SIZE OF DESIGN: 15¼ x 13¼ in. STRUCTURAL DESIGN: B.

117

BANNOCK
(*Shoshonean linguistic family*)

This design is from a parfleche collected in 1900 at Fort Hall, Idaho. The design is larger than the upper flaps and extends over both sides and the folded ends. Each panel is cut horizontally with wide green bands. A narrow band of green forms a border around the design and connects the design areas. No black or brown was used. (American Museum of Natural History)

HOLES: 1 pair. SIZE OF PARFLECHE: 60 x 13 in. SIZE OF DESIGN: 16½ x 16¼ in.

YAKIMA
(*Shahaptian linguistic family*)

This old parfleche is outlined in heavy black, and black also appears in the design. The side flaps are not decorated. The yellow in the border is unusual. No bands of color connect the decorated areas. (Denver Art Museum)

HOLES: 3 pairs in each upper flap, stake holes in the side flaps. SIZE OF PARFLECHE: 69 x 15 in. SIZE OF DESIGN: 17½ x 14½ in. STRUCTURAL DESIGN: G.

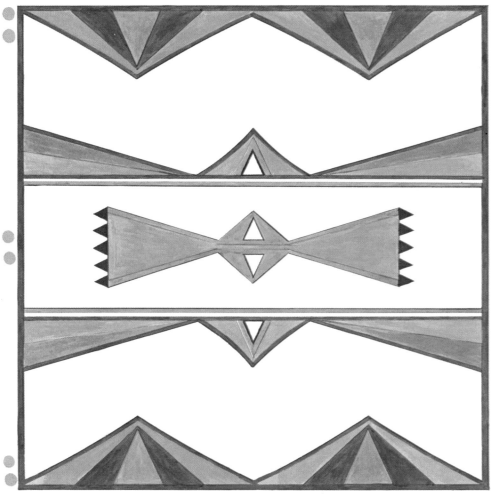

PAIUTE (Southern)
(Shoshonean linguistic family)

The basic structure of this buffalo parfleche design is three-panel vertical, with two alike panels on the sides and a different center with one free, unattached motif. The design is made up of triangles of many shapes and sizes. A few spaces are outlined in black, and five black triangles are appended to each end of the center figure. (United States National Museum)

HOLES: 3 pairs. SIZE OF PARFLECHE: 58 x 18½ in. SIZE OF DESIGN: 16¾ x 16¾ in. STRUCTURAL DESIGN: B.

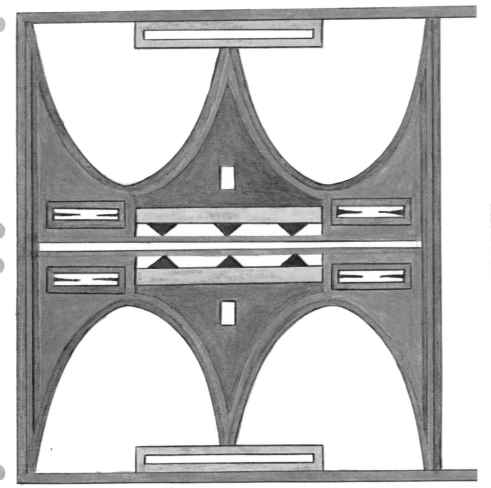

COMANCHE
(Shoshonean linguistic family)

This design, from an old buffalo parfleche, or Pa-keep, has deep curves in the center units. This type of curve is also found on Comanche rawhide bags and on the women's buffalo robes and is occasionally found on the parfleches of the Northern Utes, a linguistically related group. The design is outlined in dark brown, and incising can be seen under the brown. The wide side flaps are decorated. This parfleche had much use. The design is almost worn away, and the hide is softened. Non-Indians had sewed it into a long bag for the storage of shelled corn. (Indian Arts Fund, School of American Research, Santa Fe, New Mexico)

HOLES: single, pair, single. SIZE OF PARFLECHE: 48 x 14 in. SIZE OF DESIGN: 12½ x 13½ in. STRUCTURAL DESIGN: A.

SHOSHONI

A Fort Hall buffalo parfleche design. The design is a three-panel vertical one with simple blocks in the corners and a large double form through the center panel. No brown or black was used. (Museum of the American Indian)

HOLES: 1 pair. SIZE OF PARFLECHE: 58 x 14¾ in. SIZE OF DESIGN: 14 x 14½ in. STRUCTURAL DESIGN: B. BORDER: No. 2.

SHOSHONI
(Shoshonean linguistic family)

This Wind River design, from a parfleche that decorated Our Father's House, the Episcopal Mission church at Ethete, Wyoming, is a good example of the nine-block structure. It has a narrow green border, blue structural lines, repetition of blue in the triangular forms, a framed rectangle in the center block, and an unbroken block of rose red in each corner. No brown or black was used.

HOLES: 1 pair. SIZE OF PARFLECHE: 54½ x 12 in. SIZE OF DESIGN: 14½ x 11¾ in.

ASSINIBOIN
(Siouan linguistic family)

In this design, from an old buffalo parfleche collected on the Fort Belknap Reservation, Montana, much of the background space is painted, leaving negative design units. The color scheme is unusual: only two colors and black-brown outlining were used. Blue bands connect the two upper flaps. The custom of the Assiniboins at Lodge Pole, Montana, was to bury the possessions of the owner with his body, but one aged rawhide craftswoman told me that she wanted her parfleches handed down to her children's children.

HOLES: single, pair, single. SIZE OF PARFLECHE: 58 x 14. SIZE OF DESIGN: 14½ x 14 in.

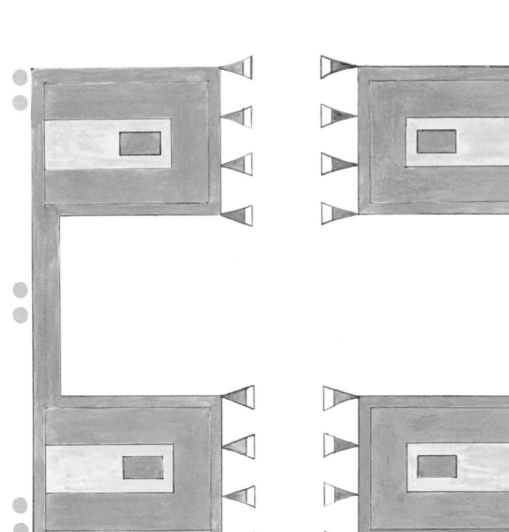

UTE (Northern)
(Shoshonean linguistic family)

This design from a Northern Ute (Uinta) parfleche, was collected at White Rock, Utah, in 1900. It has uncommon characteristics: no continuous band or border encloses the units of the design; there are no triangles except the small dark ones that are not entirely filled with brown and are attached to the large blocks by their points or apex rather than their basis; the lines are straight and are parallel to the sides of the parfleche. Green bands of color across the back of the parfleche connect the design areas. The design is outlined in brown. (American Museum of Natural History)

HOLES: 3 pairs.

121

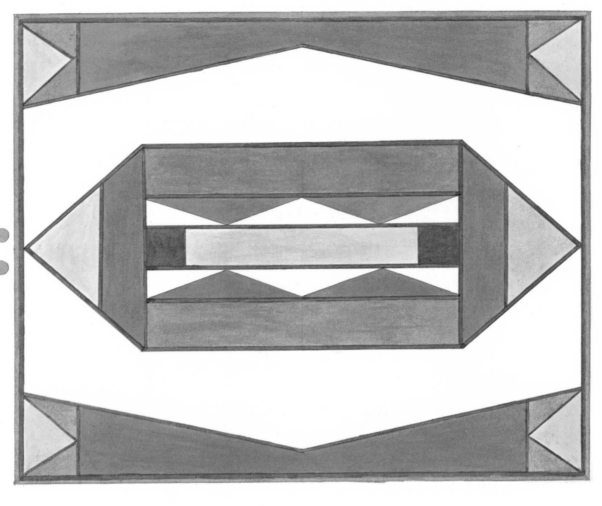

CROW
(*Siouan linguistic family*)

This design, from a buffalo parfleche collected in 1910, is an example of the Crows' use of the lozenge, symbolic of their fetish, the lizard. Note the absence of curves or outlines. The colors are typical of Crow parfleches.

HOLES: 1 pair. SIZE OF PARFLECHE: 62 x 13½ in. SIZE OF DESIGN: 16½ x 13 in. BORDER: No. 3.

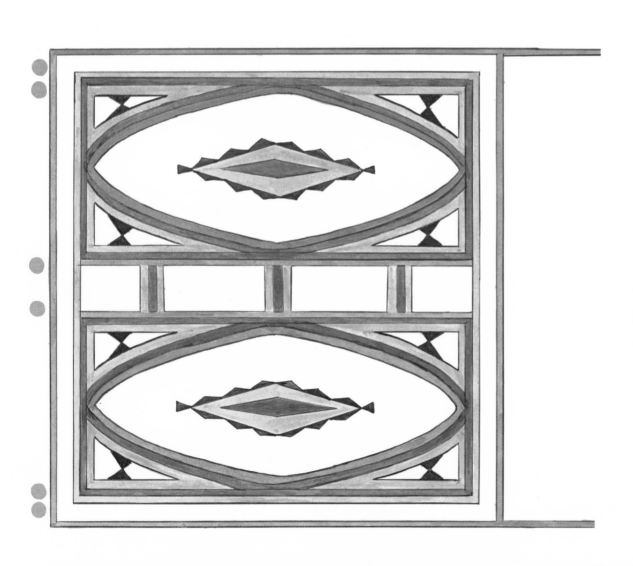

ASSINIBOIN (Canada)

This old design from a parfleche collected on the Stoney Reservation, Alberta, Canada, in 1907, is known as the Fish Design. The outline is brown-black, as are small units, and red bands connect the design areas. The curved lines are a Siouan trait. (American Museum of Natural History)

HOLES: 3 pairs. SIZE OF PARFLECHE: 48 x 13½ in. SIZE OF DESIGN: 13 x 13½ in. STRUCTURAL DESIGN: A. BORDER: No. 2.

DAKOTA (Santee)

This design is a typical two-panel design with the Dakota border and outline and small figures painted in the old brown. B. W. Thayer, of St. Paul, Minnesota, acquired this parfleche from Joe Campbell, of Prairie Island, Minnesota. It had allegedly belonged to Shakopee the Younger, a leader of the Minnesota Massacre of 1862, and was made by Mdewakanton Dakotas before 1860.

SIZE OF DESIGN: 15¾ x 12¾. STRUCTURAL DESIGN: A.

DAKOTA
(Siouan linguistic family)

This design, from a Rosebud Reservation parfleche, is outlined in dark-brown earth paint. Blue bands across the back connect the decoration on the upper flaps. The border is typical of Dakota Sioux parfleches. (Sioux Indian Museum, Rapid City, South Dakota)

HOLES: single, pair, single. SIZE OF DESIGN: 11½ x 13½ in. STRUCTURAL DESIGN: A.

123

MANDAN
(*Siouan linguistic family*)

This design is from a parfleche collected on the Fort Berthold Reservation, North Dakota, and acquired by the American Museum of Natural History in 1909. It was doubtless made much earlier. Siouan traits are evident: a wide border with a yellow background and triangles, blue bands across the back, and black outlining. The side flaps on this parfleche are wider than those of most other Siouan parfleches.

HOLES: single, pair, single. SIZE OF PARFLECHE: 59½ x 13 in. SIZE OF DESIGN: 15½ x 12½ in. STRUCTURAL DESIGN: G.

HIDATSA
(*Siouan linguistic family*)

The basic structural design of this parfleche is two-panel, with a Dakota border on two sides. Other characteristics typical of the Siouan group can be seen: heavy black outlining; single, pair, single method of closing, and blue bands across the back. This parfleche was acquired in 1909. (American Museum of Natural History)

HOLES: single, pair, single. SIZE OF PARFLECHE: 55 x 12¼ in. SIZE OF DESIGN: 15¼ x 11¾ in.

124

OTO
(*Siouan linguistic family*)

This design is outlined in black, and a few black figures are found in the design. The border is typical Siouan. (Museum of the American Indian, Heye Foundation)

HOLES: single, pair, single. SIZE OF DESIGN: 19 x 16 in.

OSAGE
(*Siouan linguistic family*)

This design, from a large parfleche that had been made into a bag, shows a two-panel vertical construction. Even after many years the yellow is almost luminous. Part of the design is outlined in dark brown. Blue bands connect the two decorated areas. (Chicago Museum of Natural History)

HOLES: single, pair, single. SIZE OF DESIGN: 18 x 17½ in. STRUCTURAL DESIGN: A.

CAYUSE

(*Waiilaptuan linguistic family*)

A design from a parfleche made before 1910. Its large size indicates that it was made to be filled with blankets. Green bands connect the two decorated areas, and the side flaps are also decorated. The under flaps are painted. (Collection of Minnie Minthorn, Umatilla Reservation, Oregon)

HOLES: 3 pairs. SIZE OF PARFLECHE: 66¾ x 17 in. SIZE OF DESIGN: 16¾ x 16¾ in. STRUCTURAL DESIGN: C.

BAGS

BLACKFOOT (Piegan)
(*Algonquian linguistic family*)

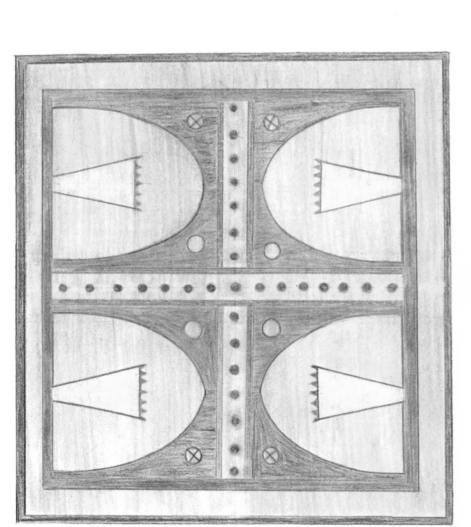

A design from a sacred bundle bag. Natural and earth colors were used. The bag was browned by the elements or by handling with sacred paint on the hands. The workmanship is excellent. The design shows the old Blackfoot characteristics. There are two thicknesses of fringe on each side, about ½ in. long. The green used on this bag is very unusual. The triangular-shaped flap is painted, and there are bands of color on the back. The following information was attached to the bag: "Painted Lodge Bundle—Water Monster—Piegan—Contains Inishims. First owner of the bundle was Big-Snake. Transferred to his son, Heavy Gun, who gave it to Yellow-Kidney. Yellow-Kidney transferred the bundle to Daniel Bull-Plume, who gave it to Wolf-Plume, who transferred the bundle to Found-a-Gun. Found-a-Gun gave the bundle to Barney Calf-Ribs as a gift; he gave it to Willie Tail-Feathers, who was the last owner." (Museum of the Plains Indians, Browning, Montana)

SIZE OF PARFLECHE: 13 x 13 in.

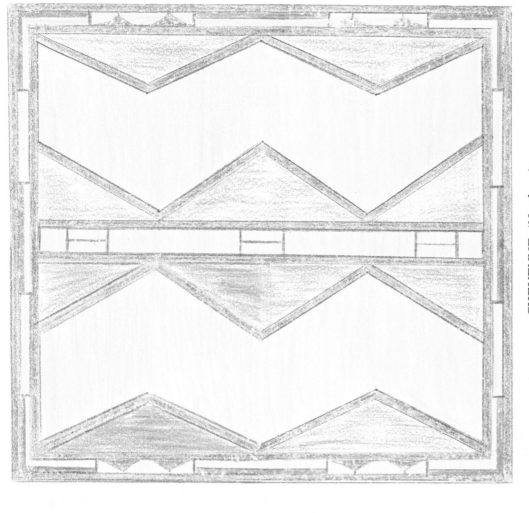

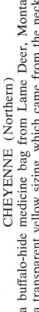

CHEYENNE (Northern)

Design from a buffalo-hide medicine bag from Lame Deer, Montana. The bag is covered with a transparent yellow sizing, which came from the neck of the buffalo, forms an important part of the bag. It has become soft, like a textile, from age and use. There are five of these bags on the reservation, one for each division of the tribe. The medicine woman who owned the bag illustrated above said that it had been made before 1870 and that she had received it from her mother, who was also a medicine woman.

CHEYENNE
(Algonquian linguistic family)

Attached to the bag on which this design appears was the following information: "Valise from the Sand Creek Massacure secured from Miles Patton by Mr. Diamond on Bear Creek. Mr. Patton was a volunteer with Clevington in the Sand Creek fight, Nov. 29, 1864.: Sometime during the 1940's, Little Woman, a Cheyenne crafts-woman living on the Cheyenne-Arapaho lands in eastern Oklahoma, was looking over a pile of rawhide designs used in compiling the information for this book. She could not read or speak English, and her daughter interpreted for her. When Little Woman came to this design, she looked at it for a long time and then asked where it had been found. She was given the above information. Little Woman then said: 'I was a little girl three years old when this happened. I hid in a sandy arroyo, and the soldiers did not find me. Now I know how old I am.': Older Cheyennes were very much interested in this design." (Denver Art Museum)

127

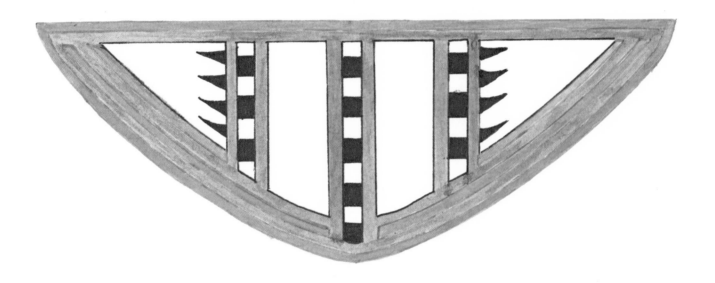

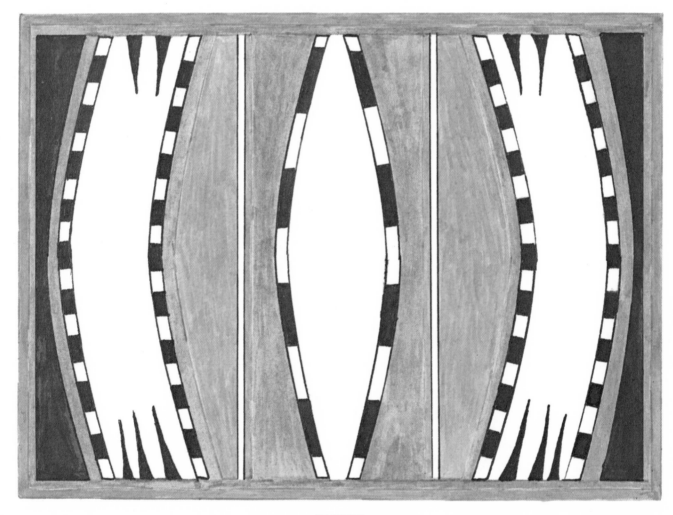

SALISH
(*Salishan linguistic family*)
This design was taken from a rawhide bag collected by Lieutenant Charles Wilkes during the expedition of 1832 to 1834 to the Cumberland Gulf on the Northwest Coast. Much true black paint was used on the flap, as well as on the front of this smooth, well-sized bag. Blue-green and rust lines extend across the back. A fringe 21 inches long hangs from the sides. (United States National Museum)

SIZE OF BAG: 10½ x 15 in. SIZE OF DESIGN: 10 x 13¾ in.

ASSINIBOIN (Canada)

(*Siouan linguistic family*)

Two designs from the front (Left:) and back (Right:) of an elliptical rawhide bag, made from moose hide, used for carrying the owner's possessions when he was on horseback. The bag was made from two pieces of rawhide sewed together at the sides. An elliptical piece of soft tanned skin was sewed into the bottom of the bag, extending it so that almost any amount of possessions could be packed in it. (Property of Charles Track, Fort Peck Reservation, Montana)

129

NAMED DESIGNS

WASCO
(*Chinookan linguistic family*)

This design, from a Warm Springs Reservation parfleche, is known as the Butterfly Design. (Chicago Natural History Museum)

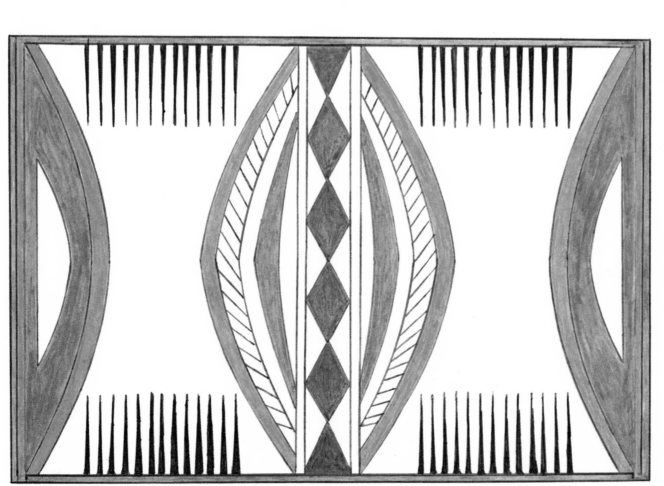

WARM SPRINGS

A design from an old envelope-type rawhide bag from the Warm Springs Reservation. Distinctive characteristics are the use of the old brown mineral paint with small amounts of orange and green and the curved lines. (United States National Museum)

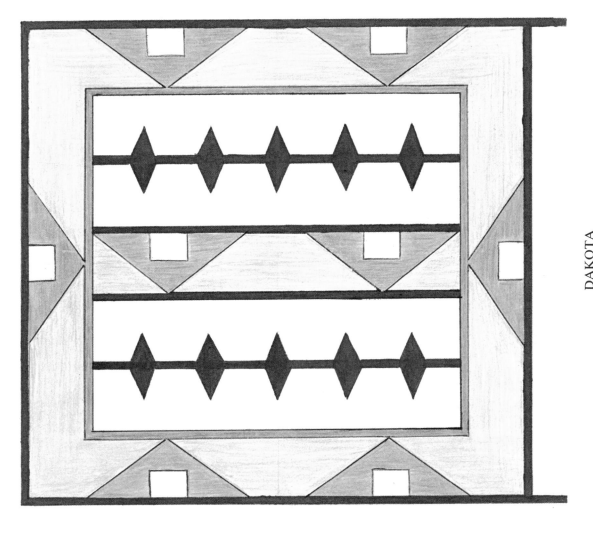

DAKOTA

This design is from a "Wakpon" parfleche made by an Oglala woman. It is a "dreamed design," Kamni-mni-la, meaning something that flutters or moves as a butterfly. It was dreamed by Begs Paint. (Contributed by Mrs. Eagle Hawk, Pine Ridge Reservation, South Dakota)

DAKOTA
(Siouan linguistic family)

This design, from a parfleche made on the Cheyenne River Reservation, South Dakota, is known as Distant View. Cactus juice was used for sizing. It was made by Mrs. Eagle Feather.

SIZE OF DESIGN: 14¼ x 14¼ in.

131

DAKOTA

This design, from a Dakota buffalo hide collected in 1900, is interpreted as representing the Four Directions. It is a typical two-panel, three-border design showing the use of curves. A diamond in each of the two panels is broken vertically and horizontally by green bands (the four directions). The small, unpainted triangles at the ends of the design are the opening through which the sun shines.

DAKOTA

This design, from an Oglala parfleche is commonly known as the Bravery Design. It was made by Ida Little War Bonnet, who died in 1934 at the age of eighty-seven. She remembered the great buffalo herds. (Pine Ridge Indian Museum)

A Northern Ute family with a parfleche in the foreground, a tipi made of elk skins, and ceremonial bundles hanging from a tripod. This photograph was made in 1873. (Bureau of American Ethnology)

pounded a despined, peeled pin-cushion cactus into the damp hide. The usual method of closing the parfleche was by the use of three pairs of holes. The Northern Ute parfleche was large, and colored bands connected the two decorated areas on the upper flaps.

SOUTHERN UTES

The Southern Ute parfleche designs were charac-terized by the use of much coloring; very little natural-colored background was seen. Their designs have much in common with those of the Dakotas; the same type of structural lines and the wide border.

A Northern Ute encampment, showing Sai-ar's tipi, in the Uinta Valley, on the eastern slope of the Wasatch Mountains in Utah. The photograph, taken during the John Wesley Powell Expedition in 1874, shows the tipi, made of elk skins, and, in the foreground, two packed painted parfleches. The horse trappings include a painted rawhide bag with a long fringe. (Bureau of American Ethnology)

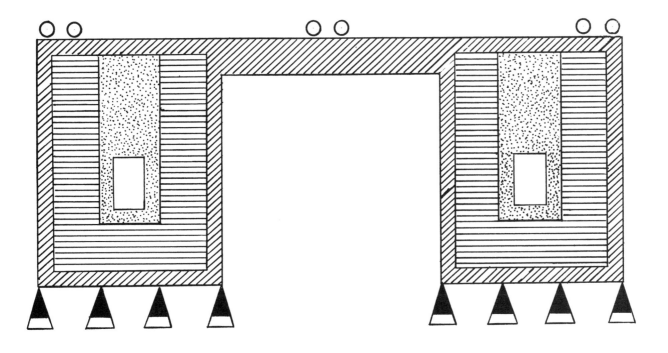

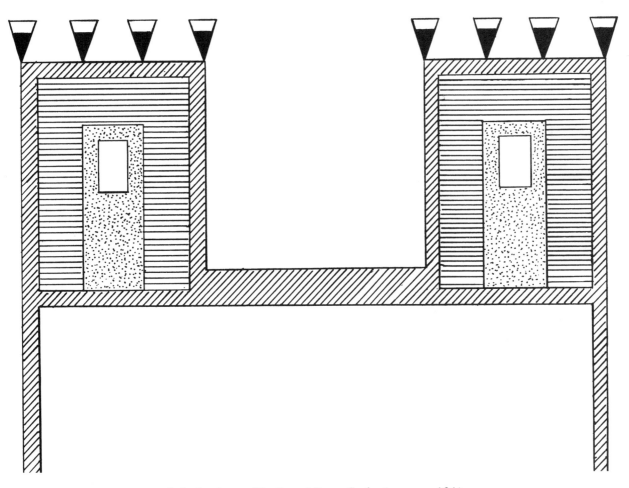

A design from a Northern Ute parfleche (see page 121).

135

10. Siouan Family

ASSINIBOINS

The Assiniboins are a Siouan group that separated from the Yanktonais before 1640. In 1658 they were living between Lake Superior and Hudson Bay. In 1744 there were two divisions of the Assiniboins in the neighborhood of Lake Winnipeg. The Plains Assiniboins now live on the Fort Peck and Fort Belknap reservations in Montana and the Assiniboins-of-the-Woods or Stoneys are on the Stoney Reserve, Alberta, Canada.

The Assiniboins lived in the north where the buffalo fed for a short season, coming late in the spring and returning south early in the fall. If enough meat and hides were to be secured to last until the return of the buffalo, it must be done in a short time. Before the Assiniboins acquired horses, guns, and ammunition, they used two methods of obtaining a supply of meat and hides. In one method, the buffalo were stampeded over a cliff; in the other, the Indians built a sort of V-shaped corral of logs; the buffalo herd was driven into the wide entrance and then the animals could be killed with bows and arrows or spears.

Since the two Assiniboin groups have lived in different environments and mingled with different people, there is quite a difference in their parfleches, though both have some Siouan characteristics. The Assiniboins in the United States said that they used many colors; black from a little seam in a bank or mountainside (it was slimy), yellow from boiled wolf's moss (*Evernia vulpina*) growing on trees in the mountains, pink earth from along the side of a cliff (a woman sent her son horseback for it), red from burning white earth, or yellow ocher. The old colors mixed with sizing were liked because they did not spread or run like the store colors. One woman said the only blue she had was from boiling a piece of blue cloth. She used a stone tool for painting and prickly pear cactus for sizing.

An old woman said that the rawhide craftswomen were particular about their rawhide. When they made rawhide, they stretched the hide inside a lodge so that they could take better care of it, and they would not allow anyone to go near it. They had a blanket stretched above the hide and dried the hide slowly and evenly. The whole process looked easy when a craftswoman did it, but it was anything but easy for a novice.

Glue was made by boiling down the hooves and thick part from the forehead of the buffalo bull in a rawhide-lined pit. The glue was cooled, broken into small pieces, and distributed among those who wanted it.

Estelle Blackbird said that her mother, Red Elk, born in 1858, made parfleches. She fleshed the green buffalo hide, threw water on it, and scraped the water off with the rough side of the animal's tongue until the hide was clean. It was pegged out about six inches above the ground and partly dried, and then Red Elk rubbed it, on the flesh side, with raw cactus juice. The design was laid out with willow sticks, and Red Elk ran the back of a knife down each side of the sticks to mark the basic division of the spaces.

Porous bones were used for painting. After painting, the hide was again sized and dried, then turned hair side up (a piece of white buckskin was put underneath the painted skin), and the hair removed by pounding with a rock. This process made the hide whiter, but much skill was required to avoid marring the design. Last, the holes for closing were burned in.

Mrs. Juanita Tucker said the women liked the skins very white, so they left them stretched outside for some time in sun and rain. The hair was pounded off with a slanting movement, not a direct blow. This also whitened the hide. Cactus juice was used for sizing while the hide was wet. At certain times of the year cactus was full of juice, but in the late summer it had little juice and had to be soaked in water, cut up, and brought to a boil in a little water in order to use it for sizing.

The old parfleches from the Stoney and Montana Assiniboins were quite different, but, as was pointed out earlier, they still showed some of the Siouan characteristics. Designs on the two upper flaps were joined across the back of the parfleche by two bands of color; they were outlined in the old brown-black. The designs on the upper flaps were almost square.

A fine old buffalo parfleche from the Fort Belknap Reservation has much of the surface covered with pigment. Only two colors, blue and red, outlined in black were used, producing a good example of negative design. White negative diamonds and triangles, outlined in black, were used to break up the red background. This parfleche had the typical Siouan number of holes for closing (single, pair, single). It had a wide Siouan border of blue and was about medium size.

The old Canadian Assiniboin parfleche was small and used the same form of closing as that of

A design from an old Assiniboin parfleche (see page 131).

the Blackfeet and Sarsis: three pairs of holes on each upper flap. The designs on the upper flaps were two panels with a large ellipse in each panel, in the center of which was a long, thin diamond made up of a number of small units. This design was known as the "Fish Design." This same de-

sign is found on the Teton Dakota parfleches. The Stoney design differed from other Dakota designs in the minor use of blue and the major use of yellow, red, and black. Yellow was important to both groups.

The Assiniboins said that when the buffalo

137

Above: Older men on Fort Belknap Reservation, photographed in the 1940's. Below: Indian craftswomen on the Fort Belknap Reservation, photographed in the 1940's. Many of these women were informants about the making of Assiniboin parfleches.

A design from an Assiniboin parfleche (see page 122).

139

Crow lodges at a Crow Indian Fair. The Crow lodge averaged fourteen hides with a maximum of eighteen hides. A medicine lodge was made from eighteen to twenty-two hides. The Crows used very long poles, about thirty to forty feet long, extending far above the cover.

could not be located and the group was near starvation, they boiled hide scrapings in water and seasoned this broth with rose hips.

The looking glass was made by the Assiniboins before the white man came. A crude mirror was made by gluing together a thin sheet of mica, some powdered mica, and a thin layer of long hair from a buffalo. These were backed by a piece of buckskin or rawhide, also glued on. It was said that these mirrors were used to flash signals from one group to another. In talking with various Indian groups, I learned that many of them used mica and polished slate for "mirrors," but that the mica was a much better reflector for signaling.

CROWS

The story of the Crow (Absaroka) parfleche is interesting. The Crows live in southeastern Montana, in much the same region where they have lived since their separation from the Hidatsas. They are a Siouan tribe, but their parfleche has little in common with parfleches of the other groups to which they are linguistically related.

They made a long, narrow parfleche, with one pair of holes for tying, and used no black outlines or small brown-black units in their designs on either the very old parfleches or the modern ones. There was no decoration on the side flaps or bands of color connecting the two decorated areas.

Simplicity of design is a distinguishing trait. The rectangular decoration on the upper flaps could be more quickly made than the decorations of any other group; many of their designs are pure division and subdivision of the given area.

The old parfleches from the Crows, made from buffalo hide, seem larger and heavier than the ones painted after 1890. The designs on the upper flaps of the modern ones measured eleven by sixteen inches while the buffalo-hide ones were thirteen by seventeen and one-half inches. The use of color was about the same. One narrow band of color or two colored bands (green on the outside, blue inside) formed a border from one-fourth to one-half inch in width around the outside of the rectangles and triangles. A large diamond in the center or two very long, narrow diamonds in a two-panel construction are characteristic of the modern Crow parfleche. A large center diamond might be split vertically, leaving two halves of the diamond separated by a narrow neutral-colored stripe.

The Crow people said that this diamond was

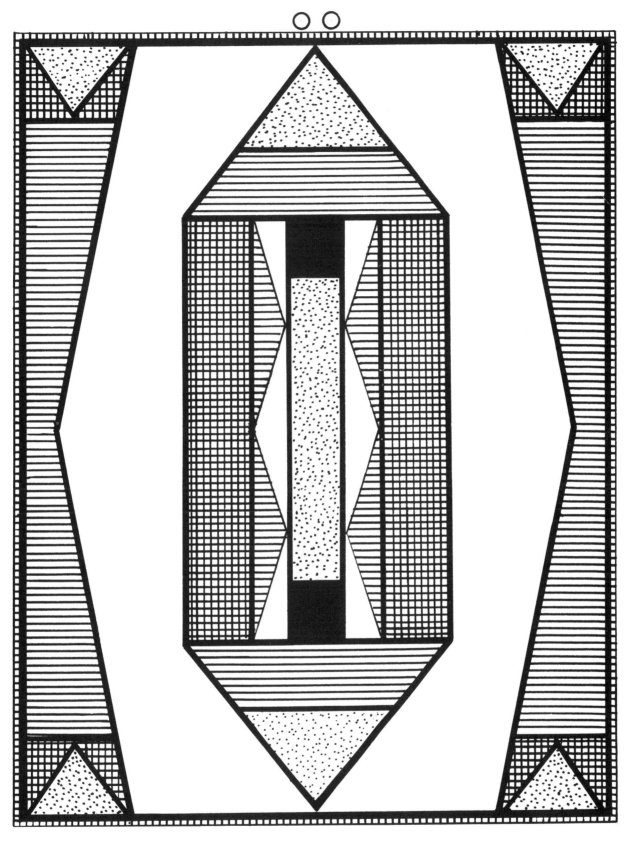

A design from a Crow parfleche (see page 122).

141

symbolic of the sand lizard, which is a talisman. They said the hunters used to find a lizard and ask it which way to go to find buffalo and that it would turn its head in the direction which they should take. An Indian judge on the Crow reservation said that the sand lizard, which looked something like a turtle, was a fetish which brought good luck to the Crows. It would not bite a Crow, but would bite other Indians. The lizard could be shown as a diamond shape; the symbol was important in protection. A baby's navel cord was enclosed in a diamond-shaped fetish made of two pieces of buckskin sewn together with bead decoration and hung from its cradle as a protection for the child. The lizard was called "ke-ple-zela."

On the old as well as the modern Crow parfleche the lines are nearly ruler straight. On a very few modern parfleches, some small circles which might have been drawn by tracing around a silver coin have been found, but these are an exception, not the rule.

The Crow parfleche has more in common with that of the Wind River Shoshonis than any other group, but it is also difficult to separate Crow from modern Nez Percé pieces. The Crows and Nez Percés made rawhide articles for trade after the buffalo were gone.

The Crows said that, besides the painted rawhide, they made the incised parfleche and that rawhide articles were made, not by a few, but by nearly all the women. The making of rawhide containers was a common occupation, and the women made quantities of them. They became so skilled that the work was not considered difficult. Many years ago the Crow women had a reputation as good craftswomen, tanning, and embroidering with quills some of the best buffalo robes as well as making fine rawhide parfleches.

An interesting aspect of the story of the Crow rawhide is that parfleches were found in nearly all collections examined. The Crows made long trips to visit and trade. (They had many horses and were skilled horsemen). At least in modern times, Crow painted rawhide has had greater distribution over this country than any other. The Crows "packed" trade goods as far west as The Dalles in Oregon even before they procured horses.

The structural divisions on the Crow parfleche were almost always painted with dark blue, and dark blue was the predominating color.

The Arapahos said that crosshatching was occasionally done by the Dakotas who came to visit them. The Dakotas admitted that they sometimes used this method of filling a space but said that

A Dakota village of the Cheyenne River group. This photograph, taken on the Yellowstone River about 1870, shows meat drying on racks after a successful buffalo hunt. (Bureau of American Ethnology)

they learned it from the Crows. None of the painted Crow parfleches examined showed this method of decoration, but the old incised parfleches, which had only light and dark, did.

The modern Crows used one pair of holes on each upper flap for tying. They did not use brown-black for outlining or for small parts of the design.

The Crows have for some time had a herd of buffalo on their reservation near Hardin, Montana.

DAKOTAS

The Dakotas are a large Siouan group now living on reservations in North and South Dakota, Nebraska, Montana, and Minnesota. Their painted parfleches have characteristics that are easily recognized as Dakota, although minor variations occur from one subdivision of the group to another, and while some of the characteristics of their rawhide parfleches differ on these reservations, there are still a number of features common to most of the Dakota group.

Their parfleches vary in size from small to large with rectangular decorated areas on the upper flaps, in which were burned holes for closing the parfleche by the single, pair, single method. The design was outlined in rather heavy old rusty

A design from a Teton Dakota parfleche. The center design is the turtle and the four cardinal points, and the squares symbolize the opening where the sun shines on the world. Blue lines connect the two upper flaps. The design is outlined in black. (Rosebud Reservation Museum, South Dakota)

HOLES: single, pair, single.

black, and occasionally a few small units of the design, such as a row of dots, were in black. A combination of curved and straight lines was found on nearly every design. Most of the designs were enclosed with a wide border of yellow or orange-yellow with triangles or skeletal triangles in blue or red. Instead of this border on four sides there might be three vertical bands, one on each of the longer sides and one through the center, leaving the ends without borders. Blue, red, or occasionally green may be the predominating color with much of the background in yellow. Two bands of color, connecting the decorated areas, were usually blue even when the structural design was red. The side flaps

A design from a Santee Dakota parfleche, made of buffalo hide (see page 123).

144

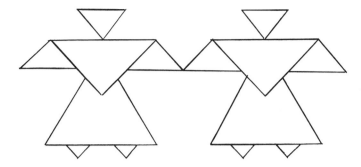

Double Woman helped the Dakota women with their rawhide designs. (Sketch by Eagle Hawk, Pine Ridge Reservation, South Dakota)

were not decorated. While many of the Indian groups wanted a natural-colored background in their designs, the Dakotas avoided it by painting much of what might have been background with yellow or yellow-orange.

Curves were laid out with willow rods by tying the two ends with a thong; the shorter the thong, the greater the curve. The Dakotas used porous bones for painting, with their paints held in turtle shells. They said that a bone with a smooth, slightly rounded point was heated over a fire and the design was traced with pressure on the bone. On the modern parfleches available for examination, the surface of the rawhide was not as smooth as that of many other groups possibly on account of the sizing used or the method of fleshing the hide.

In the modern rawhide, the Dakota and Arapaho designs have some elements in common. The fact that around the turn of the century these two groups were on visiting terms might account for similarities. There is less change in the Dakota parfleches than in the Arapaho ones.

Painted parfleches were used by the Dakotas for storage of dried meat. When they started on a trip to visit the Arapahos, they carried many parfleches filled with dried meat. These were cached along the way so that they would have food on the return journey.

One of the interesting features of the old Dakota parfleche designs was the heraldic and symbolic "significance." "Double Woman," a mythical character, helped women with designs, and anyone who dreamed of Double Woman was lucky because she would be able to make fine designs. There are many stories about Double Woman. In one, she evidently had two faces, a very old one and a young one; usually she was drawn as two women joined at the arms. Other stories tell of the only

people on earth: Iktoni, an old man, and old woman, or Double Woman.

The diamond found in the center of a parfleche design or two diamonds found on a two-panel design represent turtles. The original form had eight sides, but became simplified to four, a long diamond. Small negative squares or rectangles, usually white or unpainted hide, were said to be "the opening through which the sun shines."

There are four attributes which every Dakota man strove to attain and which he encouraged his sons to achieve. A man desired above all else to be known for bravery, fortitude, generosity, and integrity. If the head of a lodge was known for bravery or for any of the four attributes, the women of his lodge were allowed to use one bar in the diamond or the main unit of the design when they painted a parfleche. If he was recognized as both brave and generous, had distinguished himself on war parties, and had given away much of his property, the women could paint two bars or stripes in the design. Very few men could have three or four bars that might include integrity and fortitude.

Yellow was symbolic of the rocks, "the oldest things on earth, enduring for all time." The unpainted area in a design was important: some said more important than the painted area. Some designs had names, and one on the Pine Ridge Reservation is known as "the parfleche design." Other designs acquired a name after they were painted, when they reminded the worker or someone else of something that had occurred. The rainbow design is an example. A worker might see a design in a dream and try to paint it on rawhide; for example, a design used on rawhide by an Oglala woman was called "kamni-mni-la," something that moves in a circle or flutters. A headdress flutters, and the word for it is almost the same, "kami-mni-ta." The Dakotas said that the border was the most important part of this design.

Crosshatching was occasionally used on rawhide but was not held in respect; some said it was done by a woman who had only two colors of paint and that it was not Dakota. Crosshatching is a common characteristic of the incised parfleche and was not used on painted parfleches.

Among some of the Dakota groups men might work with rawhide, though usually it was women's work.

John Colhoff, a Dakota man employed at the Rapid City Indian Museum, said that "an hourglass figure [two triangles joined at their apexes, ka-pe-mini] represents a prayer. The lower part

A design from a Dakota parfleche (see page 123).

146

An Oglala Dakota woman's rawhide bag. The flap is tied with leather thongs. The design has many of the Dakota parfleche characteristics. (United States National Museum)

A design from an Oglala Dakota parfleche, called the Bravery Design (see page 132).

A design from a Teton Dakota parfleche, called Distant View (see page 131).

149

Bullboats and paddles, a sketch dated July 13, 1851, by Rudolph Friederich Kurz, an employee at Fort Berthold Post, where Mandan, Hidatsa, and other groups traded. This sketch shows flat-bottomed boats and the method of carrying them. Note the sizes of the paddles and the boats as compared with the size of the women. (Bureau of American Ethnology *Bulletin 115* [1937], plate 37a)

A bullboat and paddle (upper right), a sketch by Kurz, showing the construction of the interior of the boat. (Bureau of American Ethnology *Bulletin 115* [1937], plate 16a)

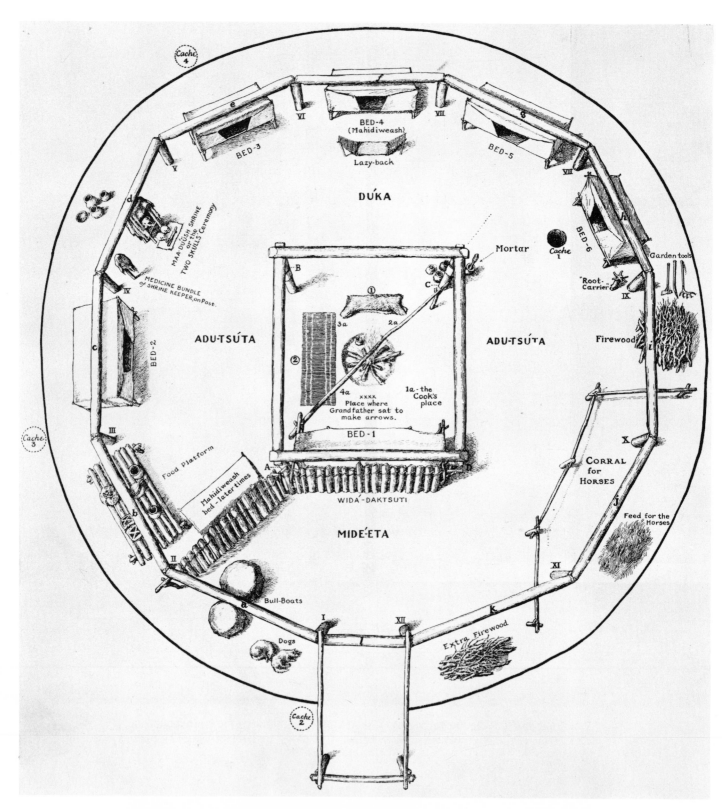

The floor plan of a Hidatsa earth lodge showing the household uses of rawhide: beds are enclosed with sheets of rawhide, bullboats of rawhide are turned upside down to dry, a sacred bundle hangs from poles, and rawhide thongs are used to tie many things, including lashing together the wattling of the room divider (Gilbert Wilson, American Museum of Natural History *Anthropological Papers*, Vol. XXXIII [1934], fig. 27)

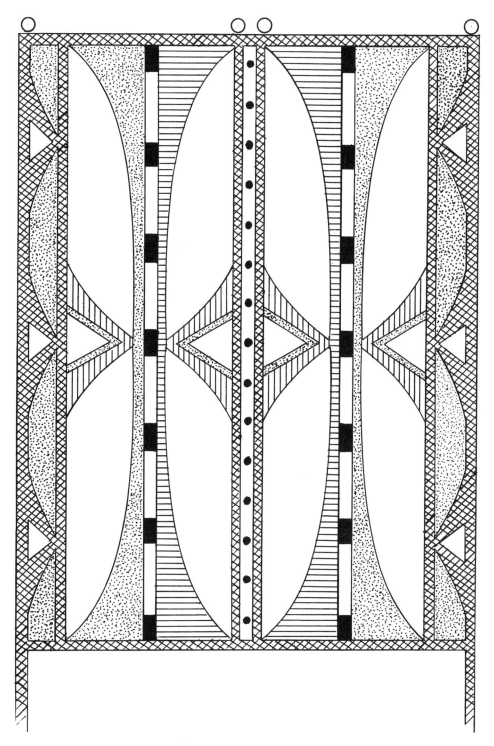

A design from a Hidatsa parfleche (see page 124).

[triangle] has to do with the earth and the upper part is the heavens. This design represents a prayer from earth going to heaven and being met halfway by the heavenly bodies." He further stated that "the Sioux have a name for each muscle of an animal and that these muscles are cut round and round nearly as thin as paper and hung out to dry. An expert will cut all of each muscle in one piece." Mr. Colhoff also said that "the Black Hills were known as 'Food Bag' because many parfleches of food were cached there."

Mrs. Ecoffy, a Pine Ridge Indian woman, said that "a parfleche might be made to commemorate an event."

The Dakota craftswomen from the Cheyenne River Reservation emphasized the fact that *timing* was very important in each step in the making of rawhide and that when staking out a hide, they used a slanting stake which would pull into the ground as the hide was drying. They also told of making their knives from elk bones.

HIDATSAS

The Hidatsas belong to the Siouan linguistic group, and all specimens of their rawhide examined show some of the characteristics common among the Dakotas. They live on the Fort Berthold Reservation on the Missouri River in North Dakota where they have been since the first non-Indians came to that region. At that time they lived in more or less permanent villages of large lodges built of logs and covered with earth. Some of the first European travelers in central North America spent a winter there. Hidatsa rawhide was probably among the best, but little of the old work exists because their villages were nearly wiped out during the smallpox and cholera epidemics in the first half of the nineteenth century. The Hidatsa lodge might be as large as forty-five feet in diameter; it was so large that horses could be brought inside.

The Hidatsas separated from the Crows some time during the eighteenth century, before horses were plentiful. They made incised pottery and may have made incised rawhide parfleche. They were an agricultural people, raising much corn and squash, and they hunted the buffalo for meat. Rawhide cases of dried meat and squash were hung up out of reach, fastened by means of rawhide thongs to the lodge poles. Caches were dug inside of the lodge and outside near the entrance. The Hidatsas used rawhide for many purposes, including enclosing their sleeping compartments with walls of rawhide.

Their parfleche decorations show curved lines, heavy dark outlines, and the single, pair, single method of closing. They used a bone stylus for painting. Blue bands across the back connected the two decorated areas. They used dots and curves combined with straight lines on their pottery. More straight lines were used in rawhide decoration, apparently because they recognized the need to follow and emphasize the structural lines of the parfleche.

In size their parfleches were medium to large, with a rectangular painted area on the upper flaps and a wide Dakota-type border. No decoration has been found on the side flaps of the specimens examined. Hidatsa parfleches were among the best, both in rawhide and in decoration.

The Hidatsa men were tattooed on the right side of the chest only, the left side and shoulder being natural. Since their robes were worn over the left shoulder and arm, the one-sidedness of the design was not apparent unless the robe was off. The type of design used was said to be very old and symbolic and may have indicated the clan.

IOWAS

The Iowas are a small Siouan group now living in northeastern Kansas and in east-central Oklahoma. The Iowas, Missouris, Omahas, and Poncas once formed a part of the Winnebago Nation. The Iowas were marginal woodland hunters and agrarians. When the buffalo were gone and after the Iowas lived in settled locations and secured wagons, they made rawhide from other large animals into Siouan-type boxes or trunks for holding their possessions. There was no longer a need for parfleches, for there was little meat to dry. Most of the old parfleches examined had been folded into Algonquian trunk-like containers. The holes for closing and the creases of the old parfleches are easily seen.

Iowa parfleches were medium in size with rectangular upper flaps and no painting on the side flaps. Blue bands connected the two decorated areas. Red was the predominating color, and curved and straight lines were used. Part of the design was outlined in old rusty black and part in red. A wide Dakota-type border enclosed a simple design.

KANSAS (KAWS)

The Kansas are a Siouan tribe, related linguistically to the Osages and Quapaws. In 1873 they moved from Council Grove, Kansas, to the Indian Territory near present Kaw City, Oklahoma. They

A design from an Iowa parfleche, which had been made into a trunk. The design is partly outlined in black, and blue bands connect the two decorated areas. (Milwaukee Public Museum)

SIZE OF DESIGN: 12 x 9 in.

155

Women gathering firewood at a Mandan village on the Missouri River in North Dakota. From an engraving of a painting by Carl Bodmer. (Maximilian, Prince of Wied, *Travels in the Interior of North America*, plate 16; Division of Photography, American Museum of Natural History)

were buffalo hunters who turned to farming only through necessity.

Few Kansa parfleches have been located for examination, but those that have been found show distinct characteristics in design. The design was not outlined in brown or black, but some units in the design were painted black. The decorated area on the upper flap was square. Design was mostly a matter of division and subdivision into many triangles which formed a heavily colored block in the center of the design and left much natural-colored background space near the simple border. The only standard Siouan characteristic was the band of color connecting the two decorated areas.

MANDANS

The Mandans are a small Siouan group now living on the Missouri River on the Fort Berthold Reservation, North Dakota, with the Hidatsas and Arikaras. They have long been agrarians who hunted the buffalo. They lived in villages of clay-covered log lodges, which were large with roofs of timber covered with earth. They built cubicles of rawhide around the outer walls of their lodges for sleeping quarters.

Before the Mandans acquired guns and horses, they hunted the buffalo by wrapping themselves in wolf skins and crawling on hands and knees until within arrow range.

156

A design from a Hidatsa Mandan parfleche (see page 124).

157

Mandan parfleches have many Siouan characteristics: the single, pair, single method of tying, the blue bands across the back of the parfleche connecting the two decorated areas, and the outlining in black. There were no small black units in the design on the specimens examined. The parfleche was medium to large with a rectangular decorated area; straight and curved lines were both present, with curves predominating in some designs. There was no decoration on the side flaps. The rawhide was well made and the decoration excellent.

Early European travelers to the Mandan country say that the women were very skillful in dyeing and painting buffalo robes, and that this work occupied a great portion of the women's time. Maximilian described the Mandan pottery and bullboat. These Indians also made a basket by covering a framework of willows with rawhide in much the same technique as that used for their bullboats.

OMAHAS

The Omahas live in Nebraska, across the river from Sioux City, Iowa. Their name means "Those going against the current." They were agrarians and buffalo hunters; the women stayed home to look after the crops while the men hunted. They are a Siouan linguistic group, and all the parfleche specimens available for study show some characteristics in common with those of other members of the Siouan family.

When used for carrying meat, the parfleches were called "we-ab-asta." The Omahas also made rawhide into a Siouan-type trunk. The craftswomen say that they needed new parfleches every two or three years when the old ones became too soft: they were then good for moccasin soles. This may account for the scarcity of old parfleches for study. Moccasins have been seen which had part of a painted rawhide design on them.

The Omaha parfleche was closed by the single, pair, single method of tying. The designs were not outlined in brown, and no small brown figures were used. The parfleche was medium in size with upper flaps only slightly longer than wide. A wide, simple border was used—bands of color connected the two decorated areas. There was no decoration on the side flaps.

The modern parfleche shows the use of "store-bought" pigment, although the Omahas knew how to make excellent red from the roots of bedstraw, a Galium, and dark blue from the bark of white maple with pulverized, roasted ocher.

The Omaha Indians used a cache for storing winter meat and all their possessions which they did not wish to carry with them on a hunt or visit. Their finest wearing apparel as well as dried food might be left in a cache, all enclosed in rawhide parfleches.

OSAGES

The Osages, a Siouan group, were agriculturalists living in permanent villages but going out at least once a year to hunt the buffalo. They now live in northeastern Oklahoma.

They probably made few parfleches after the disappearance of the buffalo. Several parfleches were seen in collections, but none of them could be called modern. The old parfleche shows most of the Siouan characteristics; some curved lines, bands of color connecting the two decorated areas, and the single, pair, single method of holes for closing the upper flaps. Some parts of the design were outlined in black, and there was an unusual yellow in narrow bands, this yellow looking more like varnish than paint. The decorated area (almost square) was enclosed by two narrow, separated bands of color.

The Osage hunting season lasted from the first of June until the first of September. Meat was dried and brought back in large quantities. Some of it was braided, a technique also used by the Kansas, and some of it was cut an inch thick, and a foot wide. It would dry in a day since the air was clear and there were no flies.

OTOS

The Otos, a Siouan family, were agrarians, buffalo hunters, and trappers who now live in eastern Oklahoma. They are related to the Iowas and Missouris and long ago were a part of the Winnebago Nation. They made rawhide parfleches until the buffalo were gone and there was no longer any dried meat to fill the parfleches, when they turned to making the Siouan type of rawhide box for storing their possessions. By this time the Indians had obtained wagons which could carry this new-shaped container which was almost useless on a horse.

The old parfleches showed many of the Siouan characteristics: the single, pair, single number of holes for closing, the heavy dark outlining of the units of design, and the wide border broken at intervals with triangles. A few small black units were found in their designs, but these were not much more than a widening of a line. The parfleche

A design from an Omaha parfleche, collected in 1930. This is probably a modern parfleche. It is decorated with four beaded rawhide strips at the closing, with metal jingles on the end. There is no black outline, and lines connect the two upper flaps. (American Museum of Natural History)

HOLES: single, pair, single. SIZE OF PARFLECHE: 28¼ x 13½ in. SIZE OF DESIGN: 13½ x 12¼ in.

A design from an Osage parfleche (see page 125).

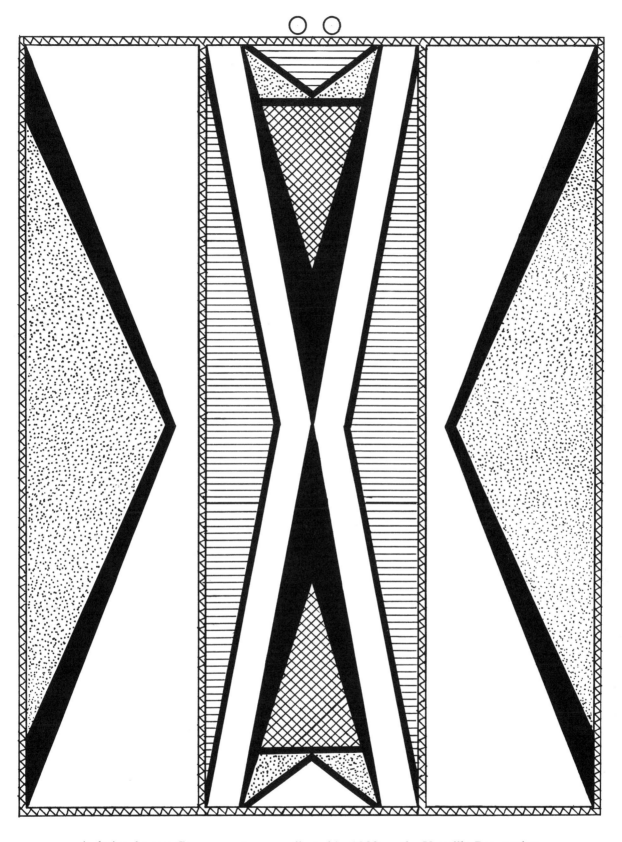

A design from a Cayuse meat case, collected in 1900 on the Umatilla Reservation. The predominant color is dark blue. The design has no black outline. (Chicago Museum of Natural History)

HOLES: 1 pair. SIZE OF PARFLECHE: 56 x 12½ in. SIZE OF DESIGN: 16¼ x 12½ in.

161

was about medium size with a rectangular design on each of the upper flaps. The designs used a combination of straight and curved lines. No decoration was found on the side flaps.

11. Waillatpuan Family

CAYUSES

The Cayuses, a Waiilatpuan tribe, have been living on the Umatilla reservation in northwestern Oregon with the Umatillas and Walla Wallas since 1855.

The painted rawhide parfleche of the Cayuses was made in much the same way as it was by the other western groups. Tamarack resin was used for sizing; the original method of closing the parfleche was with one pair of holes on each upper flap; the old incised parfleches were used to hold food and the painted ones for blankets and costumes.

A large painted parfleche, sixty-six and three-fourths inches long, found on the reservation was filled with blankets. It had been made before 1910 by a Cayuse woman. The predominating color was green, the side flap was painted, and the designs were each enclosed in a band made of two colors, narrow red outside and a wider band of green inside. A rectangular design with a band of green to enclose it was a typically western characteristic. In this instance the worker probably decided that there was too much green in the design when it was finished and added the narrow red to balance the color scheme. Dark blue was used for some of the minor units in the design.

The structural design of this parfleche was five-block, with the central block serving as the basis for a large design unit. The type of design on this case is probably more widely used than any other unless it is the two-panel vertical. Each group that used this five-block structure in design put their own trade-mark on it. The Atsinas enclosed the design within a simple border made of two bands of color with white or neutral space between. The western groups used one band, usually green. There were small blue triangles in the center design, which the Flatheads used in fours and the Cayuses in threes. On the Cayuse parfleche bands of color connected the upper flap decoration.

CHART OF PARFLECHE CHARACTERISTICS

INDIAN RAWHIDE: AN AMERICAN FOLK ART

The chart which follows is intended to summarize in condensed form what has been said in the foregoing pages about tribal design characteristics of parfleche made by thirty-nine Indian groups. Two explanations precede the chart: (1) an explanation of the characteristics noted in the chart, and (2) an explanation of the chart headings. The latter is especially important for interpreting information recorded on the chart.

EXPLANATION OF CHARACTERISTICS NOTED

Among any people a craft that is not practiced for a time and is then revived seldom achieves the excellence of the old art, and so it has been with parfleche. After the buffalo were gone (between 1880 and 1890), little or no rawhide was made for a number of years. Then the Indians secured cattle and horse hides and began to make rawhide again; but the craft reflected the change in the Indian people from a self-sustaining to a defeated group influenced by and dependent upon non-Indian people and a different culture.

In the chart the characteristics of the parfleches are those of buffalo hide or other native animals. Parfleches made of imported animals are designated as "modern." Indian rawhide was made from buffalo, elk, cow, and other available heavy hides, while thinner hides or skins from deer, antelope, sheep, goats, and smaller animals were made into buckskin and were used for clothing and towels. A shield was made from the toughest part of an old buffalo-bull hide and playing cards from the skin of a young deer or rabbit. A buffalo calf made good buckskin, but its hide was too thin for parfleches or horse bags. A beautiful buffalo robe was made by converting rawhide into leather.

The usefulness of any hide depends on the age and condition of the animal. The texture of the hides of different animals differs; each has its own characteristics and requires individual techniques and special uses.

This study of the Indian rawhide parfleche is based on the premise that any parfleche, no matter where it is found—in a museum, on a reservation, or in a private collection—has sufficient distinguishing characteristics to identify the group that made it. Parfleches made only for sale or trade and some of those made near the end of the rawhide centuries, when the buffalo and the old way of life were gone, should perhaps be excluded from this generalization.

Many persons consider the rawhide craft to be typical of the Plains Indians; they assume that other groups living on the periphery of the plains learned to make rawhide from them. In examining the truth of this assumption, several facts need to be considered. Excellent rawhide was found among the groups that lived north and west of the plains. Their rawhide craft was interwoven with their ancient legends and traditions. They were not entirely dependent upon the buffalo since hides from other large animals, elk and moose, were available in their environment. They used the old natural pigments. Designs from these groups showed distinct tribal characteristics, and the incised parfleche continued to be made and used there into modern times.

The discussion of rawhide in this book, in most instances, applies to a hide from a mature buffalo, and most of the illustrations are from buffalo rawhide, partly because it was available to so many Indian groups and can be dated since the buffalo was almost extinct by 1890. Most of the rawhide articles considered here were made before that time.

EXPLANATION OF CHART HEADINGS

Column 1. Decoration Type. Decoration may be painted, incised, or both. Many groups may have made the incised parfleches, but only those found for examination are included on this chart.

Column 2. Holes for Closing Upper Flaps. The number of holes used in closing a parfleche was fairly consistent within a group. The method of

164

tying the parfleche together and packing it on a travois or horse was a group tradition. The holes for closing the upper flaps are designated here as *one pair*; *single, pair, single* (*SPS*); and *three pairs*.

Column 3. Size of Parfleche. One size was fairly well established by each group. The words *small, medium, large, long, narrow,* and *wide* as used here are by comparison. For example, the Crow parfleche looked long and narrow compared with parfleches of most other tribes.

Column 4. Shape of Upper-Flap Decoration. The shape of the upper flaps, the decorated area, could be square, rectangular, or trapezoidal. Occasionally the decoration was longer than the flap and extended to the back of the parfleche. Many decorated areas often seem longer than they are because of the type of decoration (long, narrow divisions and seeing the decorations on the two flaps together when tied).

Column 5. Design Outline. A design may be outlined in light, medium, or dark brown, in black, or in green. A true black was used by a few tribes and a green outline by certain far-western tribes. A few parfleche designs were not outlined. Outlining is noted on the chart as *bn* (brown), *bk* (black), or *green*.

Column 6. Small Br–Bk Units. The old brown or black mineral paint was sometimes used for many small units in a design. It is more common in the old designs.

Column 7. Design Types. Nine types of design are designated, as determined by the main structural lines. They are referred to by letter in the chart.

A. Two-panel vertical division. These panels are filled in many ways.
B. Three-panel vertical division. These may be three like panels or a center with two like sides or other variations.
C. Five-block. A block, square, or rectangle in the corners and one in the center.
D. Nine-block. Two horizontal and two vertical divisions.
E. Two-panel horizontal.
F. Three-panel horizontal.
G. Center design. Center of interest without horizontal or vertical division.
H. Other methods of decoration not classified here, such as decorations on the ends of the flaps only.
I. Units of design attached to the border at sides and ends with undecorated space in the center.

Column 8. Type of Lines. Lines may be straight, diagonal, curved, or free-hand curves. A number of groups used combinations of straight and curved lines.

Column 9. Type of Border. Types of borders or bands of color are divided into six classes, designated by number on the chart.

1. A narrow band of color one-eighth to one-fourth inch wide which extends partly around the design.
2. A narrow band entirely around the design.
3. A narrow band made up of two colors.
4. Two narrow bands of color separated by a neutral space.
5. Two narrow bands of color separated by a neutral space and connected by a few small units of design.
6. A true border, three-fourths to one inch or more wide, made up of repeated units of design.

Column 10. Bands Joining Design Areas. Another distinguishing feature is the presence or absence of continuing bands of color across the back of the parfleche connecting the two decorated areas.

Column 11. Side-Flap Decoration. Some groups decorated the side flaps as well as the upper flaps. Such decoration occurs more often with the trapezoidal flaps, but may be found on others.

Column 12. Distinguishing Features. Other features which help to identify parfleches of a group.

165

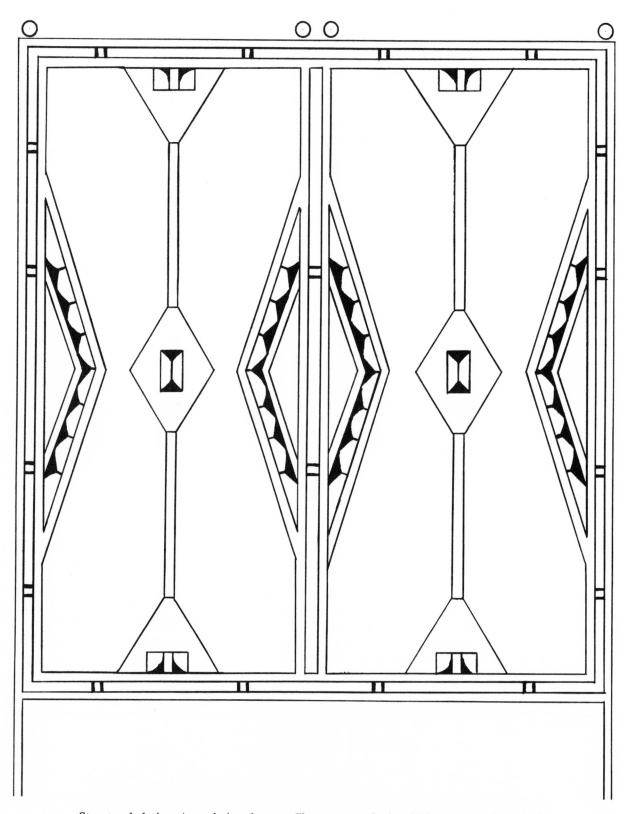

Structural design A, a design from a Cheyenne parfleche. This two-panel vertical design is the most common division of space and was used by more groups than any other structural design. It was especially common among the Arapahos, the Jicarilla Apaches, and the Crows. The two panels were filled in many ways. The design is outlined in brown, and green bands connect the two decorated areas. (Denver Art Museum)

HOLES: single, pair, single. SIZE OF PARFLECHE: 53½ x 14½ in. SIZE OF DESIGN: 14½ x 13½ in.
STRUCTURAL DESIGN: A

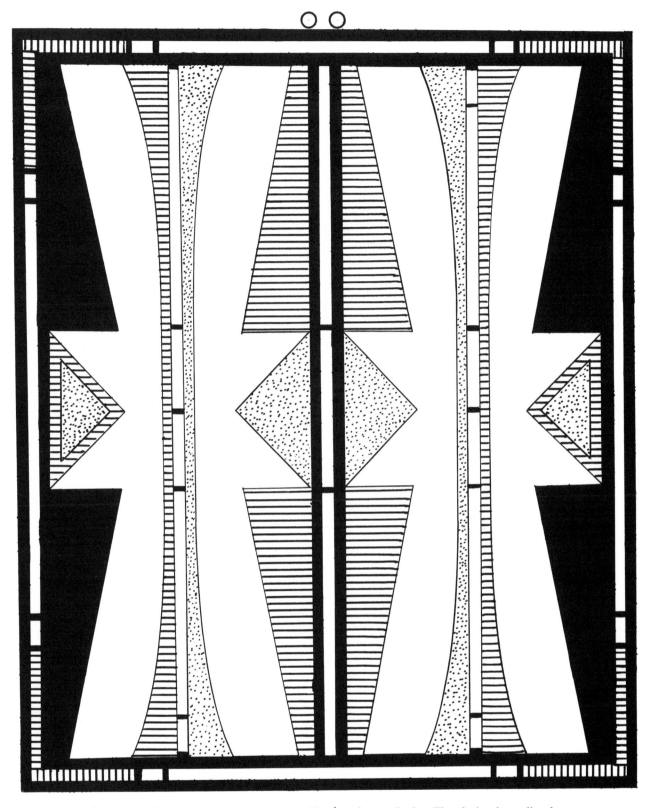

Structural design B, a design from an old Aŕapaho parfleche. The design is outlined in black. (American Museum of Natural History)

HOLES: 1 pair. SIZE OF DESIGN: 17 x 14½ in. STRUCTURAL DESIGN: B

Structural design C, a design from a Flathead parfleche. This type of design had wide
distribution, notably among the Arapahos, Atsinas, Wascos, and Flatheads. It is
distinguished by four blocks, one in each corner and one in the center. In some designs the center block may be cut longitudinally. The predominant colors in this
design are old green, old blue, and red. There is no black. (Chicago Museum of
Natural History)

HOLES: single, pair, single. SIZE OF PARFLECHE: 61 x 13½ in. SIZE OF DESIGN: 17 x 13½ in.
STRUCTURAL DESIGN: C

Structural design D, a design from a Shoshoni parfleche (see page 120).

(see page 120)

STRUCTURAL DESIGN: D

Structural design E, a design from a Crow parfleche. This rectangle was divided horizontally to form two panels, to which triangles and blocks were added, a design typical of Crow, Nez Percé, and Blackfoot parfleches. (American Museum of Natural History)

HOLES: 1 pair. SIZE OF PARFLECHE: 57 x 12 in. SIZE OF DESIGN: 15½ x 12 in. STRUCTURAL DESIGN: E

170

Structural design F, a design from a Piegan Blackfoot meat case (see page 57).

STRUCTURAL DESIGN: F

Structural design F, a design from a Nez Percé meat case from a Columbia River group. The design is slightly trapezoidal. (Property of Eliza Miller, Warm Springs, Oregon)

HOLES: 3 pairs. SIZE OF PARFLECHE: 60 x 13¾ in. SIZE OF DESIGN: 18½ x 13½ and 18½ x 14¼ in.
STRUCTURAL DESIGN: F

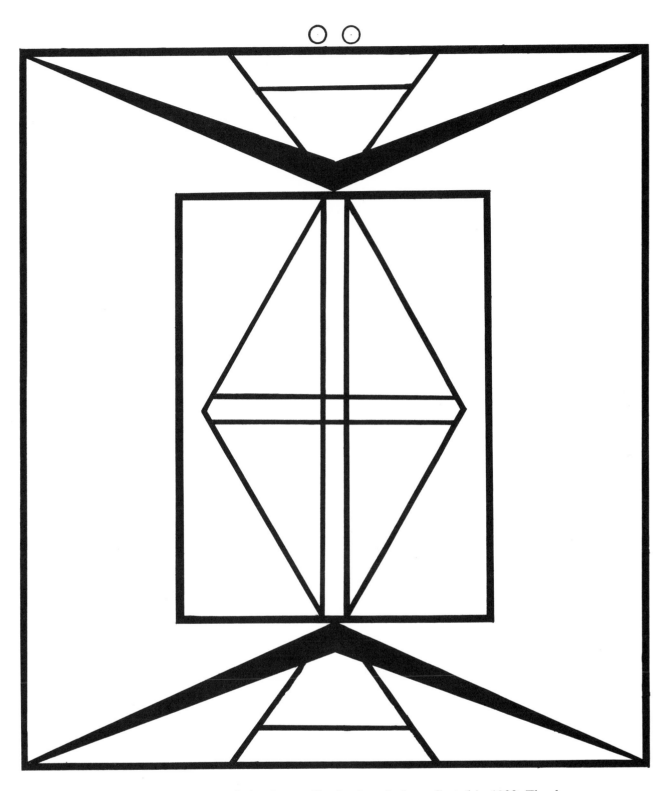

Structural design G, a design from a Shoshoni parfleche, collected in 1900. The design has no black, and the narrow lines are blue. (American Museum of Natural History)

HOLES: 1 pair. SIZE OF PARFLECHE: 28½ x 12 in. SIZE OF DESIGN: 15 x 11½ in. STRUCTURAL DESIGN: G

Structural design H, a design from a Crow parfleche illustrating the use of diagonal lines with no curves and with a few parallel lines. This design is typical of parfleches of the Crows and the Nez Percés. (Property of Eliza Miller)

HOLES: 1 pair. SIZE OF PARFLECHE: 55 x 11¼ in. SIZE OF DESIGN: 14½ x 11¼ in. STRUCTURAL DESIGN: H

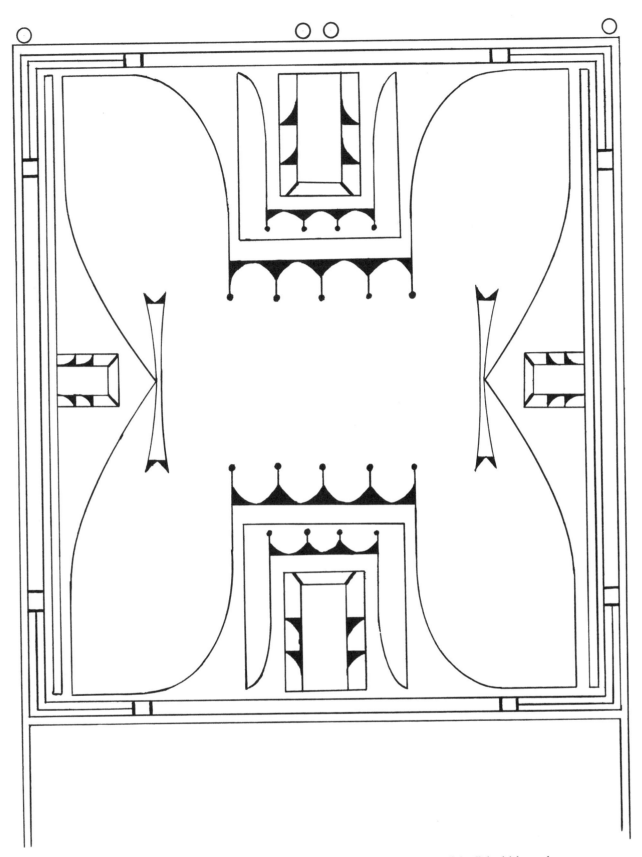

Structural design I, a design from a Cheyenne parfleche case of buffalo hide, collected near El Reno, Oklahoma, in 1899. It was made before 1890. The units of the
design are attached to the border, leaving the center free. This design was widely used
by the Cheyennes and the Utes. The design is outlined in brown, and lines connect the
two upper flaps. (B. W. Thayer Collection, St. Paul, Minnesota)

HOLES: single, pair, single. SIZE OF PARFLECHE: 25½ x 15½ in. SIZE OF DESIGN: 15½ x 14 in.
STRUCTURAL DESIGN: I

Tribe	1 Decoration Type	2 Holes for Closing Upper Flaps	3 Size of Parfleche	4 Shape of Upper-Flap Decoration	5 Design Outline	6 Small Br–Bk Units	De T-
Jicarilla Apache	painted	1 pair or stake holes	large	rectangle	br–bk	many	A
Mescalero Apache	painted	none, slits & ties	small	end decoration only	partly	few	H
San Carlos Apache	painted	1 pair	large	rectangle	yes	yes	A
Arapaho	painted	1 pair	medium to large	rectangle	br–bk	very few	C, B,
Assiniboin, Canada	painted	3 pairs	small	square	bk	yes	A
Assiniboin, Montana	painted	SPS	medium	square	bk	no	A, B,
Atsina	painted	3 pairs	medium to large	rectangle	old br	old, yes	A, C
Bannock	painted	1 pair	medium to large	square	none	none	A, H
Blackfoot (Siksika)	painted	3 pairs	medium to small	trapezoid	yes	few	A, B, E, G
Blackfoot (Blood)	painted	3 pairs	small	trapezoid	old br; modern, none	few	A
Blackfoot (Piegan)	painted	3 pairs	medium	trapezoid	none	none	B, F,
Cayuse	incised, painted	old, 3 pairs	medium to large	old, square	none	none	B, C,
Cheyenne	painted	SPS	medium to large	square	fine br	yes	A, B,
Comanche	painted	SPS	wide, medium	square	bk	yes	A
Crow	painted, incised	1 pair	long, narrow, medium	rectangle	none	none	A, B, E, G,
Dakota	painted	SPS	small to medium	rectangle	heavy bk	bk dots	A, G
Flathead	painted	3 pairs	medium to large	rectangle	green	none	C, A
Hidatsa	painted	SPS	medium to large	rectangle	heavy bk	dots and bars	A, B,
Kalispel	painted	3 pairs	medium to large	trapezoid	br	yes, br	H

8 Type of Lines	9 Type of Border (No.)	10 Bands Joining Design Areas	11 Side-Flap Decoration	12 Distinguishing Features
ight	2 narrow band	yes	yes	Many br–bk triangular units appended to edge of design. Wide side flaps.
ight, a curved	1	no	yes	Decoration on ends of upper flaps. No continuous border. Wide side flaps.
ight	2	yes	yes	Large. Wide side flaps. Designs on side flaps differ.
ight, very curved	5	no	no	Many specimens available. Outstanding color, blue. Good workmanship.
ved, ight	4	yes	no	Named design. Good workmanship.
ight, ved	6	yes	no	Excellent workmanship.
ight, curved	4	no	no	Old ones very much like old Arapaho.
ight	2	yes	no	Simple designs.
ight, ved	4, 6	yes	yes	Characteristics varied among different divisions.
ight	5	no	no	Simple, well made.
ved, ight	4, 5, 6	yes	yes	Asymmetrical use of color.
ight	2, 3	yes	yes	Design enclosed by a wide green band.
ight l curved	5	yes	no	Design indicates contents. Oldest known design shows recent characteristics. Excellent work.
ved, ight	2	yes	yes	Wide side flaps, deep curves.
ight	2, 3	no	no	Example of simple division and subdivision.
ved, ight	6	yes	no	Interesting background spaces. Typical wide border, use of orange-yellow.
ight	2	no	no	Uncluttered. Use of 4 in designs. Western use of green.
ight l curved	6	yes	no	Excellent craftsmanship.
ight	5, 6	yes	no	Heavy buffalo hides.

Tribe	1 Decoration Type	2 Holes for Closing Upper Flaps	3 Size of Parfleche	4 Shape of Upper-Flap Decoration	5 Design Outline	6 Small Br–Bk Units	De T
Kickapoo	painted	SPS	large	square	br–bk	yes	A,
Kiowa	painted	SPS	medium	square	br–bk	yes	A,
Klikitat	painted	3 pairs	medium	rectangle	none	none	A,
Kutenai	painted	3 pairs or stake holes	medium	trapezoid	br	many dots and triangles	A,
Mandan	painted	SPS	medium	rectangle	bk	none	G,
Nez Percé	painted	1 pair	medium to large	rectangle	none	none	A,
Osage	painted	SPS	very large	square	bk	none	A
Paiute	painted	3 pairs	large	square	some br–bk	very few	B
Pawnee	painted	1 pair	large	rectangle	br	few	B
Potawatomi	painted	SPS	large	rectangle	br–bk	yes	H
Sarsi	painted	3 pairs	short, wide	trapezoid	br	yes, half-circles	B
Fort Hall Shoshoni	painted	1 pair	medium	square	none	none	B
Wind River Shoshoni	painted	1 pair	small to medium	rectangle	none	none	D,
Umatilla	painted	3 pairs	medium	rectangle	none	none	B,
Uinta Ute	painted	3 pairs	large	rectangle	br	yes	I
Walla Walla	painted	3 pairs	large	square	yes	yes	H,
Wasco	incised, painted	3 pairs	medium to large	rectangle	br–bk	few	A,
Wichita	painted	three stake holes	large	rectangle	yes	few	H,
Wishram	incised, painted	3 pairs	large	rectangle	none	none	B
Yakima	painted	3 pairs	medium to large	rectangle	bk	none	G

8 Type of Lines	9 Type of Border (No.)	10 Bands Joining Design Areas	11 Side-Flap Decoration	12 Distinguishing Features
ight curved	4, 5	no	no	Browned. Color, green, red, yellow. Old parfleches folded into trunks.
ight curved	4, 5	no	no	Border colors interchanged. Use of yellow.
ight	2	yes	yes	Colors, rose-red, green, yellow. No br or bk.
ight, ved	2, 6	yes	yes	Unusual designs, varying from group to group.
ight, ved	2, 6	yes	no	Interesting curves. True Siouan border.
ight	2, 3	no	yes	Made parfleches for sale or trade in modern times.
ved, ight	5	yes	no	Colors, red, blue, accents of yellow. Definite curves.
ight	2	no	no	Many triangles of different sizes and shapes.
ight	5	no	no	Typical colors, green, red, blue, and brown.
ight, curved	5	no	no	Colors, green, red, yellow. Simple vertical designs, leaving much background.
ight curved	6, 3	yes	yes	Asymmetrical color balance.
ight	2	no	no	Blue structural lines with green, red, and yellow.
ight	2	no	no	Framed center block, unbroken block in each corner.
ight, ved	2	no	no	Old designs, combination of straight and curved lines.
ight	1	yes	no	Triangles attached by apex.
ight, curved	2	no	yes	Color illustration shows old-type design.
ight, curved	2	yes	yes	Interesting side-flap decoration.
ight	2	yes	no	Limited use of color, earth red and green.
ight	2	yes	yes	Used young buffalo and elk hides. Old symbols on side flaps.
ight	2	no	no	Much of area painted in strong colors.

OLD TYPES OF DESIGNS

BLACKFOOT
(*Algonquian linguistic family*)
(See Chart of Parfleche Characteristics)

This trapezoidal design was taken from an old browned parfleche. The simplicity of the design, which was not made by division and subdivision, the use of only two colors with brown, and the interchanging of colors in the border are characteristic of designs on some of the very old buffalo parfleches. Occasionally an old parfleche design was saved by being turned into another or a different kind of container. The old parfleche folds can easily be seen; for example, this upper flap was cut from one end of a parfleche, made into a cylindrical case, and used for storage of a ceremonial bonnet. (Collection of Amelia White, Indian Arts Fund, School of American Research, Santa Fe)

SIZE OF PARFLECHE: about 54 x 13½ in. SIZE OF DESIGN: 13½ x 13½ and 13½ x 12 in.

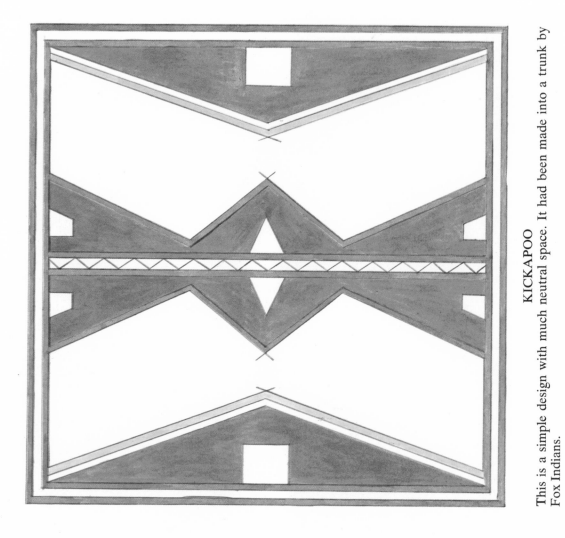

KICKAPOO

This is a simple design with much neutral space. It had been made into a trunk by Fox Indians.

STRUCTURAL DESIGN: A. BORDER: No. 4.

KICKAPOO

(*Algonquian linguistic family*)

This simple design is from an old parfleche that had been refolded into a trunk of the Sac and Fox type. The parfleche folds were visible. The design has a comparatively large amount of neutral space. (Museum of the American Indian, Heye Foundation)

STRUCTURAL DESIGN: A.

POTAWATOMI
(*Algonquian linguistic family*)
This design is from a large old buffalo parfleche. It had been refolded into a trunk-shaped container without any regard to the design. The outlining is brown.

SIZE OF DESIGN: 18 x 17 in. STRUCTURAL DESIGN: H. BORDER: No. 5.

WASCO
(Chinookan linguistic family)
The tag attached to this buffalo parfleche reads: "The Wasco borrowed the use of the parfleche from Plains tribes to the east." There is no black or brown in the design, which was painted with old natural western colors. The design was sketched from the case and was not drawn to scale. (Chicago Natural History Museum)

HOLES: 1 pair.

USE OF COLOR

BLACKFOOT (Canadian Blood)
This design shows a typical use of brown mineral paint as part of the design. The design is not outlined. (American Museum of Natural History)

KIOWA
(*Kiowan linguistic family*)
This design on a buffalo hide shows the characteristic use of color by the Kiowas. Yellow was used in the narrow bands, though most tribes used yellow to fill larger spaces in the designs. The interchanging of colors in the border is also typical. The background spaces are outlined in the old mineral paint. (Museum of the American Indian, Heye Foundation)

SIZE OF DESIGN: 13 x 13 in.

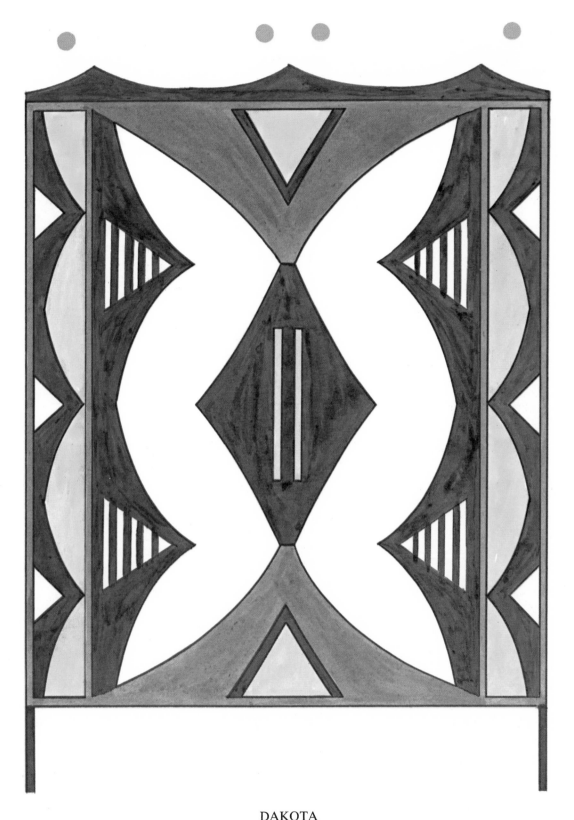

DAKOTA
(Siouan linguistic family)
This design shows the dark blue with strong yellow characteristically used by the
Dakotas. (United States National Museum)

NORTHWEST COUNTRY DESIGN

The design sketched here shows very interesting color: light and dark green, red, yellow, brown, and blue. The use of the old natural greens with only an accent of blue may indicate that the parfleche was made northwest of the Plains. The use of earth brown as part of the design and for outlining and the large area of color compared with the neutral area also indicate that this parfleche was made in the Northwest Country. It was purchased in 1938. (Denver Art Museum)

HOLES: 3 pairs. SIZE OF PARFLECHE: 58 x 15½ in. SIZE OF DESIGN: 16½ x 12 in.

 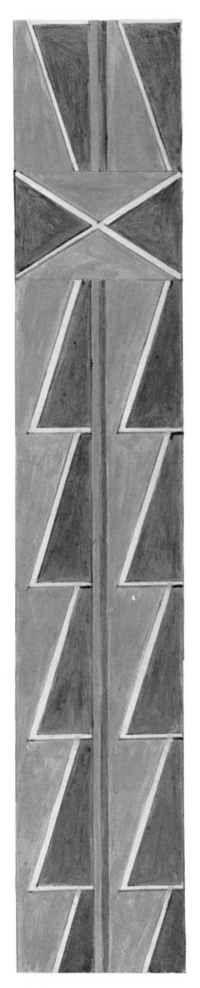

PAWNEE
(Caddoan linguistic family)
Four designs (sections from burden straps). They were made from buffalo hide,
incised, and then painted, the entire surface being covered. Such a band was placed (see overleaf)

across the forehead, and the burden, which rested on the back, was tied with long thongs attached to either end of the band. (Chicago Museum of Natural History)

TRUNKS

FOX

(*Algonquian linguistic family*)

The parfleche on which this design was painted was about 53 inches long and 37½ inches wide. The units of the design were repeated with narrow bands of unpainted hide between them. This well-browned trunk is an example of fine folk art, beautiful craftsmanship. It was collected at Black River Falls, Wisconsin. (Chicago Museum of Natural History)

FOX
This design is outlined in heavy black. It was collected in Tama, Iowa. (Museum of the American Indian, Heye Foundation)

SIZE OF TRUNK: 21½ x 10½ x 10½ in. SIZE OF DESIGN: 52 x 30¾ in.

FOX

This design is from the Fish Clan of the Fox tribe. It was painted on a folded rawhide trunk. Such a trunk was made from the hide of a whole buffalo or other large animal. The outlines and some minor units are painted in heavy genuine black. This trunk was folded without reference to the structural divisions of the design. The parfleche was brown from age and use. It was collected in Tama, Iowa. (Museum of the American Indian, Heye Foundation)

SIZE OF DESIGN: 52 x 30¾ in.

FOX

This design is from a folded rawhide trunk. It has three divisions lengthwise and five divisions crosswise.

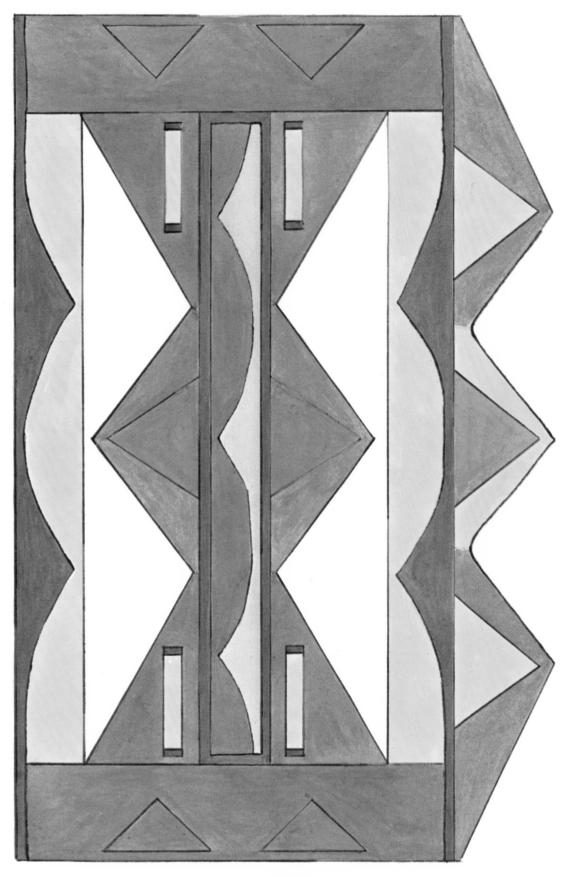

DAKOTA
(Siouan linguistic family)

This trunk is very colorful, and much of the area of the box is covered with paint. The design and the colors vary from front to sides and ends (see the next page). The top, shown here, has a blue and yellow border, while the sides and ends have blue and red borders. The colors are drawn into a whole by the use of deep-brown outlining. It is an excellent rawhide. It was made about 1912. (Owned by Mrs. Boles, of Bozeman, Montana, who purchased it from the wife of Runs-Behind)

DAKOTA
The end design of the trunk shown on the preceding page. The trunk is bound
at the corners with blue flannel.

OTHER ARTICLES FROM RAWHIDE

The lodge of the Blood Horn Society (Blackfoot Confederacy). The painted lodge is shown, with sacred bundles and containers for ceremonial headdress and other paraphernalia hanging outside the lodge. (Curtis, *The North American Indian*, portfolio 18, no. 645, E. E. Ayer Collection, Newberry Library)

1. Rawhide Bags

Until recent times the Indian women made rawhide bags of many sizes and shapes to serve many purposes.

CEREMONIAL BAGS

The first act of many Indian groups upon arriving at a temporary or fairly permanent camp was to set up a tripod of poles and to place their sacred bundles on it. These bundles usually belonged to the heads of the families. Some groups also placed the man's shield, his lance, and his pipe on the tripod with his bags. This tripod was usually placed back of the lodge. This meant that the man's paraphernalia was likely to be on the west side since many groups set up their lodges to face the east. These ceremonial articles were taken inside the lodges during bad weather, and among some groups it was customary to take them in at night and put them out again in the morning.

When these bags and other important items were inside of the lodge, they hung from the lodge poles directly over the man's place, usually at the rear, opposite the entrance. These rawhide cases were of different shapes: cylindrical, envelope, kidney, or boat, with painted or incised decoration and edged with fringe from three to thirty-two inches long.

Ceremonial bags might be used in religious or curing rites. They might be part of a ceremonial bundle or an outer covering or a container for ceremonial objects. The owner of a bundle would have been instructed in the prayers, songs, and rituals that went with that bundle. Some of these bags are very old and can be traced back through ten or more owners. These old ritual bags or cases were kept because of their sacred nature, while the utilitarian bags might finally be cut up into moc-casin soles or other items when a piece of rawhide was needed. For this reason the old ceremonial bags tell us much about the rawhide culture.

The painted, fringed cylindrical bag was never used by the Indians as a quiver. The groups who lived on the plains or hunted the buffalo there carried their bow and arrows in two cases made from the skins of small animals with the hair on the outside of the cases. The arrow case was shorter and attached to the under part of the bow case. The painted cylindrical rawhide case was used for ceremonial objects, including the headdress, feathers, whistles, and other items used in a ceremony, or, if it was used by the medicine man, herbs and fetishes. The cylindrical case was a perfect container for feathers, which could be inserted at one end and removed from the other end without damage.

Most of the sacred cases were painted, but some of the groups along the Columbia River said that cases for ceremonial use were incised. Designs on many of the cases have no symbolic meaning and were not connected in any way with the ceremony in which the bag was used, but certain bags were found with a design which was not used elsewhere and was used only in a specific ceremony.

While the making of rawhide bags was women's work, the men may have made suggestions about the designs and colors used on their sacred bags. Some women were healers or medicine women.

Many sacred bags acquired a beautiful brown finish resulting from exposure to the elements, from being given a final coating of red paint mixed with wax or other materials, or from a combination of the two. Some of the finest of these cases came from the far western groups who lived along the Columbia River or in British Columbia. These groups used fish roe for mixing with pigment and for sizing. Farther east a ceremonial bag might be covered with a yellow transparent varnish made from resin or from the gallstones of a buffalo. Much old brown earth paint was used on the western ceremonial cases in small units or as long

Top left: a sacred kidney-shaped bag. Top right: a medicine bag. Below: a mackinaw boat. The mackinaw was a flat-bottomed boat used in the Missouri River trade to carry furs to St. Louis. (From drawings made in 1851 by Kurz; Bureau of American Ethnology *Bulletin 115*, [1937], plate 16b)

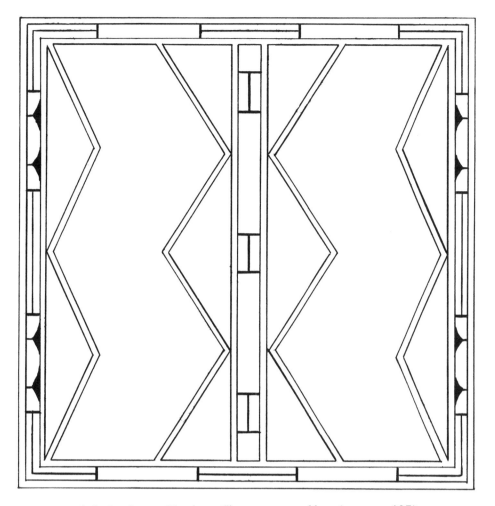

A design from a Northern Cheyenne sacred bag (see page 127).

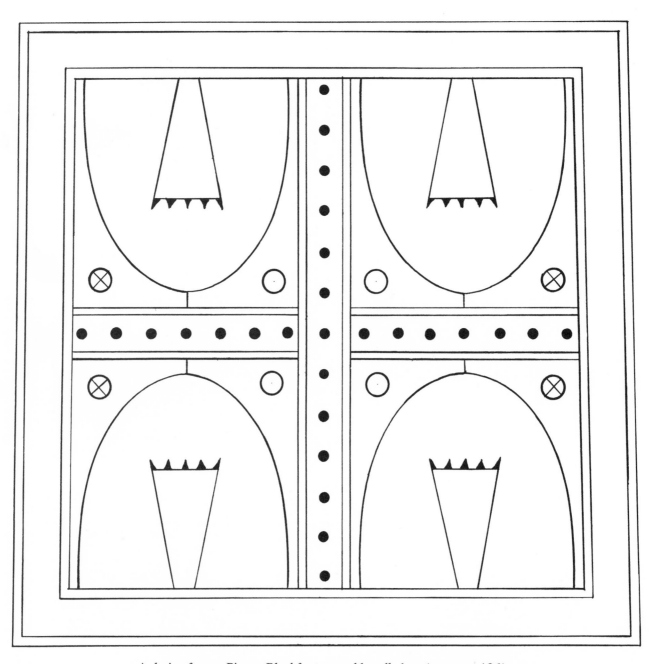

A design from a Piegan Blackfoot sacred bundle bag (see page 126).

A rawhide bag collected during the Charles Wilkes Expedition to Cumberland Gulf
in the Northwest United States, 1832–34. Both the bag and the fringe are of rawhide.
Much black paint was used in the design, which is a very old type. (United States
National Museum)

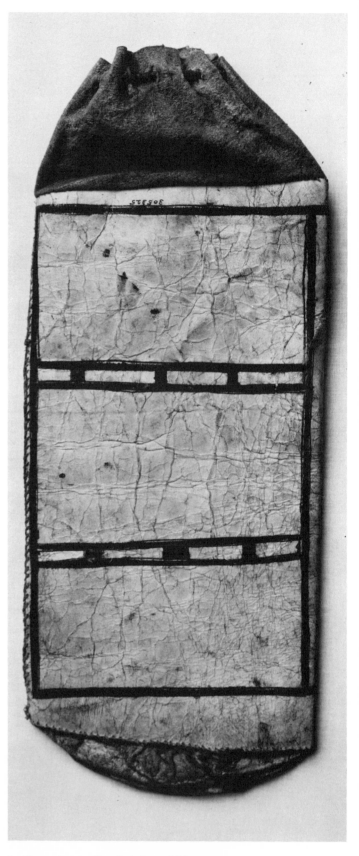

A Dakota rawhide bag: left, front; right, back. Two pieces of painted rawhide were sewed together with a drawstring and to an elliptical piece of tanned skin in the bottom and to another piece at the top. This bag could be stretched when packed. The hide is well sized, with markings characteristic of a buffalo hide. (United States National Museum)

A Cheyenne parfleche made before 1890 from buffalo hide, used for the storage of clothing. The design is outlined in brown; the other colors are delicate. Green bands across the back connect the designs on the upper flaps. (United States National Museum)

HOLES: single, pair, single. SIZE OF PARFLECHE: 54 x 13¼ in. SIZE OF DESIGN: 14¼ x 13 in.

205

A design from a Dakota rawhide bag, owned by Mrs. Foot, Fort Peck Reservation, made at Standing Rock Reservation. The bag is large and elliptical in shape, with soft buckskin at top and bottom, tied with a drawstring. There is a 5½-in. fringe around the bottom seam and another around the top. The design on the back (below) is simpler than that on the front. This bag was used as a lunch bag, which was hung from the saddle so that the rider could eat as he rode along. (Property of Mrs. Foot)

SIZE OF CASE: 19 in. long x 22½ in. in circumference. SIZE OF FRONT DESIGN: 18½ x 10½ in.

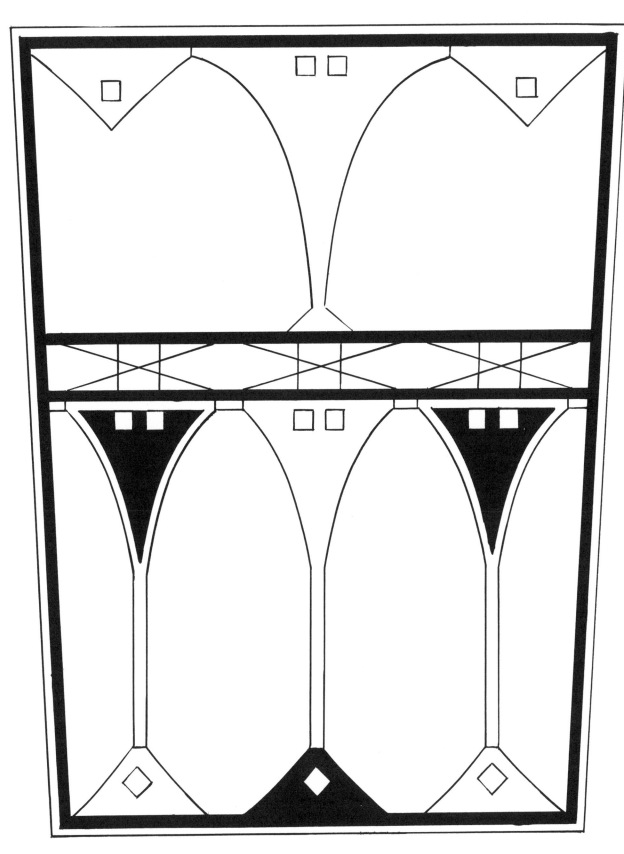

A design from a Ute cylindrical rawhide bag. There is a 15-inch fringe on the bottom. The design is outlined in dark brown. (State Historical Museum, Denver, Colorado)

SIZE OF CASE: 17 in. long x 13¼ in. in circumference at top and 11½ in. in circumference at bottom.

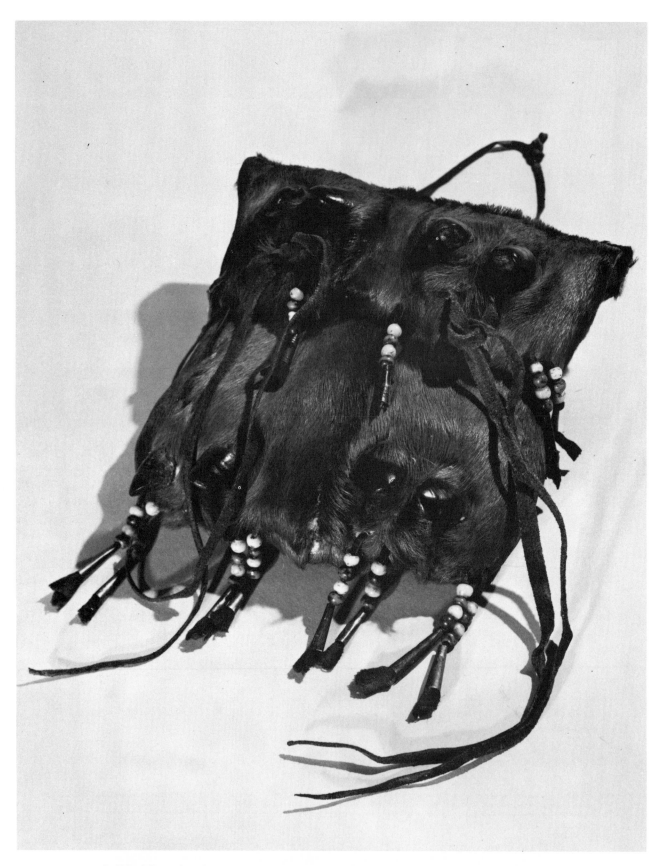

A Blackfoot dewclaw bag from Montana. (Photograph by Eyewitness, Santa Fe, New Mexico)

narrow appendages in the design. This usage on western cases had something in common with the brown or black and the browned finish of the Fox trunk, which was made on the eastern periphery of the plains. Many ceremonial bags, cases, or bundles are found on the reservations and in museums, such as horse-stealing medicine case, war-bonnet case (cylindrical), rock-medicine bag or case, and feather case or bag. From the great number of these bags which have been saved it would seem that the medicine is old and of unusual sanctity.

UTILITARIAN BAGS

Before the arrival of Europeans in North America, rawhide bags took the place of pockets, purses, boxes, and suitcases. Bags ranged from the very small paint bags to the large ones for lodge pegs. Bags made traveling and living easier because there was a bag for every item and a family could be ready in a short time to follow the buffalo.

Neatness and orderliness was accomplished at least in part by having a bag for everything and everything in its bag. Each member of the family had rawhide containers for his or her possessions. A woman's sewing bag might contain unfinished moccasins and extra moccasin soles, porcupine quills, sinews, strips of beadwork, and white earth for cleaning buckskin. In another bag were toilet articles, such as a hair brush made from a porcupine tail and red pigment for painting the part in the hair. Still another held fire-making equipment, a flint or fire steel, dry shredded bark, and a piece of punk.

Utilitarian bags were attractively decorated by painting, incising, and the use of long fringe. These painted and incised rawhide bags hung from the lodge poles when not in use and formed a colorful decoration. A family's pride was indicated by its decorated bags and, later, horse trappings.

The Dakotas made a long lunch bag which hung from the saddle and from which they could eat while riding horseback. The Atsinas had a container called a berry bag. The berry picker suspended it from her neck, leaving both hands free to pick wild buffalo berries or chokecherries. These bags were not stained because they were lined with leaves, and the contents were fresh and attractive because the fruit was layered with leaves.

These rawhide bags showed tribal characteristics. Many of them were painted on the front only, but some had simpler designs on the back. After trading posts were established in the Indian country, the women bound the edges of the bags with bright-colored woolen cloth.

The ingenious dewclaw bag was made with four pieces of hide from the lower part of the legs of the deer. The hair and claws were not removed. Two pieces were sewed together with sinew to form the front and two for the back of the bag. These, molded and shaped while still damp to form a stiff bag with a rounded bottom, were the prized possessions of the older women.

2. Boats

The first people who came to this continent may have known how to make some type of boat and how to use it. In historic times western Indian groups made a dugout canoe or a boat from a large log. The Woodland Indians made a canoe with a framework of spruce or other light wood, covered it with birchbark, and caulked it with pitch. These were light and could be carried overland between lakes and streams.

On the plains the Indians had neither large trees nor birchbark, but they constructed a boat suitable to their needs: a willow frame covered with rawhide. It was used on the Missouri and other rivers to ferry the Indian family and their possessions across the river, to gather firewood along the river banks, and to carry hides down the river; but it could not be paddled up a river.

The use of the bullboat was described by the Arikaras, Hidatsas, Mandans, and Potawatomis. The women made, carried, and propelled the bullboats. Usually only one person paddled, but two could paddle if they sat side by side in the front. A boat made of one large buffalo hide could carry four persons across the Missouri; they must sit very quietly or they would upset the craft. The women carried their bullboats along the bank to the place where they wished to cross, and on their return brought them to the village and turned them upside down to dry.

A boat of this type could be made in two or three hours and would last a year. The name bullboat came from the fact that a large, heavy hide was used in its construction and the largest and toughest hide came from the buffalo bull. The bullboat was round or slightly elliptical with a flat or rounded bottom. In crossing a wide river, the boat would be carried downstream one-fourth to one-half mile. Some old records say that the bullboat was used on the Platte River, which was shallow through most of its course. This boat drew about four inches of water, and yet it was on sandbars half of the time.

The fact that the bullboat could be made quickly was a great advantage if an enemy was only a short distance away. In that case the boat might be abandoned on the opposite shore or the hide removed and packed away for further use or staked out to dry.

The Hidatsas and Mandans made a type of good skin boat which was in constant use for crossing rivers and for gathering firewood. Such boats were flat-bottomed and so light when dry and empty that the women carried them even from one river to another. Of course, the boats were heavier when wet.

Bullboats, turned bottom up, were often carried to a river on a dog or horse travois. In such a case a dog rode across the river in the boat with the people, while a horse, led by one of the riders in the bullboat, swam across. A second bullboat loaded with luggage or meat might be lashed to the first and pulled in tandem.

The Dakota group living near Fort Thompson, South Dakota, said that they made a "hoop" boat, which would hold two to six persons. For the frame they used willow or ash saplings split through the center. These were lapped across the bottom with the large ends at the upper edge of the boat. The saplings were tied together with rawhide thongs. After the frame was finished, a green hide or a hide which had been softened was spread over the frame so that the tail of the buffalo was at the back of the boat. The hide was turned over the upper edge of the boat and fastened with rawhide thongs.

When the hair was left on the hide, it was usually the outside of the boat. The hair formed a sort of anchor or brake and also helped to keep the boat from overturning, and the buffalo tail was a steering aid. This boat was rounded at the bottom, not flat. When people sat in this boat only their heads and shoulders showed. Instead of paddling the bullboat, the Fox Indians often loaded in their possessions and children and then pulled the boat as they swam across the river.

Some of the Western Dakotas said that they never made a hoop boat or bullboat, but that they made a V-shaped frame from poles, probably their

lodge poles, and covered these with rawhide. They piled their baggage and young children on this raft. Then a good swimmer tied a rawhide thong to it and swam across the river with the thong between his teeth. Other swimmers guided the raft.

3. Burden Straps

Burden straps or carrying bands (tumplines) made from rawhide and painted must have been common many years ago, but few of them have been preserved. These straps were about one and one-half to four inches wide and fifteen to twenty inches long. A long thong of rawhide was tied to each end of the burden strap, and these ends were tied around the material to be carried, which might be firewood, robes, a baby, or food. The burden rested on the back.

A group of Pawnee buffalo-hide burden straps available for examination were incised and then painted. The incising or cutting was done before the painting. The entire surface was covered with paint.

It was important for an Indian woman to have a good-looking carrying band or burden strap.

4. Cradles

Cradles for young babies could be quickly and easily made from two pieces of rawhide, a large rectangular piece for the main part and a smaller one with two rounded corners for closing one end. The upper end extended beyond the infant's head and was open. The lower end was sewed to three sides of the rectangle. It was laced from the foot as far as the infant's shoulders, leaving the part above them open.

A Comanche woman with a baby in a rawhide cradle. Such a cradle could be easily and quickly made from two pieces of rawhide—a piece for the main part and a small rectangle with two rounded corners for closing one end. This type of cradle was generally used only for a very young baby; the infant was later given a fancier, beaded cradle. (Curtis, *The North American Indians*, portfolio 19, no. 685; E. E. Ayer Collection, Newberry Library)

211

A design from a Wind River Arapaho lodge door. Doors of lodges were often made of rawhide and painted with colored designs. These doors were almost as stiff as boards, but could be rolled up when the camp was moved. There were three pairs of holes at the top, and the door was tied over the lodge opening with thongs laced through the holes. The thongs served as hinges when the door was raised. (Chicago Museum of Natural History)

SIZE OF DESIGN: 46 x 25 in.

Yellow Kidney, a Blackfoot, teaching his great-grandson to drum and sing the old Blackfoot songs at their home on Two Medicine Creek, on the Blackfoot Reservation, adjoining Glacier National Park. The hand drum was made by stretching a wet rawhide over a wooden hoop. (Photograph by Helen Post)

5. Lodge Doors

Often doors for lodges were made of rawhide and painted with colored designs. These were almost as stiff as boards, but could be rolled when the camp moved. There were pairs of holes at the top, and the door was tied over the lodge opening with thongs laced through these holes. The thongs served as hinges when the door was lifted. One door that was examined measured twenty-five by forty-six inches.

6. Drums

Drums have played an important part in the lives of the American Indians. It would be as difficult to imagine the Indians of today without drums as drums without Indians. Some drums are used in only one type of ceremony, and the keeper of the drum is held in high esteem by his group.

Drum making is one folk art which did not decline over the years, and the Indian drum has not been exchanged for any mass-produced manufactured article. Excellent drums made at the Cochiti Pueblo, for example, are beautiful as well as functional and are sold to other Indian groups as well as to non-Indians. These drums are made from a well-seasoned hollowed log from a mature cottonwood tree. Circles of rawhide are placed over both ends and laced together with thongs. The finished drum measures about fifteen inches in diameter and twenty-seven inches in height. The Pueblo drum may weigh as much as twelve pounds, and a drummer must be physically fit to drum through a ceremony, the success of which depends to a great extent on the drummer or the drummer and the chorus.

Many types of drums are used by the different tribes: the water drum, a ceramic pot partly filled with water with a skin stretched over the top; the Algonquin drum, which is large enough to accommodate four drummers; a hand drum with a narrow hoop and one thickness of rawhide; or a hand

drum about four inches thick and twelve inches in diameter constructed of a hoop of wood, with both faces covered with rawhide. The Mandans sometimes used the shell of a turtle with hide over it for a drum. Stories of old, large turtles are found in their legends.

7. The Hat or Sunshade

The older Indians living on the reservations in the 1940's remembered the use of a rawhide hat or sunshade. These were rectangular in shape with the two back corners rounded off. The front was much longer than the back, and the front corners were usually square. The circle for the head was slashed into pie-shaped pieces. The long, pointed isosceles triangles thus made were not removed, but were bent at right angles to the brim, forming a sort of crown. The rawhide brim was painted with typical rawhide designs; the edges might be serrated, giving the hat a good finish and keeping the rawhide from curling. The Arapahos, Atsinas, and Assiniboins placed a band of fur around the crown and allowed the ends of the fur to hang over the brim. A specimen from the Kutenais has a painted brim, serrated edges, and an eagle feather at the center back, attached in the Indian manner so that it will flutter in the wind. Buckskin thongs were tied under the chin.

The Arapahos decorated the edge of the hat by slitting it every half or three-quarters of an inch and then turning up every other section at right angles to the brim. The Shoshonis used pinked edges, painted brims, and decorations of large pompons of soft feathers made by cutting out nearly all of the quill.

The Assiniboins at Lodgepole, Montana, said that the hat was worn by either men or women and that any decoration on it was purely for ornamentation or style.

A hat measured about fourteen inches from front to back and seven and one-half to nine inches in width.

When some of the Indians purchased their first felt hats from traders, they slashed the crown into pie-shaped pieces in the customary way of the old rawhide hat.

A painted rawhide hat or sunshade. The back corners are rounded off, and all edges are notched. There is a tie on each side. The eagle feathers at the back were loosely tied so that they would flutter in the wind. The design is painted on both sides of the triangular-shaped pieces, which were cut to fit the head firmly. (Denver Art Museum)

SIZE: back to front, 14½ in.; side to side, 10 in.

215

A Northern Ute woman on horseback, Uinta Valley, Utah. The horse carries a painted rawhide bag with a long fringe of elk skin. This photograph was taken in 1873 on the John Wesley Powell Expedition. (Denver Art Museum)

8. Horse Trappings

With the coming of the horse in the period between 1600 and 1800, all Indian tribes found new uses for their rawhide. The Indians may not have invented any horse trappings, but they put their knowledge of rawhide technique into making all manner of articles to be used with the horse. The skill with which they worked indicated that they were familiar with the adaptability of rawhide.

Various kinds of saddles were made by taking a piece of green rawhide and drying it over a form which had been made from wood, bone, or horn. This same technique had been used in making berry mashers, war clubs, and other implements which had been used daily for time out of mind. One saddle had a high pommel and a cantle about the same height. A prong left on an elk antler was used for the pommel. From this the woman hung some of her possessions. Stirrups of wood were covered with green rawhide and hung from the saddle by strips of rawhide.

Cruppers and martingales were made of rawhide, with painted decorations. After beads became popular, they were used in combination with painted rawhide. The industry of the family was known by their horse trappings and decorated bags, as well as by the size and decoration of their lodge.

Horse "moccasins" were sometimes made from rawhide. A very heavy circular piece of rawhide was cut from a skin before it was entirely dry. Slits were cut in the outer edge and a drawstring inserted. This partially dry rawhide was placed under the horse's hoof and the drawstring tightened to form a covering for the hoof. While these shoes would wear out in time, rawhide was plentiful and they could easily be replaced. They protected the horse's feet on rough or stony ground.

In contrast to the elaborate saddles, martingales, and cruppers, the "bridle" might consist of only a thong of rawhide or a rope of buffalo hair tied to the horse's jaw. The rider guided the horse by pressure of his knees.

Many women became excellent horsewomen, but for moving camp a gentle, patient horse was best. At this time the women's horses were so loaded that the woman, with a baby on her back, climbed up the travois to get on the horse. A folded blanket or robe on the saddle helped to raise the rider above her possessions.

Elaborate cylindrical and flat bags, intended for ornament rather than use, were made with very long, abundant fringe at the seams. When on gala occasions these bags were placed on a horse, the fringe should drop almost to the ground when the horse was dressed.

9. Knife Sheaths

A good sharp knife made from bone, flint, obsidian, or steel was a very important tool in Indian

Iowa horse trappings. The saddle was made of horn, wood, and rawhide. The bags in the upper left corner are Crow. (From a drawing made by Kurz in 1851; Bureau of American Ethnology *Bulletin 115*, [1937], plate 26b)

A Cayuse woman with horse carrying cylindrical bags with long fringes. (Curtis, *The North American Indians*, Vol. VIII, plate 60; E. E. Ayer Collection, Newberry Library)

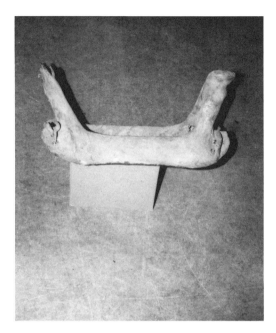

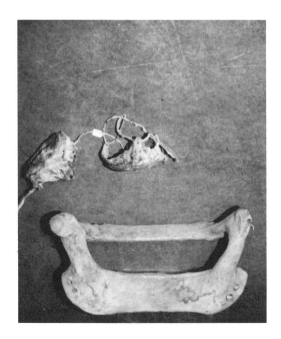

Above: A wooden saddle frame covered with rawhide. Below: a rawhide-covered saddle and horseshoes. The horseshoes are Apache. They were made from cowhide and were used on the front feet only. The diameter of the shoes—4½ in.—indicates that they were for use on a small horse. (Research Center, Museum of New Mexico, Santa Fe)

A design from a Dakota knife sheath. This design, cross-hatched in red and blue and outlined in black, is from a sheath belonging to Mrs. Lambert and was made on the Rosebud Reservation.

219

country. Decorated rawhide cases were made to sheath them. A woman might have a knife in a decorated sheath hanging from her belt as part of her costume.

:X═X═X═X═X═X═X═X═X═X═X═X═X:

10. Masks

:X═X═X═X═X═X═X═X═X═X═X═X═X:

Nearly all tribes used masks in their ceremonies. They were usually of a sacred nature and cared for

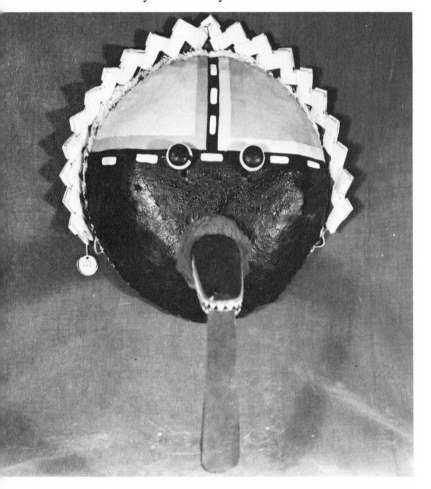

A Hopi mask of the Wupa Mok Kachina. This mask was made especially for exhibition and is not used in a ceremony. It was made like others of its type still in use in the Hopi villages of northern Arizona. The foundation is a yucca "sifter" basket, a general utility basket used in food preparation. Over the basket was stretched a damp piece of rawhide which dried tight and smooth. The beak was attached to the basket, and the rawhide was painted before it was entirely dry. (Museum of Northern Arizona, Flagstaff)

by one of the priests or the heads of the tribe. These masks were made by initiated or designated persons from many materials such as wood, corn shucks, or rawhide. Rawhide was softened and then molded to the desired shape before it dried. These were carved, painted, and decorated in many ways.

:X═X═X═X═X═X═X═X═X═X═X═X═X:

11. Mortar and Pestle

:X═X═X═X═X═X═X═X═X═X═X═X═X:

Indian women made a type of mortar, much the shape of a large vegetable dish, from green rawhide. The craftswoman first dug a hole in the ground the size and shape of the mortar which she wished to make. Next she cut a circular piece of

Grinding cherries in a rawhide mortar. (Photograph by R. R. Brosius)

220

rawhide and made slits at regular intervals near the outer edge. The rawhide was then pounded into the hole in the earth and stakes put through each of the slits around the edge. The hide was then filled with sand and allowed to dry in this shape. When thoroughly dry, it was removed from the ground. It looked like a bowl with a perforated rim. A stone was placed in the center of the mortar when it was in use. Dried berries or meat as well as dyes and paints were put on this type of large stone and pounded or crushed with a smaller stone to which a handle was fastened by shrinking green rawhide around a stone and handle.

12. Rawhide Shields

The shield was a warrior's most valuable possession. It hung outside the lodge on a tripod or inside on a pole near the place where the head of the family sat in the lodge. This was usually the opposite side from the door. Everyone had a definite place in the lodge, and his or her things were always kept there.

Shields were made in different ways. Some were constructed of three or four layers of shrunken rawhide or a single piece from the thickest and toughest part of the hide of a bull buffalo shrunken in warm water to make it even thicker and tougher. One method of shrinking rawhide was to dig a pit, put in it some very hot stones, and throw water on the stones, holding the rawhide in the steam. This process was repeated as many times as necessary to make the hide twice its original thickness. Some shields may have been as much as three inches thick at the center.

Shields were made by men. Only those who had fasted and received instructions from their guardian spirits could do the work, or a respected medicine man might make a shield and conduct the necessary ceremonial ritual. The latter would be paid a previously determined amount of horses, robes, or other material. The designs on shields were often realistic, the type used on men's possessions. Besides being painted, the shields were also decorated with eagle feathers, skins of animals, and red flannel when that became available.

The rawhide shield furnished sufficient protection from arrows, but would not stop a bullet. It is said that the warrior depended for protection more upon the painting on his shield or his "medicine" than upon the toughness of the rawhide.

Most Indian tribes used rawhide shields when on the Plains. Sometimes armor made of rawhide was worn by Indian men who lived in the wooded areas. This made it easier to get through brush than when carrying a shield.

The Pueblo groups used a shield which consisted of a very thick piece of rawhide twelve to thirty inches in diameter, with a removable cover of tanned deer or elk hide. The Pueblos had great reverence for the buffalo and used only Indian weapons, bows and arrows or spears, for killing them. Today each pueblo has a buffalo dance in the old tradition.

13. Toys

A parfleche could be cut from each side of a buffalo or other large hide. These were laid out on the hide first. The remaining spaces were used for bags of all shapes and sizes, moccasin soles, burden straps, knife sheaths, and toys for children.

Indian children's toys were small copies of articles used by adults. A little girl had a small rawhide parfleche measuring about seven and one-half by fourteen inches in which she carried her own personal articles. Her doll had a much smaller one in which doll things could be kept. These small cases were cut in the same manner as the large ones, painted with the same designs, and tied in the manner approved by the tribe.

A child's parfleche in the Chicago Natural History Museum contained the toys of a little Blackfoot girl. There were thirty-two small articles, every one made in imitation of her mother's. Among the articles were three pairs of dolls, a baby doll on a rawhide cradle, three back rests, several rawhide parfleches about two inches long and one and one-half inches wide, a rawhide case, and painted bags trimmed with flannel and fringe.

A child was taught to be orderly by being given a rawhide container in which her toys could be packed when not in use and in which they could be carried when traveling.

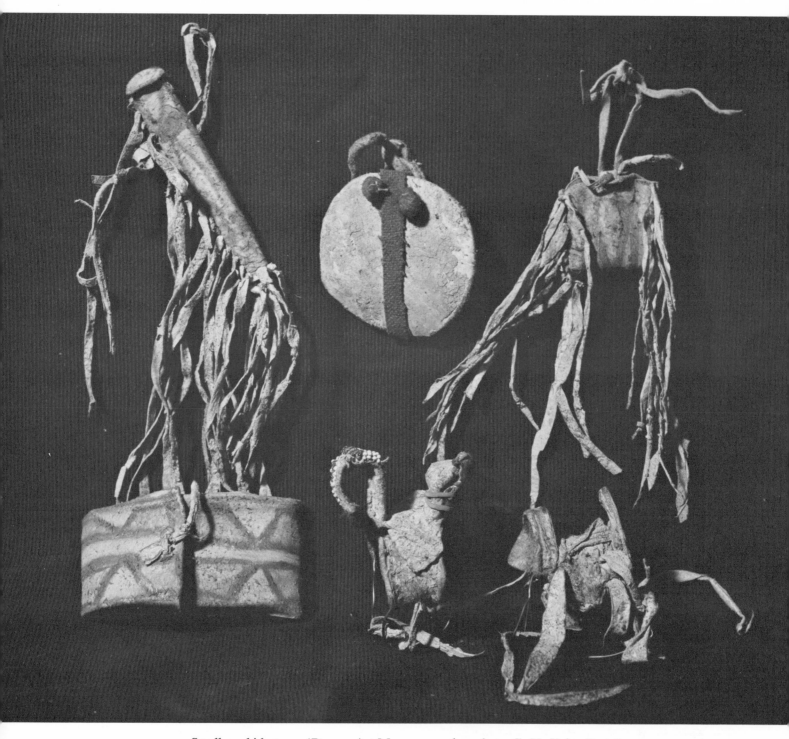

Small rawhide toys. (Denver Art Museum, on loan from G. H. Jinks, Fort Logan, Colorado)

Right: a Comanche toy rawhide cradle, made for Josephine Wapp by her grand-mother. Left: a small Sioux painted packing case. These items were collected in Comanche, Oklahoma.

An Indian girl began very young to learn to be industrious, and that industry was a quality to be admired. Her father made her small tanning tools for removing the hair and fleshing, and as she grew older, he increased the size of the tools to fit her hands. The mother or grandmother taught her to make small things for her dolls, sometimes helping her and at other times encouraging her to do it alone. Later she made articles for herself and was urged to make one after another to improve her technique. By the time she was twelve years of age she usually did creditable work, and was a skilled worker by the age of fourteen to sixteen.

A girl reared by her grandmother was apt to be a better craftswoman than one reared by her mother. The mother might feel that her child should be allowed to do as she pleased without any tasks or thought for the future. The grandmother's attitude might be that life was a serious matter and that it was best for a child to begin early to participate in reality. In this way a girl would be better prepared to meet problems and would be saved much unhappiness. The grandmother would spend much time teaching her granddaughter etiquette, craft techniques, preparation of food, such as drying meat, berries, and vegetables, and many other things.

14. The Sioux Type of Painted Trunk

Many of the Siouan groups made a painted rawhide trunk or box. These were not folded like the Algonquian trunk but were laid out on the hide with a definite top, sides, and ends, each having a full design; the bottom was not painted. When dry, this trunk was cut out of the hide in one piece and the ends and sides laced together.

The Siouan decorated trunk was a later development than the folded parfleche and women's flat bags. Trunks were used for women's possessions. The gaily colored ones were probably not used to any extent until the Indians were settled on reservations and had a fixed place of abode and traveled in wagons. These boxes were not as well suited to travel by horseback as were the parfleches and flat bags, but they were sometimes tied to each side of a horse. The Dakotas made many of these trunks, and they are also found among the Iowas, Otos, Winnebagos, Assiniboins, Poncas, and other groups.

In some ways this type of container was more

223

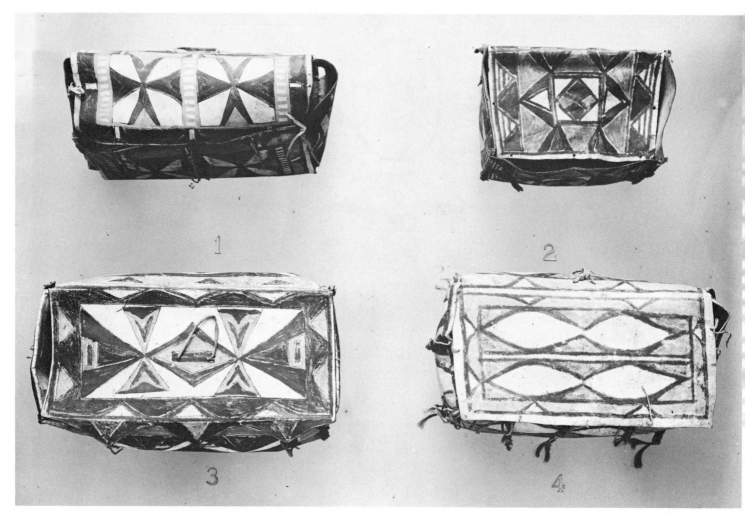

Painted Iowa trunks. (Milwaukee Public Museum)

difficult to make than the folded Algonquian type or other rawhide containers. There were five designs to paint with three different-shaped areas to fill. It took accurate, careful work to paint two or more boxes on the wet hide and dry them without having them shrink unevenly. The sides, ends, and top of the box must fit together after it was cut out. Smaller and more intricate designs were used on the boxes, and in some cases almost the whole surface, bottom excepted, was covered with pigment.

Some craftsmen did not use the same designs on all parts of a trunk—the ends might differ from the sides or top, but these were held together in some manner by borders and colors. One group, the Assiniboins, thought that the designs and colors should be the same on each unit of the box or trunk.

Designs on the boxes, or trunks, were closely related to the parfleche designs, but occasionally a conventionalized flower design was seen. The trunks were trimmed with red, blue, or green wool cloth or with fringe wrapped with porcupine quills or beads. In size these trunks varied from twenty-four inches long, twelve inches wide, and ten to eleven inches in height to miniature ones for doll clothes.

Trunks or boxes were finished by tying together with rawhide thongs, sewing two edges with sinew, or binding with red, blue, or green binding and lacing over this with strings of buckskin.

A design from a Teton Dakota rawhide trunk. This trunk was made before 1930 on Standing Rock Reservation by Her-Shawl, the wife of Chief White Buffalo, the grandson of Sitting Bull. It was collected by Harold Schunk, at one time a teacher on the Cheyenne River Reservation, who knew Her-Shawl (Schunk was later made superintendent at the Rosebud Agency). Typical Dakota borders were used to enclose a more or less realistic chokecherry design. The arrangement of details and color varied in the design from top to sides to ends. This design is an example of the evolution of Indian design. (Collection of Harold Schunk)

15. The Algonquian Trunk

The Sacs and Foxes were two related tribes, but war, cholera, and smallpox so reduced them that for some time they have been considered one tribe. Most of the Foxes, Mesquakis, live near Tama, Iowa; the group near Shawnee, Oklahoma, is mainly Sac. These two Algonquian tribes were first seen in Michigan and Wisconsin. In 1721 the Sacs were in the Green Bay area. Formerly they used birchbark and the dugout canoe. After they came to the plains, they hunted buffalo and learned to make and use the bullboat.

One of the most interesting developments in painted Indian rawhide was the Sac and Fox painted rawhide trunk. The Indians secured a buffalo hide and laid out on it a large rectangle about forty-eight to fifty-three inches long and thirty to thirty-seven inches wide; this rectangle covered most of the hide, and was usually divided into three parts lengthwise and five parts crosswise. These divisions gave the craftswoman a large number, often as many as fifteen squares and rectangles, in which to paint designs. The same design might be repeated several times. Usually the worker used a repetition of two or four patterns. The whole design gave the effect of an all-over pattern, which could have been repeated indefinitely.

When the painted hide was dry, the craftswoman cut out the rectangle and folded it into a trunk-shaped container having two sides, two ends, a bottom, and a flap which was often long enough to cover the top and extend over the front side of the trunk. When the rectangle of rawhide was folded into a trunk, it was folded entirely without reference to the design; the structural lines of the trunk had nothing in common with the basic divisions of the design. The folded corners might be tied with rawhide thongs or sinew.

The Foxes are excellent craftswomen, and they gave expression to their love of color on their painted rawhide trunks. Their brilliant colors were accentuated by deep black against a natural background, which as often as not was a part of the design.

The oldest trunks available for study show much heavy color—reds, blues, greens, and yellows, with a true rich black. The women boiled walnut root for a long time to get this black and used another root for yellow. The colors used may have significance. Green is referred to as the color of the chief's family and as the paint of the Bear clan. Undoubtedly green was an important color when these brilliant designs were painted.

The sizing was made by boiling the animal's horns until they melted. This took a long time. The designs were laid out and the outline tooled or pressed into the wet hide, and then the whole skin was covered with horn glue. Dry pigment was rubbed into the design. This method made the paint durable. A clam shell was used for a paint pan and at least one bone brush for each color.

Color was used in an interesting manner. The craftswoman might fill a number of squares, triangles, or rectangles with the same design, but the colors were interchanged from one unit to another. Some curves were used as well as straight lines.

The women did all the work on the painted rawhide; however, a trunk might belong to a man. Each clan might have a type of design, which could be varied in many ways. A woman of the Fish clan could use the fish design. Some clans left a small area in the center unpainted or with very little design.

The Sac and Foxes said that they never made the folded rawhide parfleche. They stored dried meat in long unpainted bags. Coming to the plains from the birchbark country, they substituted rawhide for their traditional birchbark folded trunk. This trunk was used for Indian clothing and finery in the past. The Indians say that the rawhide trunk itself was not a sacred object but that it might be used as a container for ceremonial materials.

The trunk continued to be made after the buffalo were gone. Sometimes a painted trunk is found which shows the original cattle brand.

The Sac trunk shows more white or neutral with less design and color than the Fox. The units of design are separated, detached, or spotty. Green was used in the designs and might outline the whole. The Fox trunk is distinguished by the heavy black outlining and more painted areas, with each unit forming a part of the larger design.

The Potawatomis, a related Algonquian group, also made the folded rawhide trunks without removing the hair and painted buffalo hides and folded them into trunks in the Sac and Fox manner.

226

Two Sac and Fox rawhide trunks. A whole buffalo or cow hide could be folded into one of these large containers. (Chicago Museum of Natural History)

227

A design from a Fox trunk (see page 192).

A design from a Fox trunk (see page 191).

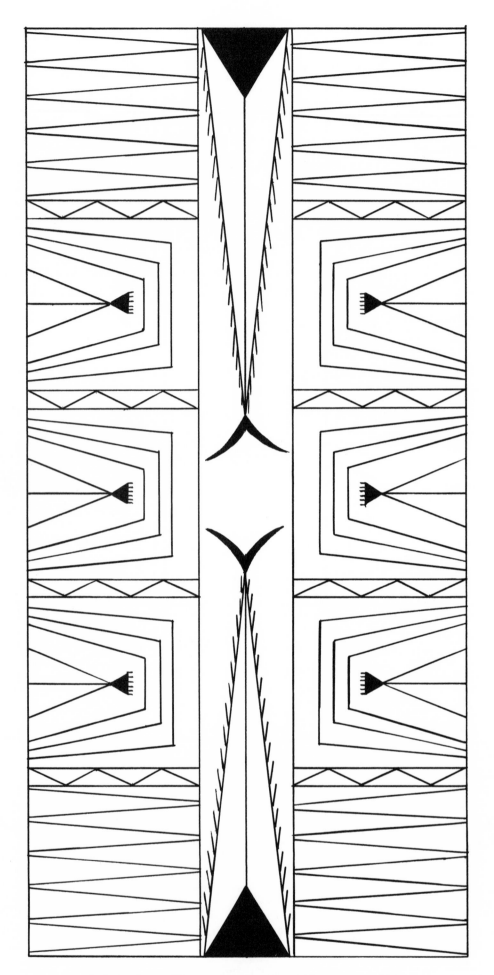

A design from a Fox trunk made of cowhide (see page 193).

A design from a Sac trunk. The design is characterized by three divisions crosswise and four divisions lengthwise. The design is outlined in dark green. (Milwaukee Public Museum)

SIZE OF TRUNK: 19½ x 10 x 10 in. SIZE OF DESIGN: squares, 12¼ x 12¼ in.; center, 7 in. wide.

APPENDICES

Appendix 1

MUSEUM COLLECTIONS STUDIED

American Museum of Natural History, New York City

Chicago Natural History Museum (Field Museum), Chicago, Illinois

Denver Art Museum, Denver, Colorado

Hamilton Collection, Yellowstone National Park

Indian Arts Fund, School of American Research, Santa Fe, New Mexico

L. D. Box Collection, Denver

Milwaukee Public Museum, Milwaukee, Wisconsin

Minnesota Historical Museum, Minneapolis

Montclair Art Museum, Montclair, New Jersey

Museum of the American Indian, Heye Foundation, New York City

Museum of Northern Arizona, Flagstaff, Arizona

Museum of the Northern Plains Indians, Browning, Montana

National Museum of Canada, Toronto

New Mexico State Museum, New Mexico Research Center, Santa Fe, New Mexico

Oklahoma Historical Society Museum, Oklahoma City, Oklahoma

Pine Ridge Indian Museum, Pine Ridge, South Dakota

Roy Robinson Collection, Chicago

Sioux Indian Museum, Rapid City, South Dakota

South Dakota Historical Museum, Rapid City, South Dakota

Southern Plains Indian Museum, Anadarko, Oklahoma

The Southwest Museum, Los Angeles, California

Taos Museum, Millicent Rogers Foundation, Taos, New Mexico

Taylor Museum, Colorado Springs, Colorado

United States National Museum, Washington, D.C.

The University Museum, University of Pennsylvania, Philadelphia

University of New Mexico Museum, Anthropological Museum, Albuquerque, New Mexico

Wyoming State Museum, Cheyenne, Wyoming

Appendix 2

INFORMANTS AND CONSULTANTS

This book could not have been completed without the assistance of craftsmen and craftswomen on the reservations. My information came from persons who were held in high regard by their tribes. When I interviewed them, I encouraged them to talk without prompting or interruption of thought patterns.

During my visits with each group, I asked the following questions, to record information about specific parfleches, and I later verified the answers through observation and study.

Was the design made by incising or painting or both?

What combination of holes was used for closing the parfleche: one pair; single, pair, single; three pairs? Were stake holes used in closing the parfleche?

Is the parfleche large, medium, small? Is it long, narrow, short, wide? Was it made from buffalo, elk, cow, or other hide? What type of sizing was used? Is the outer surface smooth? Is the flesh side outside? Was the hair pounded or scraped off? Does the decorated area coincide with the folds?

Are the upper flaps square, rectangular, or trapezoidal?

Are the designs outlined? If so, in what color? Is the outline fine or heavy? Were the lines burned in? Was the design outlined before or after it was painted?

Are there any brown-black minor units of design?

What is the type of design? Is the design large and bold or composed of many small units? How much of the surface is painted?

Are there curved lines, or are all lines straight or of a type that might be called "freehand straight"?

Is there a small, simple border around the whole area? Is the border painted on all four sides? Are the painted areas on the upper flaps connected across the back by bands of color? If so, what type of band or border encloses the design?

Are the side flaps narrow, average, or wide? Are there painted designs on the side flaps?

What is the color combination? How was each color used? Which color or colors predominate? Are the pigments natural or "store-bought"? Is the workmanship good, and is the parfleche well finished? For what was the parfleche used—for storage of food, clothing, medicine? Was it used to hold ceremonial paraphernalia or other materials? Do the designs have names? Are symbols used, and, if so, what significance do they have?

It would be impossible to list all those persons who helped me in my research for this book. The following informants deserve special mention, however, for their assistance and for their knowledge of the parfleche craft:

Assiniboins: Two Woman; Mary First Raised; Brown Hair; Mrs. West, Fort Peck Reservation; Estelle Black Bird and her mother, Red Elk; Mrs. Gone, Fort Belknap Reservation; Mrs. Takes-Them; Mrs. Foot; Mr. Long, Frazier, Montana; Mrs. Two Kill, Lodgepole, Montana; Juanita Tucker, Lodgepole; Mrs. Thinker.

Atsinas: Mrs. Julia Shultz, Fort Belknap Reservation, Montana; Takes-a-Prisoner, Hays, Montana; Gros Ventre Johnny, Montana; Rattle Snake Woman (medicine woman), Lodgepole; Mrs. White Weasel, Montana; Garter Snake Woman (wife of Jim Shortman), Hays, Montana; Fred Gone; Grandma Thick, Hays; Mrs. Little Shield, Hays; Grandma-Takes-the Bow, Montana.

Bannock: Daisy St. Clair.

Blackfeet: Louise Berry Child Croft; Mrs.

Wades-in-Water; Good Victory (Agnes Rose); Mrs. Yellow-Kidney, and her daughter, Katie Home-Gun; Mae Williams; Annie Flat Tail; Violet Williamson, Browning, Montana; Agnes Mad Plume.

Cheyennes and Arapahos: Marguerite Walker (Cheyenne-Arapaho); Three Fingers (Cheyenne); Magpie (Northern Arapaho); Little Woman (Cheyenne); Lena Brown (Arapaho); Cordelia Yellow Plume (Arapaho); Bruce Grosbeck (Arapaho); Ida Wise; Jessie Hadley; Esther Horn (Arapaho); Cassie Little Ant (Northern Arapaho); Mrs. Elizabeth Friday (Northern Arapaho); Mrs. Old Man (Northern Arapaho); Irene Bearing (Northern Arapaho).

Comanche: Mrs. Lena Myers.

Dakotas: Mrs. Agnes Eagle-Hawk (Oglala), Pine Ridge Reservation, South Dakota; John Colhoff, Pine Ridge Reservation; Mrs. Two Bonnet High Back (Oglala); Nellie Buffalo Chief, Rosebud Reservation, South Dakota; Mrs. Plum Man, Rosebud Reservation; Mrs. Lambert, Rosebud Reservation; Mrs. Eagle Feather, Cheyenne River Reservation, South Dakota; Mrs. Bad Warrior, Cheyenne River Reservation; Afraid-of-Hawk, Pine Ridge Reservation; Elsie Bonner, Pine Ridge Reservation; Mrs. Bordeaux, Rosebud Reservation; Mrs. Crow Eagle, Cheyenne River Reservation; Crow Eyes; Mrs. Runs-Behind.

Flatheads: Mary Kaiser; Mrs. Eneas Granjo, Arlee, Montana; Temna Pierre, Dixon, Montana. Carrie Lyford, supervisor, B.I.A.

Nez Percé: Phil George.

Rocky Boy's Reservation, Montana: Buffalo Child, Day Child, Dan Belgarde.

Shoshonis: Annie Washakie; Ethel Wadda; Mrs. Emma Aragon, Wind River Reservation, Wyoming; Pandora Pogue, Wind River Reservation; Lynn St. Clair, Wind River Reservation.

Sioux: Thomas Genick, Minnesota.

Warm Springs Reservation, Oregon: Ruby Davis; Josie McCorkle; Eliza T. Miller; Hazel Webster.

Other persons who gave me valuable assistance are M. G. Chandler, Southwest Museum, Los Angeles, California; Joe Sherbourne, trader, Browning, Montana; Mr. Demers, trader, Arlee, Montana; B. W. Thayer, Minnesota Historical Society, Minneapolis; Josephine Wapp, Comanche, Oklahoma; Reese Kincaid, Clinton, Oklahoma; Alice Marriott, Oklahoma City, Oklahoma; Frederic Douglas, Denver, Colorado; Mr. Martell, trader, Wind River Reservation, Wyoming.

Bibliography

Beckles, Willson. *The Great Company, 1667–1871: An Account . . . of the Hudson's Bay Company . . . .* London, 1900.

Boas, Franz. "Decorative Art of the North American Indian," *Popular Science Monthly*, October, 1903.

———. *Primitive Art.* Cambridge, Mass., 1927.

Brackenridge, Henri Marie. *Views of Louisiana; Together with a Journal of a Voyage up the Missouri River, in 1811.* Vol. VI in Reuben Gold Thwaites, ed., *Early Western Travels.* Cleveland, 1904.

Brackett, Albert G. "The Shoshonis, or Snake Indians: Their Religion, Superstitions, and Manners," Smithsonian Institution *Annual Report for 1879.* Washington, D.C., 1880.

Bradbury, John. *Travels in the Interior of North America.* Vol. V in Reuben Gold Thwaites, ed., *Early Western Travels.* Cleveland, 1904–1906.

Bradley, James H. "Affairs at Fort Benton," Montana Historical Society *Contributions*, Vol. III (1851).

Bushnell, David I. "Ethnological Material from North America in Swiss Collections," *American Anthropologist*, N.S., Vol. X (1908).

———. *Use of Buffalo Hair by the North American Indians.* London, 1906.

Campbell, Walter Stanley. "The Cheyenne Tipi," *American Anthropologist*, N.S., Vol. XVII, No. 4 (October–December, 1915).

———. "The Tipis of the Crow Indians," *American Anthropologist*, N.S., Vol. XXIX, No. 1 (January–March, 1927).

Catlin, George. *Letters and Notes on the Manners, Customs, and Conditions of the North American Indians.* 2 vols. London, 1841.

Chittenden, Hiram Martin, and Alfred T. Richardson. *Life, Letters, and Travels of Father Pierre Jean De Smet, S.J., 1801–1873.* 4 vols. New York, 1905.

Curtis, Edward S. *The North American Indians.* 20 vols. New York, 1907–30.

Deloria, Ella. *Speaking of Indians.* New York, 1944.

Denig, Edwin Thompson. "Indian Tribes of the Upper Missouri," ed. by J. N. B. Hewitt, Bureau of American Ethnology *Forty-sixth Annual Report.* Washington, D.C., 1930.

Dixon, J. K. *The Vanishing Race.* New York, 1913.

Dorsey, James Owen. "Omaha Clothing and Personal Ornament," *American Anthropologist*, O.S., Vol. III (1891).

———. "Omaha Dwellings, Furniture, and Implements," Bureau of American Ethnology *Thirteenth Annual Report.* Washington, D.C., 1896.

———. "Omaha Sociology," Bureau of American Ethnology *Third Annual Report.* Washington, D.C., 1884.

———, and Alfred L. Kroeber. "Traditions of the Arapaho," Chicago Museum of Natural History *Publications in Anthropology*, Ser. V (1903).

Douglas, F. H. "An Incised Bison Rawhide Parfleche," Denver Art Museum *Material Culture Notes, No. 6.* Denver, 1936.

———. "Parfleches and Other Rawhide Articles," Denver Art Museum *Leaflet 77–8.* Denver, 1936.

———, and Réné d'Harnoncourt. *Indian Art of the United States.* New York, 1961.

Drucker, Philip. *Indians of the Northwest Coast.* New York, 1955.

Ewers, John C. *Plains Indian Painting.* Stanford, 1939.

———. *The Story of the Blackfeet.* Washington, D.C., 1944.

———. *Teton Dakota Ethnology and History.* Washington, D.C., 1938.

Gregg, Josiah. *Commerce of the Prairies*. Ed. by Max L. Moorhead. Norman, 1954.

Grinnell, George B. *The Cheyenne Indians*. 2 vols. New Haven, 1923.

————. "The Lodges of the Blackfoot," *American Anthropologist*, O.S., Vol. VIII, No. 1 (1901).

————. *Pawnee, Blackfoot, and Cheyenne*. Ed. by Dee Brown. New York, 1961.

Haeberlin, Hermann, and Erna Günther. "The Indians of Puget Sound," University of Washington *Publications in Anthropology*, Vol. IV, No. 1 (1924).

Haines, Francis. *The Nez Percés: Tribesmen of the Columbia Plateau*. Norman, 1955.

Haupt, Herman, Jr. "The North American Indians," unpublished manuscript, E. E. Ayer Collection, Newberry Library, Chicago.

Hayden, Ferdinand V. "Contributions to the Ethnography and Philology of the Indian Tribes of the Missouri Valley," American Philosophical Society *Transactions*, N.S., Vol. XII (1862).

Hodge, Frederick Webb, ed. *Handbook of American Indians North of Mexico*. 2 vols. Washington, D.C., 1910.

Inverarity, Robert Bruce. *Art of the Northwest Coast Indians*, Berkeley, 1950.

Jones, William. "Ethnography of the Fox Indians," Bureau of American Ethnology *Bulletin 125*. Washington, D.C., 1939.

Kroeber, Alfred Lewis. "The Arapaho," American Museum of Natural History *Bulletin*, Vol. XVIII, Part 1 (1902).

————. "Decorative Symbolism of the Arapaho," *American Anthropologist*, O.S., Vol. III (1901).

————. "Ethnology of the Gros Ventre," American Museum of Natural History *Anthropological Papers*, Vol. I, Part 4 (1908).

Kurz, Rudolph Friederich. *Journal of Rudolph Friederich Kurz*. Trans. by Myrtis Jarrell, ed. by J. N. B. Hewitt. Bureau of American Ethnology *Bulletin 115*. Washington, D.C., 1937.

Laut, Agnes Christina. *The Story of the Trapper*. New York, 1902.

Lewis, Meriwether, and William Clark. *Original Journals of the Lewis and Clark Expedition, 1804–1806*. Ed. by Reuben Gold Thwaites. 8 vols. New York, 1904–1905.

Lowie, Robert H. "The Assiniboine," American Museum of Natural History *Anthropological Papers*, Vol. IV, Part 1 (1909).

————. "Cradles of the American Aborigines," United States National Museum *Special Report*. Washington, D.C., 1887.

————. "Crow Indian Art," American Museum of Natural History *Anthropological Papers*, Vol. XXI, Part 4 (1922).

————. "The Northern Shoshoni," American Museum of Natural History *Anthropological Papers*, Vol. II, Part 2 (1909).

————. "A Note on Aesthetics," *American Anthropologist*, N.S., Vol. XXIII (1921).

————. "Notes on Shoshonian Ethnology," American Museum of Natural History *Anthropological Papers*, Vol. XX, Part 31 (1924).

————. "Riding Gear of North American Indians," American Museum of Natural History *Anthropological Papers*, Vol. XVII, Part 1 (1915).

McClintock, Walter. *Old Indian Trails*. London, 1923.

————. *The Old North Trail*. London, 1910.

McCracken, Harold. *Portrait of the Old West*. New York, 1952.

Mallery, Garrick. "Pictographs of the North American Indians," Bureau of American Ethnology *Fourth Annual Report*. Washington, D.C., 1886.

————. "Picture Writing of the North American Indians," Bureau of American Ethnology *Tenth Annual Report*. Washington, D.C., 1893.

Mason, Otis T. "Aboriginal Skin Dressing," United States National Museum *Report for 1889*. Washington, D.C., 1889.

————. "Human Beast of Burden," Smithsonian Institution *Annual Report for 1887*. Washington, D.C., 1887.

Maximilian, Prince of Wied. *Travels in the Interior North America*. Trans. by Hannibal Evans. Vols. XXI–XXIV in Reuben Gold Thwaites, ed., *Early Western Travels*. Cleveland, 1906.

Michelson, Truman. Smithsonian Institution *Miscellaneous Collections*, Vol. LVII, No. 2 (1924).

Mooney, James. "The Cheyenne Indians," American Anthropological Association *Memoirs*, Vol. I, Part 6 (1907).

————. "The Ghost-Dance Religion and the Sioux Outbreak of 1890," Bureau of American Ethnology *Fourteenth Annual Report*. Washington, D.C., 1896.

————. "The Siouan Tribes of the East," Bureau of American Ethnology *Bulletin 22*. Washington, D.C., 1894.

Morgan, Lewis Henry. *The Indian Journals, 1859–1862*. Ed. by Clyde Walton. Ann Arbor, 1959.

Murphy, Robert. "Tales of the Buffalo," *Saturday Evening Post*, June 14, 1952.

Owen, Mary A. *Folklore of the Musquakie Indians*. London, 1914.

Parkman, Francis. *The Oregon Trail: Sketches of Prairie and Rocky Mountain Life*. Boston, 1883.

Peterson, Willis. "The Plainsman: The Story of the Buffalo," *Arizona Highways*, June, 1964.

Poesch, Jessie. *Titian Ramsay Peale, 1799–1855, and His Journals of the Wilkes Expedition*. New York, 1961.

Ray, Verne F. "The Sanpoil and Nespelem: Salishan Peoples of Northeastern Washington," University of Washington *Publications in Anthropology*, Vol. V (December, 1932).

Rodnick, David. *The Fort Belknap Assiniboine of Montana*. Philadelphia, 1938.

Ruzenthalsler, Robert. "The Kickapoo Indians of Mexico," Milwaukee Public Museum *Publications in Anthropology*, 1956.

Sandoz, Mari. *The Buffalo Hunters*. New York, 1954.

Sapir, Edward, ed. *Wishram Texts, Together with Wasco Tales and Myths*. Coll. by Jeremiah Curtin. Leyden, 1909.

Skinner, Alanson. "Cultural Position of the Plains Ojibway," *American Anthropologist*, N.S., Vol. XVI, No. 1 (January–March, 1914).

———. "Ethnology of the Ioway Indians," Milwaukee Public Museum *Bulletin*, Vol. VI, Part 1 (1924).

———. "The Mascoutens or Prairie Potawatomi," Milwaukee Public Museum *Bulletin*, Vol. VI, Part 1 (1924).

———. "Material Culture of the Menomini," Museum of the American Indian, Heye Foundation, *Indian Notes and Monographs, Miscellaneous No. 20*, 1921.

———. "Notes on the Eastern Cree and Northern Saulteaux," American Museum of Natural History *Anthropological Papers*, Vol. IX, Part 1 (1911).

———. "Notes on the Plains Cree," *American Anthropologist*, N.S., Vol. XVI, No. 1 (January–March, 1914).

———. "Notes on the Plains Cree," *American Anthropologist*, N.S., Vol. XXI (1919).

———. "Observations on the Ethnology of the Sauk Indians," Milwaukee Public Museum *Bulletin*, Vol. VI, Nos. 1–31 (1923–25).

———. "A Sketch of Eastern Dakota Ethnology," *American Anthropologist*, N.S., Vol. XXI (1919).

Smith, Huron H. "Ethnobotany of the Forest Potawatomi Indians," Milwaukee Public Museum *Bulletin*, Vol. VIII, No. 1 (1933).

Speck, Frank G. "Art Processes in Birchbark of the River Desert Algonquin, a Circumboreal Trait," *Anthropological Papers*, No. 17, Bureau of American Ethnology *Bulletin 128*. Washington, D.C., 1941.

———. "The Double-Curve Motive in Northeastern Algonkian Art," Department of Mines (Ottawa) *Memoir 42*, 1914.

———. "Montagnais Art in Birchbark, a Circumpolar Trait," Museum of the American Indian, Heye Foundation, *Indian Notes and Monographs*, Vol. XI, No. 21 (1937).

Spier, Leslie. "An Analysis of Plains Indian Parfleche Decoration," University of Washington *Publications in Anthropology*, Vol. I, No. 3 (1923).

———. "Klamath Ethnography," University of California *Publications in American Archaeology and Ethnology*, Vol. XXX (1930).

———. "Plains Indian Parfleche Designs," University of Washington *Publications in Anthropology*, Vol. IV, No. 3 (1931).

———, and Edward Sapir. "Wishram Ethnography," University of Washington *Publications in Anthropology*, Vol. III, No. 3 (1930).

Spinden, H. J. "The Nez Percé Indians," American Anthropological Association *Memoirs*, Vol. II, Part 3 (1908).

Starr, Frederick. *American Indians*. Boston, 1899.

Strong, William Duncan. "Indian Tribes of the Chicago Region," Chicago Museum of Natural History *Anthropological Leaflet 24*, 1926.

———. "An Introduction to Nebraska Archaeology," Smithsonian Institution *Miscellaneous Collections*, Vol. XCIII, No. 10 (1935).

Teit, James A. "The Middle Columbia Salish," University of Washington *Publications in Anthropology*, Vol. II, No. 4 (1928).

———. "Painted Rawhide Bags, the Shuswap," American Museum of Natural History *Memoirs*, Vol. IV, Part 7 (1909) [*Publications* of the Jesup North Pacific Expedition, Vol. II, No. 7].

———. "The Salishan Tribes of the Western Plateaus," Bureau of American Ethnology *Forty-fifth Annual Report*. Washington, D.C., 1930.

———. "The Thompson Indians of British Columbia," American Museum of Natural History *Memoirs*, Vol. II, Part 4 (1900).

Thayer, B. W. "A Santee Dakota Buffalo Hide

Parfleche Bag," *Minnesota Archaeologist*, January, 1942.

Turney-High, H. H. "The Flathead Indians of Montana," American Anthropological Association *Memoirs*, Vol. XLVIII (1937).

Webb, Walter Prescott. *The Great Plains*. Boston, 1931.

Wedel, Waldo R. *An Introduction to Pawnee Archaeology*, Bureau of American Ethnology *Bulletin 112*. Washington, D.C., 1936.

Willoughby, Charles C. "A Few Ethnological Specimens Collected by Lewis and Clark," *American Anthropologist*, N.S., Vol. VII (1905).

Wilson, Gilbert. "The Hidatsa Earth Lodge," American Museum of Natural History *Anthropological Papers*, Vol. XXXIII, Part 5 (1934).

Wissler, Clark. *The American Indian*. 3d ed. Washington, D.C., 1938.

———. *Boas Anniversary Volume*. New York, 1906.

———. "Ceremonial Bundles of the Blackfoot Indians," American Museum of Natural History *Anthropological Papers*, Vol. VII, Part 2 (1912).

———. "Costumes of the Plains Indians," American Museum of Natural History *Anthropological Papers*, Vol. XVII, Part 2 (1915).

———. "Decorative Art of the Sioux Indians," American Museum of Natural History *Bulletin*, Vol. XVIII, Part 3 (1904).

———. "The Influence of the Horse in the Development of the Plains Culture," *American Anthropologist*, N.S., Vol. XVI, Part 2 (1914).

———. "Material Culture of the Blackfoot Indians," American Museum of Natural History *Anthropological Papers*, Vol. V, Part 1 (1910).

———. *North American Indians of the Plains*. Washington, D.C., 1927.

———. "Some Protective Designs of the Dakota," American Museum of Natural History *Anthropological Papers*, Vol. I, Part 2 (1907).

———. "Symbolism in the Decorative Art of the Sioux," International Congress of Americanists *Report, 13th Session*, New York, 1902.

Index